JAPANESE ART

POTTERY AND PORCELAIN

PLATE XXVII

JAPANESE POTTERY

FROM THE COLLECTION OF POTTERY AND PORCELAIN PREPARED ESPECIALLY BY THE TOKYO IMPERIAL HOUSEHOLD MUSEUM

1. Square dish designed by Ogata Kenzan, one of the most famous potters of Japan, and painted by his brother, Ogata Korin (c. 1657–1716). Given to the Imperial Household Museum by the Dowager Empress Shoken
2. Water jar used in the tea ceremony (*q.v.*), by Nomura Ninsei, one of Japan's greatest ceramists. He worked chiefly at Awata in Kyoto and produced beautiful examples of jewelled faïence. 17th century
3. Octagonal bowl by Sakrida Kakiemon, noted for his enamelled porcelain. Height, 13.6 cm. 17th century
4. Teapot used in *Sen-cha*, or steeped tea, by Aoki Mokubei, a celebrated Kiyomizu artist. 17th century
5. Incense case of Iga ware, used in the tea ceremony (*Chan-no-yu*). The incense often consists of small chips of wood or ground-up wood burnt in the charcoal fire which heats the water for making the tea

BRITANNICA BOOKLET No. 6

JAPANESE ART

A SELECTION OF ARTICLES FROM THE
NEW 14TH EDITION OF THE

Encyclopædia Britannica

BY THE FOLLOWING AUTHORITIES

Laurence Binyon	George Pearse Ennis	Benjamin March
Warren E. Cox	Daniel Garber	Alan R. Priest
Stewart Culin	Jiro Harada	Eleanor B. Saxe
George Walter Dawson	Robert Lockhart Hobson	Lieut.-Colonel Edward
Sir Charles Norton	Younghill Kang	Fairbrother Strange
Edgcumbe Eliot	A. F. Kendrick	Kojiro Tomita

WITH MANY FULL PAGE PLATES IN COLOUR AND HALFTONE

A Brief Survey of the Various Arts and
Their Periods in Japan

ENCYCLOPÆDIA BRITANNICA, Inc.   THE ENCYCLOPÆDIA BRITANNICA CO., Ltd.
NEW YORK   LONDON

COPYRIGHT

IN ALL COUNTRIES SUBSCRIBING

TO THE BERNE CONVENTION

BY

THE ENCYCLOPÆDIA BRITANNICA COMPANY, LTD.

COPYRIGHT

IN THE UNITED STATES OF AMERICA, 1929, 1930, 1932, 1933

BY THE

ENCYCLOPÆDIA BRITANNICA, INC.

JAPANESE ART

A SELECTION OF ARTICLES FROM THE NEW
14TH EDITION OF THE

ENCYCLOPÆDIA BRITANNICA

PREFACE

Heretofore the student of art has been taught that "Classic Art" meant Greek and Roman Art; that the classic periods were those of the height of the Greek and Roman urges for beauty, and, as a correlative, he was informed that the art of the Far East was merely "Decorative." This was undoubtedly due to the inception of our western conception of Eastern Art based upon porcelains and other decorative objects imported, in the eighteenth and nineteenth centuries, from China and Japan, into France and England. Recently we have begun to be acquainted with the earlier and more serious arts of the countries of the East; the tomb sculptures, the early bronzes, the paintings which show a superb understanding of nature, and the great temples, have taught us that in the Far East there is also classic greatness to be found.

The understanding of the art of Japan has suffered not only under this incubus, along with that of China, but under another quite as heavy: that of considering Japanese Art mere copying of the great things of China. Thus many western students have believed Japanese Art to be nothing more than a facile copy of the "Decorative" art of China. Now, however, this misapprehension has been corrected and western museums are forming important collections, western collectors are vying with one another to make acquisitions and western students of art are finding much satisfaction in the study of the masterful works of old Japan.

Whistler is not the only artist who has acknowledged a considerable debt to the makers of Japanese prints. Many of our wiser western painters have made careful study of this small branch of Japanese Art, and found to their amazement a wholly new understanding of composition, of colour, of contrast and of many elements of art which had never occurred to them before and which, without a doubt, help to make things more beautiful.

I promise you, therefore, a new and vital intellectual and emotional enjoyment, if you study Japanese Art seriously. I promise fundamentals quite as important and "Classic" as those to be found in Greek Art. I suggest that there have been few peoples in this world who have so perfectly learned to make a unit of art and life; to put art into every smallest task of daily living and, therefore, to create a really living art. Oh, very, very much do we of America need this lesson! We who, as a nation, are afraid to admit an enjoyment of the beautiful for fear of not being thought "regular fellows." We who think of the artist as effeminate and queer and not particularly to be trusted, if not actually crazy, and who, through such wrong thinking, have actually made a number of crazy men think that they are artists. We need the lesson that the artisan, the merchant, the housewife and even the soldier can be artists; that "Only the man who knows the sword can appreciate the cherry blossom and only he who has handled the branch of cherry blossoms can understand the sword." What a lesson in fencing is that, for I remember my French master saying that the foil should be held as lightly as though one were holding a small bird in the hand and keeping it from getting away without crushing it!

But there is a deeper lesson than the mere casting off of such youthful ideas in the close association of life and art in Japan. It is the lesson of living beautifully. Few Americans do. We all know the chief reasons why there is no chance to begin so to live. The greediness, the struggle for money, the hurry and the restless, youthful urge to the vaguest of ideals. I need not go further into them, but I would like to say that a very average Japanese can get more beauty from the appreciation of a piece of old drift wood in his home than an American can get from the "most expensive carved mahogany" in his; a Japanese can have more real pleasant enjoyment with his friends over a few cups of tea than an American can over a "flock of cocktails," and it is in such understanding that happiness lies.

This little book is designed primarily for the uninitiated; though it will serve also as a very helpful guide to those who have studied Japanese Art, it will be found to be so simply and directly written that any school child can understand it. Such writing can be had only from those who know perfectly their subjects—men like A. F. Kendrick, Laurence Binyon, Jiro Harada, R. L. Hobson, Kojiro Tomita, Benjamin March, and Alan R. Priest. Japanese authorities in every field of art in which Japan has been active, cover it briefly and yet with remarkable comprehensiveness. The articles are exceedingly well illustrated with the finest examples of art which could be selected, regardless of the cost of making the plates. In the article "Pottery and Porcelain," as an instance, there is a plate from the Tōkyō Imperial Household Museum which was prepared especially for the 14th Edition of the Encyclopædia Britannica. In the article "Screen," Plate V, there are two fine examples from the Boston Museum, which would have probably been rendered in halftone in any other book as they are in shades of grey. We have, however, at some considerable cost, used the four colour process in printing them, as well as actual metallic gold, because we wished to bring out all of the beautiful gradations of shade and hue which the originals possess. Though this is a small book and sold at a low price because we can use the plates already in our hands, it is a book which combines the greatest and most diverse authority in the world to-day, with colour plates, drawings and halftones which are the best money can buy.

Some articles in this booklet have appeared also in other booklets of this series because we felt they would prove useful. One such is my own short article "Periods of Art" with its three graphic tables. Another is "Flower Painting" by George Walter Dawson who like Whistler is another of our great artists who says that he has learned much from Japan and whose whole article shows this appreciation. A few of the articles tie together the arts of Japan and China in such a way that we think it best to give them entire. Others which could be divided we have reproduced only in those parts which concern us here.

I have said that the Japanese are not solely copyists of the Chinese and that is very true; but I do not mean that Japanese Art is not strongly influenced by Chinese. Buddhism swept from India into China where it and its art results were tempered and changed, moved from there into Korea, where it was changed again, and finally arrived in Japan, a very different thing from what it was. But Buddhism ties together over long periods of time the thoughts and, of course, the arts of all these various countries. China, in the olden days, being the great nation of the mainland and the link between Japan, her seas and her islands, and the rest of the world, was undoubtedly a great influence, but just as China herself has maintained her personality in spite of invasions of many different sorts, so too has Japan, over periods of thousands of years and in spite of all vicissitudes. Thus it is interesting, when you set out to read the arts of these countries, to attempt to fix in mind what influences were foreign and what inspiration sprang from native genius. Some such contrasts are presented in the articles which cover both arts together.

We have also included in this booklet a section of Japanese history against which background the student should embroider his conception of the arts. No art can be properly understood in the abstract. A knowledge of the ideals, the civic struggles, the customs and all that goes to make up everyday life will give an insight which cannot otherwise be gained. It is difficult for us to realize that in just one generation Japan has changed from a feudal state into a democratic empire very much like those of the west. The feudal period of our own middle ages seems very distant and we find it hard to place ourselves in the mental attitude of people living under that system. A very good friend of mine whose father was a Samurai, or as we would say a knight of the old régime, has told me that it was considered a great insult in his boyhood days for one lad to say to another, "You know the value of money." These people were not supposed to deal with money; they had the power of life and death over those beneath them and merchants were by no means of their class. Japanese art is founded upon aristocracy of the highest and most distinctive sort. Perhaps it was this attitude which made for that tasteful economy practised in their work, an economy of line and colour which the west has had little knowledge of through all the ages. Many stories are told of the master's use of this economy.

One which I have always remembered is related of the man who first brought the morning-glory flower to Japan. He was a master of the tea ceremony and a gardener. A prince having heard of the beautiful flower sent word that he would like to see it and so set out upon a journey of many miles to reach the garden. When he arrived, what was his dismay to see that all the plants had been removed and the beds strewed with plain white sand. So wroth was he that he was about to turn back when he bethought himself that perhaps he had best go on and take tea with this impertinent gardener and then chastise him as was deserved. The prince was made welcome and finally entered the room where tea was to be served and there in the tokonoma, or small alcove, in a very plain room, stood a vase with one beautiful blossom of the morning-glory and a few leaves and tendrils arranged with the greatest care. The gardener knew that the best appreciation could be found in the one complete flower and not in a garden of many.

It is the regular custom of Japan to show only a few works of art at a time. These are changed for different seasons and occasions and really enjoyed, for each time they are brought out there is a certain newness about them and they may be viewed afresh in many different moods. This is a far better custom than ours of putting every picture we own on the walls of our homes and soon becoming so accustomed to them that after the first few weeks of ownership we seldom really look at them at all.

With the article on the history of Japan there are four halftone plates which show the mode of life and natural aspects of the country. These should be studied with those in the article on Japanese Architecture for they give some idea of how well the Japanese know nature and how well they are able to build their homes and gardens and temples into nature without harming the beauty of the landscape. Theirs is one of

PREFACE

the most beautiful countries in the world, and they have done much to make it even more beautiful. Let us hope that the influences of the west will not ruin these lovely vistas as the westerner seems to take delight in ruining his own. But the influences of Zen Buddhism have done much to instruct the artist of Japan in a very excellent conception of his own place in nature and to give him a fine balance between his subjective part in a work of art and his debt to all glorious surrounding nature. I have always loved the arts of Koyetsu, Korin and his brother Kenzan and I believe there is one thing, among many others, which makes their work stand out: It is that rather than distort nature, as do many of our western painters, to the purposes of their designs, they seem to arrive at their designs by a careful and what must be very painstaking process of selection. In other words they hunt for the beautiful designs actually to be found in nature, rather than try to bend any part of nature to their own carelessly unrelated purposes. This is a very fundamental method in art and could never lead them to make the mistakes of Picasso, Van Gogh and other practisers of the schools of distortion. It has been said that a beautiful piece of pottery should be such that you could put it down in the forest at some time of the year and later pass it by thinking that it was some natural lichen, mushroom or other growth. Such a conception gives one a new way of looking at the potteries of Sung China and of Japan. The potters of Japan have not revolted against nature but have added the beauties they could conceive of to those of the original gourd which was used before pottery came into being. A similar attitude is held by the painters, sculptors and architects. Art does not begin where nature leaves off as has been said in the west; art begins with a profound understanding of nature, an understanding such as that which has been shown by Leonardo da Vinci and by Korin.

I have tried to give in a few words some idea of what is in store for the student of Japanese Art. Read this little book, then read "The Book of Tea" and "The Laws of Japanese Painting" by Kukuzo Okakura and Henry P. Bowie, respectively; they are small books and very pleasant and interesting. Then turn to Laurence Binyon and Ernest F. Fenollosa and you will have set sail on strangely azure seas and be in the way of discovering beautiful, enchanted islands.

WARREN E. COX.
Art Director of the Encyclopædia Britannica

PUBLISHERS' NOTE

Since the publication of the New 14th Edition of the Encyclopædia Britannica, we have received thousands of requests to publish in separate form the articles in certain fields of knowledge so that these articles may be the more available for continuous reading, for students' use, etc. Accordingly we have prepared books containing all the Britannica articles on Painting; Mammals and Birds; Chinese Art; The Earth, the Sea and the Heavens; Graphic Arts; Botany, the Science; Botany: Plants and Gardening; The Theatre and Motion Pictures; Fishes, Reptiles and Insects; and Japanese Art, and expect to follow these with many others. We trust they will prove useful, not only in themselves but also as evidence of the wide scope and the fullness of information in the Britannica itself.

The articles in this book are all taken *verbatim* from the New 14th Edition of the Encyclopædia Britannica except that material not essential to the subject has been omitted and in a few unimportant instances certain material has been condensed for mechanical reasons. The plates, too, are reproduced unchanged, but the numbering is not always consecutive because the original numbering has been retained in order to agree with the text. A number of cross references to articles not in this booklet have also been retained for the benefit of those who possess the Britannica.

Following the Britannica custom, we have retained at the end of signed articles, the initials and not the full name of the author. The reader, however, can always identify the author by referring to the Table of Contents where the full names of the authors are given together with the initials.

CONTENTS

		PAGE
1.	JAPAN—*History*, SIR CHARLES NORTON EDGCUMBE ELIOT, G.C.M.G., P.C., C.B., M.A. (**C. El.**); BRITISH AMBASSADOR TO JAPAN, 1919–26	1
2.	PERIODS OF ART, WARREN E. COX (**W. E. Cx.**), ART EDITOR, 14TH EDITION, ENCYCLOPÆDIA BRITANNICA	26
3.	ART—*Far Eastern Methods*, KOJIRO TOMITA (**K. T.**), KEEPER OF JAPANESE ART, MUSEUM OF FINE ARTS, BOSTON	26
4.	LANDSCAPE PAINTING—*Far East*, DANIEL GARBER (**D. Ga.**), PAINTER; MEMBER OF FACULTY, PENNSYLVANIA ACADEMY OF FINE ARTS	34
5.	WATER-COLOUR PAINTING—*Japanese Art*, GEORGE PEARSE ENNIS (**G. P. E.**), MEMBER, AMERICAN WATER COLOR SOCIETY, GUILD OF AMERICAN PAINTERS	34
6.	JAPANESE PAINTING AND PRINTS, LAURENCE BINYON, HON. LL.D. (**L. Bi.**); AUTHOR AND DEPUTY KEEPER OF SUB-DEPARTMENT OF ORIENTAL PRINTS AND DRAWINGS, BRITISH MUSEUM	35
7.	IRON IN ART—*China and Japan*, BENJAMIN MARCH (**B. Mar.**), CURATOR OF ASIATIC ART, THE DETROIT INSTITUTE OF ARTS	40
8.	FLOWER PAINTING—*The Art in China and Japan*, GEORGE WALTER DAWSON (**G. W. D.**), DEPARTMENT OF FINE ARTS, UNIVERSITY OF PENNSYLVANIA	40
9.	JAPANESE SCULPTURE, JIRO HARADA (**J. Har.**), OF THE IMPERIAL HOUSEHOLD MUSEUMS, JAPAN	41
10.	LACQUER OR LACKER, LIEUT.-COLONEL EDWARD FAIRBROTHER STRANGE, C.B.E. (**E. F. S.**); LATE KEEPER OF WOODWORK, VICTORIA AND ALBERT MUSEUM, LONDON	42
11.	IVORY CARVING—*Japanese*, JIRO HARADA (**J. Har.**), OF THE IMPERIAL HOUSEHOLD MUSEUMS, JAPAN	45
12.	BON-KEI, ANONYMOUS	46
13.	BON SAI, ANONYMOUS	46
14.	BON SEKI, JIRO HARADA (**J. Har.**), OF THE IMPERIAL HOUSEHOLD MUSEUMS, JAPAN	46
15.	WOOD-CARVING—*Far Eastern*, JIRO HARADA (**J. Har.**), OF THE IMPERIAL HOUSEHOLD MUSEUMS, JAPAN	47
16.	POTTERY AND PORCELAIN—*Japan*, ROBERT LOCKHART HOBSON (**R. L. Ho.**), KEEPER OF DEPARTMENT OF CERAMICS AND ETHNOGRAPHY, BRITISH MUSEUM	48
17.	INTERIOR DECORATION—*Japanese*, JIRO HARADA (**J. Har.**), OF THE IMPERIAL HOUSEHOLD MUSEUMS, JAPAN	49
18.	JAPANESE ARCHITECTURE, JIRO HARADA (**J. Har.**), OF THE IMPERIAL HOUSEHOLD MUSEUMS, JAPAN	51
19.	FAN—*Japan*, ELEANOR B. SAXE, A.M. (**E. B. Sa.**); ASSISTANT, DEPARTMENT OF DECORATIVE ARTS, METROPOLITAN MUSEUM OF ART, NEW YORK	52
20.	DOLLS, STEWART CULIN (**S. Cu.**), BROOKLYN INSTITUTE OF ARTS AND SCIENCES, BROOKLYN, N. Y.	52
21.	NŌ DRAMA, JIRO HARADA (**J. Har.**), OF THE IMPERIAL HOUSEHOLD MUSEUMS, JAPAN	53

CONTENTS

22. HAKO–NIWA, Anonymous 53

23. DANCE—*Japan*, Jiro Harada (**J. Har.**), of the Imperial Household Museums, Japan, and Younghill Kang (**Y. K.**), instructor, comparative literature, New York University 54

24. SEALS—*Japanese and Chinese*, Alan R. Priest (**A. R. Pr.**), curator of Far Eastern art, Metropolitan Museum of Art, New York 55

25. DRESS—*Far Eastern*, Younghill Kang (**Y. K.**), instructor, comparative literature, New York University 56

26. TEA CEREMONY, Jiro Harada (**J. Har.**), of the Imperial Household Museums, Japan . . . 56

27. SCREEN—*Screens of China and Japan*, Kojiro Tomita (**K. T.**), keeper of Japanese art, Museum of Fine Arts, Boston 56

28. TEXTILES AND EMBROIDERIES—*The Far East*, A. F. Kendrick (**A. F. K.**), keeper in the Victoria and Albert Museum, South Kensington, of textiles, 1897–1927, ceramics 1899–1902, and woodwork, 1904–8 58

29. JAPANESE GARDENS, Jiro Harada (**J. Har.**), of the Imperial Household Museums, Japan . 59

30. FLOWER ARRANGING, Jiro Harada (**J. Har.**), of the Imperial Household Museums, Japan . 61

31. ENAMEL—*Chinese and Japanese Enamels*, Lieut.-Colonel Edward Fairbrother Strange (**E.F.S.**) late keeper of woodwork, Victoria and Albert Museum, London 61

32. JAPAN—*Weapons—Armour*, Anonymous 63

X. The initial used for anonymous contributors.

LIST OF PLATES
COLOUR PLATES

FACING PAGE

1. POTTERY AND PORCELAIN, Plate XXVII
   JAPANESE POTTERY (Frontispiece)

2. JAPANESE PAINTING AND PRINTS, Plate I   34
   KORIN AND KOYETSU SCREENS

3. JAPANESE PAINTING AND PRINTS, Plate II   34
   PORTRAIT OF YORITOMO

4. JAPANESE PAINTING AND PRINTS, Plate III   36
   18TH CENTURY JAPANESE PRINTS

5. FAN, Plate IV   52
   JAPANESE FOLDING FANS

6. SCREEN, Plate II   58
   JAPANESE "WAVE SCREEN" OF THE 17TH CENTURY, *painted by Ogata Korin*

7. SCREEN, Plate V   58
   TWO JAPANESE SCREENS

HALFTONE PLATES

FACING PAGE

1. JAPAN, Plate I   8
   THE GROUNDS OF TWO JAPANESE TEMPLES

2. JAPAN, Plate II   9
   ASPECTS OF JAPANESE LIFE

3. JAPAN, Plate III   18
   ASPECTS OF LIFE IN JAPAN

4. JAPAN, Plate IV   19
   NATURAL SCENERY IN JAPAN

5. ART, Plate I   26
   JAPANESE ARTISTS AT WORK

6. ART, Plate II   27
   A JAPANESE WATER-COLOUR ARTIST AT WORK

7. JAPANESE PAINTING AND PRINTS, Plate IV   38
   JAPANESE PICTURE ROLLS AND SCREENS

8. JAPANESE PAINTING AND PRINTS, Plate V   38
   JAPANESE PAINTERS OF THE ASHIKAGA PERIOD—THE CHINESE RENAISSANCE

9. JAPANESE PAINTING AND PRINTS, Plate VI   38
   PAINTINGS OF THE KANŌ SCHOOL

10. IRON IN ART, Plate V   40
    CHINESE CAST IRON WORK

11. IRON IN ART, Plate VI   40
    GROUP OF CHINESE IRON PICTURES WITH PAPER OR SILK BACKGROUNDS AND JAPANESE SWORD GUARDS

12. FLOWER PAINTING, Plate II   40
    JAPANESE AND CHINESE FLOWER PAINTING

13. JAPANESE SCULPTURE, Plate I   42
    JAPANESE SCULPTURE OF THE TEMPYO AND KAMAKURA PERIODS

14. JAPANESE SCULPTURE, Plate II   43
    BUDDHISTIC IMAGES IN CLAY, WOOD AND DRY-LACQUER

15. LACQUER, Plate   44
    CHINESE LACQUER WORK OF THE 16TH, 17TH AND 18TH CENTURIES

16. IVORY CARVING, Plate VII   44
    IVORY CARVINGS OF JAPAN

17. IVORY CARVING, Plate VIII   45
    JAPANESE IVORY ORNAMENTS AND WORKS OF ART

18. BON-KEI, Plate   46
    MINIATURE LANDSCAPES MODELLED ON TRAYS OF BRONZE, CONCRETE OR PORCELAIN

19. BON-SAI, Plate I   46
    THE JAPANESE ART OF DWARFING TREES FOR ORNAMENTATION

20. BON-SAI, Plate II   46
    DWARF TREES TRAINED INTO VARIOUS SHAPES BY PRUNING AND FERTILIZATION

21. BON-SEKI, Plate I   46
    JAPANESE TRAY LANDSCAPES AND THE PARAPHERNALIA FOR MAKING THEM

22. BON-SEKI, Plate II   47
    AN ARTIST IN BON-SEKI AND SOME ARRANGEMENTS OF STONES AND SAND ON TRAYS (KI SEKI)

23. WOOD-CARVING, Plate IV   48
    EXAMPLES OF FAR EASTERN WOOD-CARVING

24. POTTERY AND PORCELAIN, Plate XLII   48
    JAPANESE POTTERY

25. INTERIOR DECORATION, Plate XVI   50
    JAPANESE HOUSE INTERIORS

26. INTERIOR DECORATION, Plate XVII   50
    JAPANESE INTERIORS AND FURNISHINGS

27. JAPANESE ARCHITECTURE, Plate I   50
    TEA PAVILION, A SHRINE AND OTHER JAPANESE BUILDINGS

28. JAPANESE ARCHITECTURE, Plate II   50
    JAPANESE TEMPLES, AND OTHER BUILDINGS

29. JAPANESE ARCHITECTURE, Plate III   50
    NIKKO SHRINE

30. JAPANESE ARCHITECTURE, Plate IV   51
    VARIOUS FORMS OF JAPANESE ARCHITECTURE

HALFTONE PLATES

FACING PAGE

31. FAN, PLATE III 52
    JAPANESE AND INDIAN FANS OF THE NINETEENTH CENTURY

32. DOLLS, PLATE 52
    ASIATIC AND EGYPTIAN DOLLS

33. NŌ DRAMA, PLATE I 52
    CHARACTERS IN THE NŌ DRAMA

34. NŌ DRAMA, PLATE II 52
    SCENES FROM THE NŌ DRAMA

35. NŌ DRAMA, PLATE III 52
    MASKS WORN IN THE NŌ PERFORMANCES

36. DANCE, PLATE II 54
    JAPANESE DANCES AS DANCED BY GEISHAS AND ACTORS

37. DANCE, PLATE III 54
    CHARACTERISTIC DANCES OF JAPAN

38. SEALS, PLATE II 54
    CHINESE SEALS

39. TEA CEREMONY, PLATE I 56
    TEA SET AND SCREENS USED IN THE TEA CEREMONY

40. TEA CEREMONY, PLATE II 56
    METHOD OF PREPARING TEA FOR THE TEA CEREMONY

41. TEA CEREMONY, PLATE III 56
    ETIQUETTE OBSERVED BY HOST AND GUEST IN THE TEA CEREMONY

FACING PAGE

42. TEA CEREMONY, PLATE IV 57
    ETIQUETTE OBSERVED BY HOST AND GUEST IN THE TEA CEREMONY

43. SCREEN, PLATE IV 58
    A CHINESE AND A JAPANESE SCREEN IN THE T'ANG STYLE

44. TEXTILES AND EMBROIDERIES, PLATE IV 58
    EMBROIDERERS AT WORK

45. TEXTILES AND EMBROIDERIES, PLATE XII 58
    JAPANESE COVERS

46. JAPANESE GARDENS, PLATE I 60
    CHARACTERISTIC JAPANESE GARDENS

47. JAPANESE GARDENS, PLATE II . . . 60
    IMPERIAL AND OTHER JAPANESE GARDENS

48. FLOWER ARRANGING, PLATE 60
    JAPANESE STYLES OF FLOWER ARRANGING

49. ENAMEL, PLATE III 62
    THE PROCESS OF CLOISONNÉ

50. ENAMEL, PLATE IV 62
    FIRING THE ENAMELS

51. ENAMEL, PLATE V 62
    PAINTED, CLOISONNÉ AND CHAMPLEVÉ CHINESE ENAMELS OF THE XVIII AND XIX CENTURIES

52. ENAMEL, PLATE VI 63
    THE CLOISONNÉ PROCESS AND CHINESE CLOISONNÉ ENAMELS OF THE XV–XVIII CENTURIES

JAPANESE ART

JAPANESE ART

A Selection of Articles from the New 14th Edition of the
Encyclopædia Britannica

JAPAN

HISTORY

THE early history of Japan is indistinguishable from mythology and consists of legends collected in the two chronicles called Kojiki and Nihongi or Nihonshoki. Both were composed in the 8th century: the first ends about 500, but the second closes with the year A.D. 697, and the latter portion of it is more or less historical, though the chronology is not trustworthy. The legends contained in these works are so nebulous and disconnected that they cannot be summarized in a coherent narrative but they tell how the land and people of Japan were produced by the Gods among whom the Sun goddess Amaterasu and her brother Susanoo play a principal part. It is noticeable that in the earliest stories there are two centres. Susanoo descends to Silla in Korea and sails thence to Izumo in Japan where his posterity rule, but the child sent by the Sun goddess to rule Japan descends, after negotiations with the rulers of Izumo, to the province of Hyūga in Kyushu. This confirms the theory, which is probable for other reasons, that the Japanese are a mixed race. The oldest known stratum of population is represented by the Ainus, whose bones are said to show some of the characteristics found in European prehistoric skeletons. There is no record, even legendary, of their arrival in Japan, but the evidence of place names shows that they once occupied the entire country, including Kyushu. They were gradually driven to the north by invaders who came partly from Korea, and perhaps ultimately from Central Asia, and partly from the south. Recent discussions tend to emphasize the importance of a Malay-Polynesian element in the Japanese language and customs and the legend also dwells on the activity of the descendants of the Sun goddess who reigned in Kyushu rather than on the doings of the rulers of Izumo.

According to the chronicles the first human sovereign of Japan was Jimmu Tennō who, starting from Kyushu, proceeded to conquer the east. He halted on the northern shores of the Inland sea and then, after much fighting, established his rule in the province of Yamato, which now becomes the centre of Japan. It is doubtless true that at some period before the Christian era there was a movement of population from the west to Yamato, but the details seem entirely legendary. Jimmu was not really the ancient name of the leader (Kami Yamato Ihare-biko) but a posthumous title invented by scholars in the 8th century, and the date of his accession, February 11, 660 B.C., is a similar invention. But in 1889 the leaders of Japan wished the nation to believe in the continuity of Japanese history and the antiquity of the imperial lineage, and with this object promulgated the new constitution on the supposed date of Jimmu's accession and made it a public holiday. In the same spirit they erected in 1890 a mausoleum on the plains of Yamato near a tumulus where he is said to have been buried. The chronicles give the names of Jimmu's successors, but ascribe to them impossibly long reigns, and there also appears to be an error in chronology by which the dates are 120 years too remote. Although the record is mainly genealogical it contains points of interest: (1) Women hold an important position and are the heroines of many tales. (2) Irrigation works are mentioned and the Emperor Suinin is said to have constructed more than 800 ponds and channels. (3) The imperial harem was large. Thus the Nihongi tells us that the Emperor Keikō gave "fiefs of provinces and districts" of 77 of his children and each child proceeded to his own province. In this way, no doubt, arose the territorial nobility which plays such a conspicuous part in subsequent history. (4) In an edict ascribed to 81 B.C. ships are stated to be of cardinal importance, because of the difficulty of land transport, and every province is ordered to build them. (5) About the time of our era the practice of burying men alive with princes was discontinued and clay figures were substituted. (6) Several expeditions against savages, that is, probably, Ainus, are mentioned, the principal being ascribed to Yamato-takeru, son of the Emperor Keikō and first of the picturesque young heroes of Japan. He subdued first the land of Kumaso in Kyushu (so called from the Kuma and So, two tribes which inhabited it) and then successfully attacked the north and east, penetrating as far as Shimosa and Shinano. But he fell ill and died at the age of 30 on "the moor of Nobo," regretting in his last words that he could not report his victories to the emperor. "Alone I lay me down on the waste moor with none to say a word to me. But why should I regret the loss of this body? My only grief is that I cannot meet thee." His son or descendant, Chūai, became emperor and sent another expedition against the Kumaso, but it was not victorious.

TENNOJI PAGODA, AT OSAKA, A TYPICAL EXAMPLE OF THE FIVE-STOREYED TEMPLE BUILT OF WOOD TO BE RESILIENT TO EARTHQUAKE SHOCKS

Invasion of Korea.—We now come to an important legend, the conquest of Korea by the Empress Jingō, for which the traditional date is A.D. 200. Apparently it did not belong to the Yamato cycle, for the Kojiki transfers the scene abruptly to Kyūshū. The Nihongi makes a more coherent though still very strange story by telling how the court removed to Kyushu and how the empress, after invading Korea, regained possession of Yamato which had revolted during her absence. But it is fairly clear that there were two cycles of legends, one having Kyushu, the other Yamato as its centre. After this period Yamato definitely becomes the seat of the emperor and of government. The Empress Jingō appears to have been a real person, for the Chinese annals, though they do not mention her name, say that Japan was ruled by a woman at this period. The Nihongi recounts how she invaded

Silla, how the neighbouring kings of Koryo (or Koguryo) and Pakche spontaneously tendered submission, and how during many years tributary missions were sent at intervals to Japan and occasionally punitive expeditions despatched to Korea. Whether at this period the Japanese subdued any considerable part of Korea may be doubted, but the Korean annals mention many incursions of Japanese pirates and also the exchange of missions. There must have been considerable intercourse, both peaceful and hostile, between the two countries. In A.D. 284 the Emperor Ōjin summoned from Pakche a learned man called Wang-in, who became tutor of the heir apparent and the ancestor of "the chiefs of writing." Ōjin was succeeded by Nintoku who is one of the romantic figures in Japanese history. The throne remained vacant for three years because he wished his brother to occupy it. The latter refused and at last solved the question by committing suicide. Nintoku made Naniwa, the modern Osaka, his capital. A celebrated story relates how he ascended a tower and looking over his country observed that no smoke was rising from the houses. Inferring that his people were poor and had no rice to cook, he abolished forced labour for three years. His palace fell into disrepair, but "the people had plenty, the praise of his virtues filled the land and the smoke of cooking was also thick." The Nihongi states that in this reign an official named "Kino Tsuno was the first to distinguish the boundaries of provinces and districts and to commit to writing in detail the products of the soil in each locality." We also hear that it became the custom to store ice in ice-houses for use during the summer.

Beginning of History.—The first date given by the Nihongi which is confirmed by external evidence is equivalent to A.D. 461 and the reign of the Emperor Richu, which is reckoned as beginning in A.D. 400, is generally considered to mark the commencement of the historical period. The appearances of deities become less frequent, but the chronology is still confused, but, as few important events are recorded, this defect is not of much moment. The Government is represented as a monarchy inherent in one family of divine descent but with somewhat irregular succession and subject to frequent usurpation. The emperors are generally represented as beneficent and beloved of their subjects, with two exceptions Yuriaku (456–471) and Buretsu (498–506) who are described as monsters of cruelty and injustice. The nobles are called Omi and Muraji, the former apparently claiming divine, that is remote imperial lineage, and the latter content with a merely human pedigree and probably descended from the old nobles of Kyushu and Izumo. At the beginning of each reign a great Omi and a great Muraji were appointed who seem to have corresponded to a chancellor and a commander-in-chief. Besides these there were personages, Kuni-no-Miyakko or chiefs of provinces, who were heads of clans owning the territory in which they resided. There were also numerous corporations called *Be*, such as the *Bes* of the mountain warders, seamen and carpenters. It is not clear how these corporations fitted into the clan system, but they included many immigrants from Korea. The most important feature of the period from A.D. 400–550 is the growth of relations with this country. The chronicles contain many admissions that the Japanese learned from it various arts of life and, on the other hand, if the language used about conquest and tribute is unduly patriotic, it is clear that they had some sort of special sphere in the peninsula. Between the two little kingdoms of Silla (or Shiragi) on the coast facing Japan and Pakche (Kudara) to the west, lay a territory called Imna or Mimana, to the west of the modern Fusan. Here the Japanese had a settlement and we hear from time to time of a Japanese garrison and Japanese governors or perhaps residents, for a king of Imna is also mentioned. The relations of Imna and Pakche were generally friendly but the rulers of Silla were from the Japanese point of view unsatisfactory and insubordinate. With the aid of the northern kingdom of Koryo they invaded Pakche and in 562 they "destroyed the Miyake of Imna."

Introduction of Buddhism.—But meanwhile an event of the utmost importance occurred. A mission from the king of Pakche asking for armed assistance recommended Buddhism to the attention of the emperor of Japan as the religion of the civilized world, and presented an image of the Buddha and sacred books. This incident is justly selected by historians as marking the introduction of Buddhism and Chinese civilization, for the Japanese Government were confronted with the immediate problem of what to do with the presents, but naturally the ground had been prepared by immigration and intercourse. In 540 we read that the men of Ts'in (China) and Han, etc., were "assembled and enrolled in the registers of population": that the men of Ts'in alone numbered 7,053 houses and that one of them was made director of the Treasury. The emperor and his court were probably not wholly ignorant of Buddhism, and Soga, perhaps the greatest personage in the aristocracy, is represented as asking whether Japan was to be alone among the nations in not worshipping the Buddha. Other councillors objected, but at last it was agreed that the Soga family should worship the image as an experiment. A pestilence which broke out at this time was regarded as a sign of the anger of the native gods and Buddhism was forbidden but, as the pestilence then grew worse, this was with equally good reason interpreted as the anger of the Buddha. As a compromise Buddhism was tolerated as the family cult of the Sogas, but since that family was very much to the fore and rising in importance it became the established church in a few decades. On the death of the Emperor Yomei there was a dispute as to the succession which led to war between the Sogas and their rivals, the Mononobe, opponents of Buddhism who championed the institutions of old Japan. The Sogas were completely victorious and after further dynastic troubles in which the Emperor Sujun was assassinated Soga no Numako's niece, known as the Empress Suiko (593–628), was summoned to the throne in her own right, although there was no lack of male heirs. At the same time Shōtoku Taishi, a son of the Emperor Yōmei who had fought with Soga against the Mononobe, was declared heir apparent and though he did not live to reign himself became one of the best known figures in all Japanese history. He was also called Umayado, or Prince Stable-door, because he was born unexpectedly while his mother was inspecting the imperial stables. He was entrusted with the government from 593 to 621 and when he died, says the Nihongi, the old wept as if they had lost a child, the young as if they had lost a parent. His name is associated with the establishment of Buddhism in Japan and he built the temple of Hōryūji which still exists. He was a lover of art and the greatest scholar of his time, the author of commentaries on several Buddhist scriptures and of a history of his country. But more than this; he seems to have introduced good administration and humane customs into a land which sadly needed them. The Nihongi, speaking of the year 562, observes "at this time between father and child, husband and wife, there was no mutual commiseration." Shōtoku Taishi "prepared for the first time laws." They consist of 17 clauses which are moral maxims rather than legal enactments and are inspired by Confucianism, though Buddhism is held up for admiration as the universal religion. The power of the throne is emphasized, the duties of ministers defined, the provincial authorities are forbidden to levy exactions and forced labour is to be required only at seasonable times. Japan had now official relations with China as well as Korea. In 607 an envoy was sent to the Emperor Yang-Ti of the Sui dynasty and next year a return mission arrived. The two potentates were not quite agreed as to their respective rank, for while the Chinese despatch began "The Emperor greets the sovereign of Wa" (the old name of Japan), the reply said "the emperor of the east respectfully greets the emperor of the west." But there was no doubt that Japan wished to learn from China all that was useful.

The Sogas.—Shōtoku Taishi, as practical ruler of Japan, had maintained good relations with the great Soga family, but after his death their power and arrogance became excessive and provoked the suspicion that they intended to usurp the throne. The story of their downfall is one of the best known episodes in early Japanese history. They had placed on the throne the Empress Kōgyoku, widow of the Emperor Jomei, but Soga no Iruka governed the country and kept almost imperial state. There was at that time a certain young man called Kamatari, who afterwards received the name of Fujiwara and became the founder of that illustrious house. He belonged to the family of Nakatomi, hereditary guardians of the great Shinto shrines and rivals of the Soga. "He was indignant with Soga no Iruka," says the Nihongi, "for breaking down the order of prince and vassal, senior and junior and for cherishing veiled designs on the State." He was offered the post of head of the Shinto religion but refused it and, keeping away from court, entered into a conspiracy with the empress's brother, Prince Karu, and also secured the friendship and assistance of Prince Naka, her son, by his politeness in a game of football. As Soga was always guarded when out of doors it was decided to kill him at court in the presence of the empress. When the critical moment arrived the swordsmen appointed to strike the blow were afraid and Prince Naka himself cut Soga down. He fell at the feet of the empress, who was greatly shocked, but Naka said to her—"He wished to destroy utterly the Heavenly House and subvert the Solar Dignity. Is he to take the place of the Heavenly House?" This ended the pre-eminence of the Soga family. The empress thought it prudent to abdicate. Naka was content to be prince imperial and Karu succeeded her in 645 under the name of Kōtoku.

The Reforms of Taikwa.—He decided that the beginning of his reign should be known as Taikwa, great civilization or development, and the changes he introduced are spoken of as the Reforms of Taikwa. This is the first instance of the use of a *nengō* or year name, which became the regular method for fixing dates in Japan. Instead of using an era which covers many centuries, a special name is given to a few years. In quite modern times this period coincides with an emperor's reign; thus 1904 was the 37th year of Meiji and 1927 the second year of Showa. But formerly any remarkable event was considered a sufficient reason for a new *nengō*. In later Japanese history events are commonly referred to in terms of nengō, as for instance the Wars of Ōnin (1467–9), the Code of Kemmu (1334–6), where Ōnin and Kemmu are names not of people or places but of periods. From Taikwa down to the present Showa there have been 247 nengō. Kōtoku was not a personality like Shōtoku Taishi, but he was assisted by Kamatari, who proved one of the ablest statesmen that Japan has produced. Under his guidance the Government was reorganized and Chinese institutions were adopted on a scale which can only be paralleled by the deliberate imitation of European methods under the Emperor Meiji. The Nihongi says that "he honoured the religion of Buddha and despised the way of the Gods," that is, Shintoism or the ancient worship of Japan. The development of Japanese religion does not come within the province of this article, but it may be mentioned that though there was naturally a struggle between the imported faith and old institutions, the contest was comparatively gentle and had little of the violence which attended the Reformation in Europe. It is only occasionally and mostly quite late in history that we hear of troubles arising between the two creeds. At the time of which we are treating the triumphal progress of Buddhism was remarkable; we hear continually how images were cast and temples built in a magnificent style unknown to Shintō, which favoured simplicity; how teachers and priests arrived from Korea and China; how Japanese eagerly received ordination as monks and nuns and how an important precedent was set by a prince who retired to a monastery to avoid political complications. But all this did not mean merely an influx of foreign piety or superstition. Kōtoku and his advisers saw that the existing system of government and society was radically wrong and set themselves to reform it, taking China as their model. The central power was weak and had no machinery by which it could exert its authority far from the capital; the great mass of the people were ignorant peasants, victims of the tyranny of numerous local magnates, who were not appointed by the crown but owed their position either to birth or, very often, to their unscrupulous use of their opportunities. The system of forced labour was abused; the administration of justice and the collection of taxes were both purely local and corrupt; the families of serfs were distributed as their masters chose and provincial chiefs appropriated both lands belonging to private persons and the estates of the crown. To remedy such abuses the regulations of Taikwa appointed three great officials styled ministers of the left, right and interior; provincial governors were ordered to prepare registers showing the number of free men and serfs and the area of cultivated land in their jurisdiction. It was further ordained that the common people should have equal share in the advantages of irrigation: that the acceptance of bribes should be punished: that a box for receiving petitions should be placed in the imperial court and a bell be hung for the use of those who had complaints to make: that the absorption of land into great estates should cease: that officials should receive by way of emolument "sustenance fiefs," that is to say, the taxes of a certain number of homesteads: that in cities and townships (defined as 50 houses) aldermen should be appointed for "the superintendence of the population and the examination of criminal matters": that officials should have as assistants "men of solid capacity, skilled in writing and arithmetic." Also the whole soil of the empire was supposed to be surrendered to the central Government and was theoretically at least distributed among peasants in equal holdings of a few acres, subject to a six-yearly redistribution. The old taxes and forced labour were abolished and a system of commuted taxes instituted. Many matters of detail which cannot be here enumerated, are dealt with at length. For instance, the practice of constructing enormous tombs diverted labour from more profitable work. It was now enacted that the tomb of a prince must not require the labour of more than 1,000 men for a week, and that the grave of an ordinary official must be completed by 50 men in one day. In 649 the emperor ordered the establishment of eight departments of State, though perhaps this central organization was not really completed until somewhat later. Of these eight ministries which were modelled on the six boards of the Tang dynasty, four were concerned with the court, but their province included questions which we should now call education and public worship. The other four were the Home Office (Minbushō), the War Office (Hyōbushō), the Treasury (Ōkurashō) and the Ministry of Justice. The intention of Kōtoku's reforms was evidently to arrest feudalism, but in this they were not successful, though they did much for the improvement and civilization of his country. In China there were few great families and public opinion found selection by merit and even by public examinations natural. But the subsequent history of Japan shows that the tendency to consider office and influence as hereditary was not easily eradicated.

On the death of the Emperor Kōtoku, Prince Naka, though recognized as the heir apparent, again stood aside and allowed his mother to have a second reign under the style of Saimei. It was not till her decease in 661 that he at last came to the throne as Tenchi. At this period an important change occurred in Korea: with the assistance of the Chinese, Silla conquered the other States of the peninsula. The Japanese sent a force to help their old ally Pakche but it was annihilated by the Chinese fleet in 663, and until the time of Hideyoshi at the end of the 16th century Japan had to keep her hands off Korea. But after the fall of Pakche and Koguryu large numbers of Koreans emigrated to Japan and were hospitably received by Tenchi. He was an able and enlightened monarch but on his premature death in 671 the country was thrown into confusion by civil war between his son Ohotomo, who had been set aside, and his younger brother who had been named prince imperial. The latter won and ruled till 686 as the Emperor Temmu. The Kojiki and Nihongi which were compiled by his orders, though not completed until after his death, give a long and sometimes imaginative account of the struggle.

When he died there was again a difficulty about the succession: his son Ohotsu was put to death and his widow came to the throne as the Empress Jitō. She abdicated in 697 and for the first time in Japanese history a minor was made emperor, a practice which afterwards became very frequent. He was known as the Emperor Mommu and was both grandson and nephew of the late empress. Coming to the throne when only fourteen he died at the age of twenty and was succeeded by his own mother the Empress Gemmei. In 697 the Nihongi comes to an end, but the chronicles of old Japan are continued in the Shokunihongi, Nihon-Kōki and other official histories. The Civil Code of Taiho also throws much light on the condition of Japan at this period. It is the oldest extant body of Japanese law, but what has come down to us is not the original text which was published in the year of 702 but the edition of 833, in which a commentary is incorporated.

THE NARA PERIOD

Up to this time there had never been a fixed metropolis. The court had moved about from one town to another in the five home provinces (Gokinai), the provinces of Yamato, Yamashiro, Settsu, Kawachi and Izumi) or to Otsu on Lake Biwa, the capital being always changed on the death of the sovereign and often at other times. This habit had many inconveniences and caused great hardship to the labouring classes who were called upon to construct new palaces at frequent intervals. So in 710, in the reign of the Empress Gemmei, Nara was selected as a fixed capital and with brief intervals continued to be the imperial residence for three-quarters of a century. Except for a campaign in the north conducted by a Fujiwara general against the Ainu, the Naran period was eminently peaceful and marks an epoch in the history of art, literature and religion. The city was laid out on the plan of the Chinese capital and was visited by learned men and artists not only from China and Korea but from India, Cambodia and Central Asia. Many Japanese also went to China to study. It was the fashion to imitate everything Chinese, in art and letters, in costume and amusements; but in many religious carvings and ornaments, Indian influence is also apparent. But though this cultivated society had not much originality, it was not wanting in force and power of expression, for the Naran sculpture is remarkable for its vigour and beauty. It was at this time that the first anthology of poems (the Manyōshū) was compiled and the poets Hitomaru and Akahito wrote. Nara was pre-eminently a Buddhist centre. There were seven monasteries in or near the city and, as ecclesiastical property paid no taxes, it tended to increase, for the peasants were quite ready to surrender their land to the church and then hold it as tenants in return for a rent smaller than the imposts levied by the Government. At this period the private ownership of land began to be recognized, for it was found that the uncertain tenure and frequent redistributions prescribed by the regulations of Taikwa deterred improvements. In 708 copper was discovered and a mint established, but its operations were seriously impeded because so much of the new metal was required for the casting of bells and images. The greatest of these was the Daibutsu in the Tōdai-ji of Nara, a gigantic image weighing more than 550 tons. It was dedicated in 749 by the Emperor Shōmu who appeared before it with all his Court and declared himself the servant of the Three Treasures—the Buddha, the Law and the Church. In fervour of devotion he may rank with the Indian emperor Asoka, and like him he constructed hospitals and almshouses, roads and bridges. In all these enterprises, whether appertaining to religion or public works, he was assisted by the eminent Korean priest, Gyōgi Bosatsu, who was made head of the hierarchy. Shōmu took the tonsure and abdicated in favour of his daughter Kōken, who was also a zealous Buddhist and followed her father's example by becoming a nun in 752, a young prince succeeding her as the Emperor Junnin. But she continued to control the more important affairs of the empire and there was thus a dual monarchy consisting of a retired and a reigning sovereign, a position which often reappears in Japanese history.

The emperor's chief adviser was Emi no Oshikatsu, of the Fujiwara family, which was growing powerful, and the empress was under the influence of a handsome and ambitious monk called Dōkyō. Oshikatsu attempted to make away with him, but the empress took vigorous action in her favorite's defence and civil war broke out. Oshikatsu had many enemies on account of his sudden rise to eminence at court and was overpowered and executed. The empress then banished the young emperor to the island of Awaji where he was strangled and, emerging from her retirement, again ascended the throne in 756, changing her name to Shōtoku. Dōkyō became chancellor and practically ruler of the empire, but his ambition knew no bounds and he spread a report that the God of War wished him to be made emperor. Even his devoted mistress raised objection to this and insisted that the oracle must be consulted officially. When this was done, his enemies arranged that the divine reply should be a decided negative. Dōkyō, however, did not fall at once and even had time to take personal vengeance on his opponents. But, when the empress died in 769, he was banished. Nothing remarkable happened for the moment, but it is significant that no empress was allowed to reign again until 1630. An elderly prince came to the throne and ruled for twelve years as Kōnin Tennō, under the guidance of Fujiwara Momokawa and was then succeeded by a really able emperor, Kwammu (782–805).

THE FUJIWARA PERIOD AND WARS OF GEMPEI

Kwammu removed the court to Nagaoka, Yamashiro; then in 794 to the new city of Kyōto, which continued to be the imperial residence until 1869. The chief reason for the change was no doubt the fear that at Nara the Government might be made subservient to the Buddhist church, and the incident of Dōkyō shows that there were ambitious prelates who dreamt of a state analogous to the Papacy or the Lamaist hierarchy of Tibet. At Kyōto the Government was for the time being at any rate not exposed to undue ecclesiastical influence. Not that Kwammu in any way quarrelled with the Buddhist church: he built many temples himself, but he made an enactment that imperial sanction was necessary for the construction of new ones. Kwammu also tried to abolish, though without permanent success, the hereditary tenure of office enjoyed by provincial governors. These officials owned large tax-free estates called shōen which, like those of the monasteries, continually increased by absorbing the neighbouring land owned by peasants. This system had two most important consequences: first it created a class of quasi-independent territorial magnates and secondly it impoverished the exchequer by increasing the extent of areas which paid no taxes. Kwammu's reign was also remarkable for a long campaign against the Ainu. At this time the extreme outpost of the Japanese empire was the fortress of Taga about 50 miles to the north of Sendai. The Ainu seized it in 780 and it was not till 802 that the fighting was over. The hero of these wars was Sakanoe Tamuramaro, whom Japanese romances represent as the ideal soldier, most terrible to his enemies but gentle and unassuming among his friends. He was the first to receive the title of Sei-i-tai-Shōgun, or Barbarian-subduing-Generalissimo, which was the name by which the later rulers of Japan were known.

The sovereigns who immediately succeeded Kwammu were not without ability and have been called the learned emperors. But from this point onward a most remarkable and persistent feature makes its appearance in Japanese history. This is the constant tendency to separate titular and real authority, to preserve a venerable hereditary office but to set up beside it a recognized and efficient power which was also generally hereditary. Not only was the Government during many centuries administered by a Shōgun but the effective power of the Shōgun sometimes passed to a deputy and at other times an emperor who had nominally abdicated in favour of a minor retained the real control of the State. The history of Japan from Kwammu to Meiji is not a history of emperors but of certain great families of whom the Fujiwaras were the first. Yet the really remarkable fact is the continued existence of the imperial house and the veneration in which it was held through all these vicissitudes. The period from the beginning of the 9th century to the middle of the 11th is commonly known as the period of the Fujiwaras. They were not like the later Shōguns, a military power which brought pressure to bear on the court: they ruled by identifying themselves with the imperial family. For instance, Fujiwara Michinaga (966–1027) who governed the country for thirty years, was the father-in-law of three emperors and the grandfather of four more. The emperors married Fujiwara ladies and their children were educated in Fujiwara palaces. Very often the emperor was a minor and in that case his maternal grandfather acted as regent. If he was of full age, a Fujiwara filled the office of Kwambaku, a sort of chancellor. If the emperor showed any inclination to assert himself, he generally had to retire to a monastery. During 200 years of Fujiwara rule there were fifteen emperors, of whom seven were minors and eight abdicated.

The Fujiwara or Heian period as it is sometimes called (Heiankyō, or capital of peace, being another name of Kyōto) was a peaceful time. There were, indeed, some disturbances, such as piracy and the short-lived attempt of Masakado (939) to make himself emperor in the Kwantō and there was in the north some fighting with the Ainus and with the Japanese family of Abe which had established itself there. But such distant troubles did not much affect the court at Kyōto. Literature, art and gallantry flourished. Buddhism also flourished and the great monasteries on Mount Hieizan began to acquire a dangerous importance in politics, as those of Nara had done before. Scholars like Kōbō Daishi and Dengyō Daishi visited China and brought back with them novelties in art and religion. As at Nara, everything Chinese was fashionable. The fault of this pleasant and cultured society was that being engrossed with its own refined amusements, it neglected the provinces where great estates continued to grow and attract the military spirit of the country.

Tenjin.—A picturesque figure of this period is Sugawara no Michizane, known to every Japanese as Tenjin. Though not of the Fujiwara stock, his talents and learning gained him high office early in life and the confidence of the Emperor Uda, who however retired to a monastery in 897 and abdicated in favour of his son Daigo, aged fifteen. He entrusted the youth's education to Michizane and intended to retain control of the Government with his assistance. This was more than the Fujiwaras could stand: the young Emperor had to sign an edict appointing Michizane viceroy of Kyushu, then regarded as a remote province, and the ex-Emperor protested in vain. But after Michizane's death at his distant post some years afterwards the country was visited with droughts, fires, floods and other calamities, in which popular imagination saw the vengeance of his indignant spirit. He was canonized as Tenjin Sama, the god of calligraphy, and his temples, marked by plum trees, of which he was specially fond, are to be found in most Japanese towns.

The first check to the power of the Fujiwara family was the reign of the Emperor Go-sanjō (1068–1072) who came to the throne because the Fujiwara bride selected as Empress for his predecessor was childless and who ruled with considerable independence. He seriously attacked the evils of provincial administration, ordered that no governor should hold office for more than one term and confiscated many *shōen* which could produce no title deeds. Unfortunately he reigned only four years. The next period, 1073–1156, is sometimes called the rule of the Cloistered Emperors, because the two sovereigns Shirakawa and Toba, though they became monks and nominally retired from the world, managed to keep the real power with a court and a council of their own, whereas the Fujiwara could only control the titular emperor, who was a minor. But the system did not work well. There was a natural conflict of authority between the two courts and the Cloistered Emperors, having become nominal monks, allowed the church to acquire great temporal power. Enormous sums were spent on building and adorning temples, and the monasteries of Hieizan, which had established the practice of keeping mercenaries, became veritable fortresses whence, if any ecclesiastical interest was at stake, armed forces used to descend into Kyōto to over-awe the Government. Even Shirakawa complained that, though he was emperor, there were three things he could not control: the inundations of the river Kamo, the hazards of the dice and the monks of Hieizan. The evils of provincial administration increased, for the court stultified its own edicts. It prohibited the extension of *shōen* but at the same time, being in need of money, it sold appointments and prolongation of office.

Taira and Minamoto.—Two great clans came specially to the front, the Taira and Minamoto: both were of imperial descent but both rose to power through the military services which they rendered, the first in western Japan, the second in the extreme north against the Ainu. Also the Cloistered Emperors established for their own protection a new body of guards in which both clans were employed, though special confidence was placed in the Taira. The contest between the two clans is often called the wars of Gempei.

Troubles about the succession in 1156 and a conspiracy in 1160, for taking part in which many Minamoto lost their lives, made the Taira supreme and Kiyomori, the head of the house, was practically a dictator until his death in 1181. The brief rule of the Taira does not seem to have been inspired by any original policy or to have had any special consequences for the history of Japan and it was unpopular. Kiyomori was haughty and exacting: he distributed all the great offices of state among his kinsmen: he made enemies of the Buddhist clergy, although when he was ill he took the tonsure according to the custom of the time and, strange to say, recovered: at great expense and inconvenience to both nobles and commoners he made the court remove for a time to Fukuwara near the modern Kobe where he had his private residence. Besides this, evils for which he was not responsible, pestilence, fire and famine ravaged Kyōto and though he died in peace himself, the rule of the Taira came to an end four years after his death and gave way to the Minamoto, led by Yoritomo.

Yoritomo.—Though the issue at stake was the supremacy of one or other family, Yoritomo began by having the support of many of the Taira, for Kiyomori had favoured only his own section of the clan and had made enemies of others. His first attempts during the life of Kiyomori were unsuccessful. He was captured and narrowly escaped being killed but was banished to Izu. Subsequently in the battle of Ichi-no-tani near Suma (1184) and the great sea-fight of Dan-no-ura (1185), the power of the Taira was completely crushed. These victories were mainly due to the genius of Yoshitsune, Yoritomo's younger half brother, and it is melancholy to relate that when Yoritomo's power was established he was not merely ungrateful but determined to remove his brother as a dangerous rival. Yoshitsune fled to northern Japan and when pursued by Yoritomo's assassins committed hara-kiri. But he lives in military history as one of the greatest Japanese strategists, and in art and romance he and his faithful henchman Benkei are still among the most popular heroes of the Japanese public.

THE KAMAKURA PERIOD

Instead of trying to rule the court at Kyōto as the Fujiwara and Taira had done, Yoritomo with the help of his celebrated counsellor, Oye Hiromoto, set up at Kamakura a new military government called the Bakufu with a council, home office, treasury and supreme law court of its own. The owners of *Shōen* were no longer allowed to appoint their own stewards. In each province was placed a High Constable (*Shugo*) whose duty was to raise troops and keep order, and a Land Steward (*Jito*) who collected taxes and superintended the administration of justice. Both officers were responsible to the Bakufu and not to the emperor or the owners of estates. Unlike Kiyomori, Yoritomo was careful to conciliate the Buddhist clergy and to show due deference to the emperor and court. The titles and property of the Kyōto nobles —called *kuge* or courtly houses as distinguished from *buke* or military houses—were duly respected and he himself obtained from the emperor the title of Sei-i-tai-Shōgun, which was equivalent to giving him a permanent commission to see to the defence and tranquillity of the empire. The title had been granted before to Tamuramaro (as mentioned above) and to others, but hitherto it had been limited in time and place whereas Yoritomo's mandate was permanent and for the whole empire. It is difficult to exaggerate the importance of the changes introduced by Yoritomo. Before his time, Japan means Kyōto and the neighbouring provinces. We hear of the west and the north-east as regions in which rebellions occasionally occurred and to which troublesome persons were banished. But now the size of the country seems more than doubled and the Kwanto emerges as an integral part of the empire, a civilized land with a great capital. Secondly, the Japanese character has at least two sides—one artistic and one military. The civilization of Nara and Kyōto and the open imitation of Chinese culture developed the former, not without danger of encouraging effeminacy. There was plenty of turbulence, it is true, even among the clergy but in reading the earlier chronicles one does not receive the impression that the Japanese were a nation of soldiers. But under the institutions of Yoritomo they became so. Except at the Court of Kyōto, the administration and social life were controlled by the military class. Yoritomo died in 1199. Though he founded a system of government, he did not found a dynasty. It is true that the Minamotos remained prominent in Japanese history, for both the Ashikagas and Tokugawas were branches of that family, but his own descendants did not rule.

Rule of the Hōjō.—The real power passed into the hands of the house of Hōjō, to which his wife belonged. They assumed the title of *Shikken*, constable or regent, and for about a century governed in the name of puppet Shōguns, much as the Fujiwaras had governed in the name of the emperor.

Yoritomo's two sons and nephew were allowed to succeed but after that the Shōguns were generally minors and chosen from among imperial princes. For some time the court at Kyōto had a certain independence. The chief power was in the hands of the ex-emperor Go-Toba, a man of ambition and some talent, who realizing that it was very hard for a titular sovereign to have much influence in Japan, had abdicated and was allowed to manipulate the succession among his sons as he pleased. In 1221 he made an attempt, in which he relied to a considerable extent on the military strength of the great monasteries, to break the power of the Kamakura Government. The attempt seems to have been premature and the exceedingly prompt action of the Hōjōs had no difficulty in crushing it immediately but it had important consequences. Go-Toba was banished, the Hōjōs took charge of the court and the imperial succession as the Fujiwaras had done and two of them were installed in Kyōto as military governors. More than this, 3,000 estates belonging to Go-Toba's adherents were confiscated and distributed among the supporters of the Bakufu, which materially strengthened the feudal system.

Mongol Invasion.—The most remarkable and creditable event in the Hōjō administration was the repulse of the Mongol invasion. In the 13th century the Yüan or Mongol dynasty seized the throne of China and also subdued Korea. This conquest brought them almost into contact with Japan and Khublai Khan came to the conclusion that it ought to accept his authority. So in 1268 he sent a patronizing letter addressed to the "King" of Japan, pointing out what had happened in Korea and asking that a mission might be sent to China. No answer was sent and in 1274 an attempt of the Mongols to land at Hakozaki in Kyushu was repulsed. Further envoys sent by Khublai were executed, so in 1281 he decided to despatch a really great expedition and chastise the Japanese. This aroused an outburst of patriotism in which the Buddhist Church took part. The forces of nature aided the Japanese: a great typhoon destroyed Khublai's armada and no more was heard of the Mongol peril.

But, in spite of this success, the Government of Kamakura became unpopular and inefficient. Takatoki, the ninth Hōjō Regent, was conspicuously debauched and extravagant. The central administration lost its hold on the provinces, and the old evil of independent fiefs, large and small, against which Yoritomo had legislated, reappeared. The military class were sinking deeper and deeper into penury and debt and their only hope was a successful war.

Go-Daigo.—Bad harvests and pestilence had brought the peasantry close to starvation. It had been the custom of the earlier Hōjōs to store grain and distribute it in times of need at low prices, but their successors, instead of following this wise custom, endeavoured to make money by selling it to the highest bidder. At Kyōto the practice of putting on the throne minors who abdicated early became increasingly frequent and at one time (1298-1304) there were no less than five ex-emperors alive. Go-Daigo, however, who succeeded in 1318, was of mature age and in a few years' time quarrelled with the Government of Kamakura because they refused to recognize his son as Prince Imperial on the ground that he was ineligible by the terms of a will made by the Emperor Go-Saga (1272). In the dispute which ensued the emperor was banished to the island of Oki but it was soon clear that the Hōjōs could not rely on the support of the country or even of their own nominal adherents.

Go-Daigo managed to escape from Oki in 1333: Ashikaga Takauchi who was sent against him went over to his side and in the east Nitta Yoshisada, another eminent general of the Bakufu, turned against them and burnt Kamakura. With the suicide of Hōjō Takatoki and 300 followers the rule of the Hōjō came to an end. The interesting events of the stormy half century which followed form the theme of many historical romances but are so complicated that they can only be summarized here very briefly. The period 1334-35 is often called the Restoration of Kemmu and it may seem that Go-Daigo, being left master of the situation, could have permanently restored the ancient imperial régime, especially as his own son was named titular Shōgun. But he evidently lacked the ability to do this, and he refused to follow the wise and cautious advice of his devoted follower Kutsunoki Masashige, celebrated as a model of self-sacrificing loyalty. The man who emerged as victor was Ashikaga Takauji. He proclaimed himself Shōgun in 1335. Go-Daigo refused to recognize him and fled with the regalia. On this Takauji deposed Go-Daigo and appointed to the throne an imperial prince who reigned as the Emperor Kōmyō and in return recognized him as Shōgun.

THE ASHIKAGA PERIOD

Thus began the Ashikaga line of Shōguns (1338-1565) and also a period of divided sovereignty which lasted 56 years, the Emperor Go-Daigo and his descendants reigning at Yoshino as the southern court and the Emperor Kōmyō and his descendants at Kyōto as the northern court. Though the former court is generally considered as legitimate, it ultimately had to yield and handed over the regalia to the court of Kyōto in 1392, when the double sovereignty ceased.

This arrangement was effected by Yoshimitsu, the third and ablest Shōgun (1367-1395) of the Ashikaga house, for he saw that the struggle between the rival courts was demoralizing authority, ruining the peasantry and giving over the whole country to lawlessness and brigandage. During most of the Ashikaga period the imperial dignity descended regularly from father to son: few sovereigns abdicated and the country was not distracted by ex-emperors ruling *de facto* without any constitutional warrant. The Shōguns resided in Kyōto but did not attempt to govern by making matrimonial alliances with the imperial family. The court simply subsided into the second place, chiefly because hardly any revenue reached it. Yoshimitsu also checked piracy and restored some sort of order in Kyushu. He re-established commercial and diplomatic relations with China and the results were lucrative, though he had incurred much censure from patriotic Japanese because in his official correspondence with the Ming emperor he tolerated and even used phrases which implied that Japan was a vassal state. Towards the end of his life he retired and became a monk, but continued to govern the country from his palace Kinkakuji (the golden temple) in Kyōto. After Yoshimitsu's death and especially from the rule of Yoshimasa the eighth Shōgun (1443-1474) onward, things went from bad to worse, but in reading the melancholy annals of the Ashikaga—one long catalogue of individual debauchery and tragedies and of ruinous wars between the great feudal houses—we must not forget that this was also the golden age of Japanese painting, when some of the best literature was produced and the Nō drama was invented. Art, it is true, flourished chiefly in monasteries and its inspiration, largely Chinese, was due to the intercourse with China promoted by Yoshimitsu's policy. Still, this art was by no means devoid of vigour and originality and the monasteries could not have produced such talent had the general intelligence of the age been stagnant. Disastrous as was the strife of noble houses, it at least stimulated the spirit of adventure and offered a career to men of ability, regardless of birth. The system of serfdom which had prevailed for more than a thousand years was broken up, and no chieftain could hope to hold his own unless he could attract men to his service and maintain a moderately just and efficient administration within his own domains.

Nevertheless, it is impossible to give a favourable account of either the capital or the provinces during the Ashikaga rule of 15 Shōguns. Eleven were minors at their accession, nine abdicated, five died in exile, and at least two came to violent ends. Just as the Hōjō regents had ruled instead of the Minamoto Shōguns, so officials called wardens (Kwanryō) took the power from the Ashikaga Shōguns and fought for it among themselves. This arrangement became so much a matter of course that the three houses (Shiba, Hosokawa and Hatakeyama) who claimed the right to hold the office were called Sankwan, or the three warden families. By the middle of the 15th century Kyōto was in ruins and reduced to a population of 22,000.

Nor were things any better in the provinces. Taxation is said to have amounted to 70% and the unfortunate cultivators had to pay not only regular imposts but also extraordinary taxes called Dansen levied for special purposes sometimes more than once in a year. This resulted in frequent popular tumults demanding a Tokusei or benevolent act of the Government, that is, cancellation of debts. In the time of Yoshimasa alone there were 13 such Tokusei. The Kwantō was governed by regents taken from another branch of the Ashikaga family, but after about 1440 their authority became precarious. The whole region was practically independent of Kyōto and the chief power was in the hands of the Uyesugi family. Disastrous dissensions in the great houses of Shiba and Hatakeyama known as the wars of Ōnin (from the name of the period when they began in 1467) wasted the country for ten years. Soon afterwards another war broke out, occasioned by internal jealousies of the Hosokawa family. But, long as the struggle lasted, it ended in nothing: the antagonists wore themselves out and in the 16th century both Ashikagas and Hosokawas disappeared. In this century, one of the most eventful in the history of Japan, two features are especially remarkable. The first is the almost simultaneous rise of three great men, Nobunaga (1534-1582), Hideyoshi (1536-1598) and Iyeyasu (1542-1616) whose successive efforts, though they consisted of little but war, ended by giving their country unity and peace. The second feature is the discovery of Japan by the Portuguese in 1542 and the arrival of European merchants and missionaries.

NOBUNAGA, HIDEYOSHI AND IYEYASU

It now becomes comparatively easy to follow one main thread in the history of Japan. An account of Nobunaga's conquests is an account of the successive withdrawal of various territories from chaotic feudalism to form the basis of a new Japanese empire. At the time that he was born, there was no central government. Though the emperors remained the fount of honour, they did not make a single public appearance between 1521 and 1587: the Shōguns were puppets in the hands of contending chieftains: the provinces ceased to be administrative areas and the only effective government was that exercised by the heads of the principal feudal houses in the lands—often comprising several provinces— which they had acquired by force of arms. The free city of Sakai near Osaka was an interesting but unique phenomenon. It had expelled its feudal lord, and the Jesuit Vilela says it was "governed by its own laws and customs in the fashion of Venice." An important factor in the situation was the temporal power of the Buddhist Church. Even more than before the larger monasteries became fortresses with lands, troops and secular ambitions. In spite of this worldly tendency Buddhism had shown itself in the preceding centuries by no means deficient in religious vigour. The preaching of Nichiren stimulated patriotism in the time of the Mongol invasions and out of the monasteries of Kyōto, wealthy foundations devoted to art and political intrigue, there arose in the 12th century sects analogous to Protestantism which preached with signal success simple doctrines intelligible to the masses. One of these sects called Shinshū allowed the clergy to marry, with the result that abbots became hereditary and even more like feudal lords than celibate prelates had been. In Echizen, Echigo, Kwantō and Kaga, the vast tracts ruled by religious establishments of this sect were hardly distinguishable from ordinary baronies, and Kennyō, the eleventh abbot, was accused of wishing to supplant the emperor.

Nobunaga.—Oda Nobunaga belonged to the Taira family and inherited a small fief in the province of Owari. He was a brilliant military genius and at that time the natural career for a man of his calibre was to extend his lands by conquest and, if possible, penetrate to Kyōto and get the Shōgun into his power. In executing this programme he had the assistance of Hideyoshi, a simple peasant said to have been remarkably ugly, who entered his service as a groom, and after his death surpassed his achievements and ended by administering the whole empire. Nobunaga also acted in concert with Iyeyasu, a rising young warrior of the Tokugawa family which was a branch of the Minamoto. By 1568 Nobunaga had taken possession of all Owari with the neighbouring provinces of Mino, Ise and Omi, had entered Kyōto and installed Yoshiaki, the last of the Ashikaga Shōguns.

Arrival of Portuguese and Jesuits.—It was in 1572 that Nobunaga first made the acquaintance of the Jesuits, to whose doings we must now turn. Thirty years earlier the hazard of a storm had driven a Portuguese ship which was bound for Macao to the coast of Tanegashima, an island lying off the extreme south of Kyushu. They were well received, and when the news of the discovery spread among the Portuguese establishments in the East seven expeditions were equipped in the next few years to exploit the new market. They traded in the ports of Kyushu and even visited Kyōto. In 1549 the first missionary, Xavier (*see* article XAVIER), landed at Kagoshima, accompanied by two Portuguese priests, and by a Japanese called Anjiro or Yajiro who had somehow found his way to Malacca. He was most favourably received by the Daimyō of Satsuma, who saw in his arrival a prospect of opening a lucrative trade with foreign markets. But the ships which were expected at Kagoshima, went to Hirado instead. In 1550 the disappointed Daimyō issued an edict in which he forbade Christianity, and the missionaries thereupon moved to Hirado. Here they were well received by the Portuguese merchants, who recommended them to the Japanese, and their preaching had some success. Xavier paid a fruitless visit to Kyōto, but his stay at Yamaguchi in western Japan and in the province of Bungo in Kyushu had more result. When he left, after spending about two years in Japan, it is said that he had baptized 760 persons. In the year following Xavier's departure more Jesuits arrived in Bungo, which was for some time the principal Christian centre. It was from there that they began to send to the General of their order in Rome the series of reports called *Annual Letters* which give a most valuable picture of contemporary Japan. The head of the Otomo family, the ruling house in the province, assisted them not only by encouragement in his own territories but by his influence among his neighbours. In Hirado the fortunes of Christianity varied: sometimes the desire to encourage trade at any price prevailed, but sometimes indignation at aggressive propaganda, and such outrages as burning temples, provoked restrictive legislation. Sumitada, chieftain of Omura, a fief near Hirado, became a most zealous Christian. He gave land and residences to the Jesuits, forced Christianity on his vassals by drastic means, and in 1567 built a church at Nagasaki, then an obscure fishing village. His object was to provide a centre for Portuguese trade and religion and he succeeded so well that in five years Nagasaki grew into a town of 30,000 inhabitants, while he himself became one of the most important feudal lords of Kyushu. His neighbour, the chieftain of Arima, thought it well to follow this example and became known to the Portuguese as Prince Andrew. In Arima and other places there were many vicissitudes, but on the whole the progress of Christianity was astonishing. The *Annual Letter* of 1582, only thirty-two years after the landing of Xavier, reports that there were 150,000 converts. In this year, too, at the suggestion of the Jesuit Valegnani, an embassy of four Japanese youths was despatched from Kyushu to the Pope and also visited Lisbon and Madrid. The vast majority of the conversions mentioned took place in Kyushu, but the propaganda of a Jesuit called Vilela had considerable results in Kyōto, and its success is interesting because his converts cannot have been actuated by commercial motives. In 1564 a chieftain called Takayama Yushō challenged Vilela to a public disputation and, admitting that he was vanquished, embraced Christianity with all his household and vassals. But in Kyōto too, the aggressiveness of the missionaries irritated the Buddhist clergy, who as early as 1565 and 1568 induced the emperor to issue two anti-Christian edicts, and it would probably have fared ill with the new religion but for the constant support of Nobunaga, who was now the most powerful man in Japan and who ruled 30 out of the 66 provinces. He assisted and protected the Jesuits in every way he could and even built a house and church for them in the new city of Azuchi which he constructed on the shores of Lake Biwa. Nobunaga never showed the slightest sign of becoming a Christian himself but, like many Japanese, he was anxious to learn all he could from Europeans, and he was also actuated by violent hatred of the Buddhist priesthood. In his early struggles they had taken sides against him and in 1570 they were a menace to his rule in Kyōto. In that year the Miyoshi family threatened the city in conjunction with the Shinshū priests of Osaka, whose temple there was one of the strongest fortresses in Japan, and while he was occupied with them his enemies, the nobles of Echizen and Omi, planned another attack with the help of the monasteries of Hieizan. As soon as he had disposed of his lay enemies Nobunaga made a sudden attack on this holy mountain and, after perpetrating an appalling massacre, burnt the monasteries of which there are said to have been 3,000. He was not quite so successful in dealing with the temple fortress of Osaka which, under the command of the abbot Kennyō, a most capable soldier, withstood a long siege until both parties agreed to accept the mediation of the emperor, who evidently regarded this open war with a religious body as a public scandal. Nobunaga's stormy career now came to an unexpected close. He had sent Hideyoshi to the west in order to subdue the powerful Daimyō of Chōshū near the straits of Shimonoseki. In June 1582 a body of troops under Akechi Mitsuhide which was meant to reinforce this expedition suddenly turned on Kyōto. The motives of Mitsuhide, who was killed in the struggle, have never been satisfactorily explained. Possibly he was avenging some ancient insult. At any rate he attacked Nobunaga's house and the latter, being unable to escape, committed suicide.

Hideyoshi.—Nobunaga was a considerable military genius but not of any administrative ability. He had, however, made his age familiar with the idea that supreme authority under the emperor was vested in one man, and Hideyoshi, the peasant who had been his groom, who had become his trusted lieutenant, and who now took his place, made the most of this idea and in eight years' time became both military and civil master of the whole country. At first the question of succession presented some difficulty. Hideyoshi supported the claims of the child of Nobunaga's deceased eldest son and constituted himself the infant's guardian. Nobunaga's other sons objected and one of them, Nobuo, ultimately took the field and had the support of Iyeyasu. But when Iyeyasu and Hideyoshi, who had formerly worked together, found themselves pitted against one another, they thought that the question at issue was not worth a conflict and made a compact which they confirmed by a matrimonial alliance. None of Nobunaga's descendants ultimately played any political rôle of importance and Nobuo subsequently fought for Hideyoshi. In the first years of his rule Hideyoshi conducted a vigorous and successful campaign against Echizen and, as a result, four provinces on the Sea of Japan submitted to him. He also subdued the island of Shikoku which had become a practically independent principality under Chōsokabe of Tosa. But, more than this, he began to organize an efficient system of central government supervised by five ministers called Bugyō, and to reform the administration of justice and the coinage. In 1585 he received from the court the title of Kwampaku and was master of all Japan except Kyushu and the Kwantō with the provinces to the north of it. He now turned his attention to these two regions, beginning with Kyushu. The warlike Shimazus of Satsuma had been advancing towards the north and threatened Bungo among other provinces. The chieftain of Bungo asked Hideyoshi to intervene. He gladly did so and when he received a defiant answer to his representations from Satsuma, he invaded the island and reduced it to submission, but was careful to show a wise clemency to the powerful house of Shimazu.

Christianity.—This expedition brought Hideyoshi into contact with Christianity as a political power and led to the restrictive edicts which caused the Jesuits to execrate his name. Up to this time he had shown no animus against them and he certainly was not prejudiced in favour of Buddhism, for he had an old quarrel with the monastery of Negoro, which he burnt in 1584. In the main island the Jesuits had confined their activity to religious matters, but what Hideyoshi saw and heard in Kyushu evidently convinced him that they were not merely a new sect but that they aimed at establishing an *imperium in imperio* and were a danger to the State. He was careful to complete his campaign before making new enemies, but when on his return journey he reached Hakata in the north of the island he unexpectedly caused five questions to be put to the vice-provincial of an order which sufficiently indicate the nature of his suspicions. On what authority, he asked, do the Jesuits constrain Japanese subjects to become Christians? Why do they incite their disciples to destroy temples? Why do they persecute Buddhist priests? Why do they eat animals useful to men, such as cattle? Why do they allow Portuguese to carry off Japanese and make slaves of them in the Indies? The answers to these questions were not considered satisfactory and an edict was immediately published (1587) ordering foreign priests to leave the country within 20 days on pain of death. Portuguese merchants, however, were allowed to remain. But this ordinance was not put into force. A certain

BY COURTESY OF THE Y.W.C.A.
JAPANESE GIRLS IN NATIVE GARB

number of churches were destroyed, but Hideyoshi was clement by nature and desirous to reap the advantages of foreign trade. He winked at the infractions of his edict and in the years following it, though the Christians were obliged to behave with more moderation, their numbers seem to have increased, for in 1595 we are told there were 137 Jesuits in Japan and 300,000 converts. But in 1597 he became uncompromisingly severe, the reason for this change of attitude being apparently the arrival of Spaniards.

Spaniards.—In virtue of a papal bull, accepted by both Spain and Portugal, the latter enjoyed a monopoly of religious propaganda and trade in Japan. But in 1593 a party of Franciscans, describing themselves as envoys, arrived from Manila and were well received. They quarrelled with the Jesuits, against whom they made accusations to the Japanese authorities. About the same time a Spanish ship was stranded on the coast of Tosa and, according to the story, the pilot being anxious to impress the Japanese, dilated on the Spanish conquests and when asked how they had been made replied that "the Catholic king first sent ministers of the Gospel to convert the natives, who afterwards uniting with the captains of his majesty made their work of conquest easier." This remark, whether historical or not, is no doubt a correct epitome of Hideyoshi's suspicions. He was seized with a fury against missionaries: 26 Christians, native and foreign, were executed, many churches were destroyed: feudal chiefs were forbidden to become Christians, and all Jesuits were commanded to leave the country. But they managed to evade the order for some time and before it could be rigorously enforced Hideyoshi died. We must now return to his other doings.

After his successful expedition to Kyushu, only the east and north remained to be subdued. The northern districts were not in a position to offer much resistance but the provinces called Kwantō were practically a powerful independent kingdom ruled by Hōjō Ujimasa. This family of Hōjōs had nothing to do with the great but now extinct house of Kamakura. They had come from Ise about a century before and established themselves at Odawara in a strong position. As they refused to come to Kyōto and do homage to the emperor, who was still recognized as the nominal sovereign, Hideyoshi, Iyeyasu and Nobuo marched against them in 1590 with an army of 250,000 men and received their submission before the end of the year. The castle of Odawara

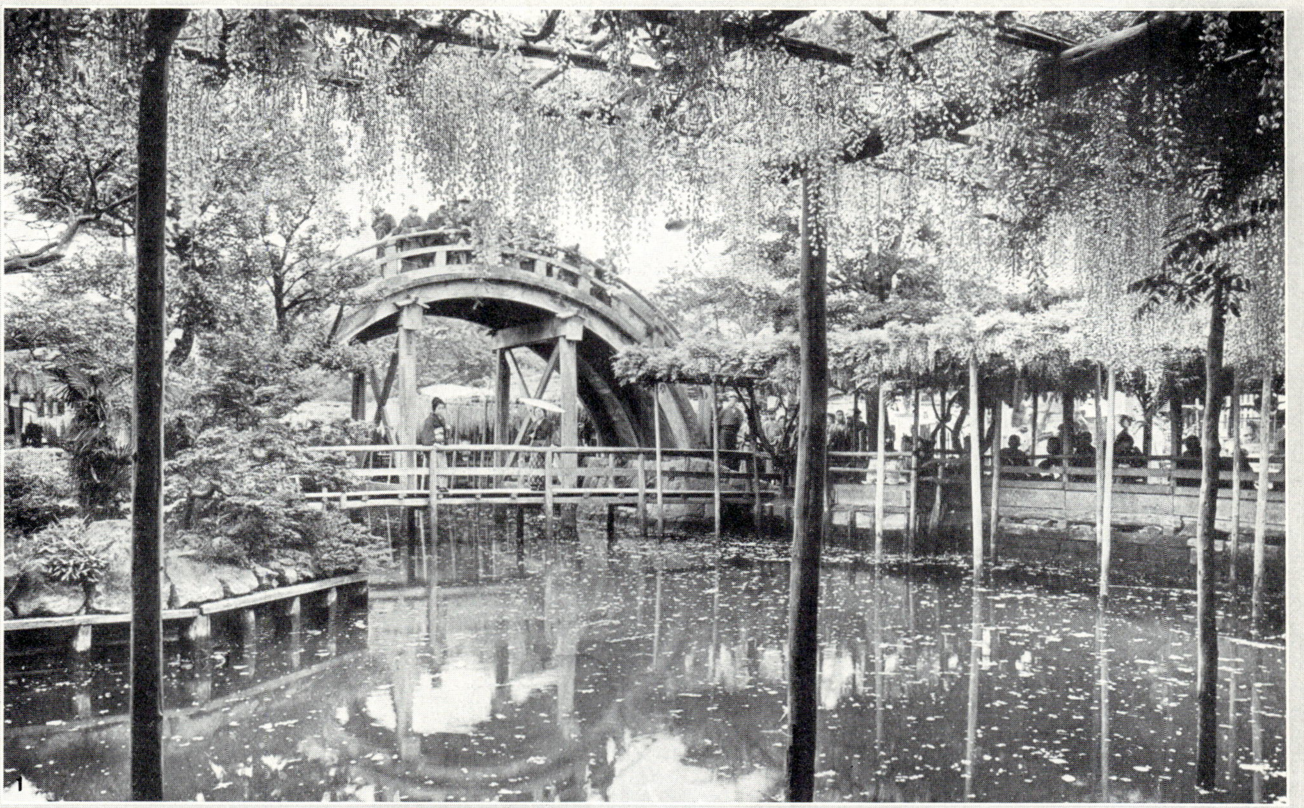

BY COURTESY OF HERBERT G. PONTING, F.R.P.S.

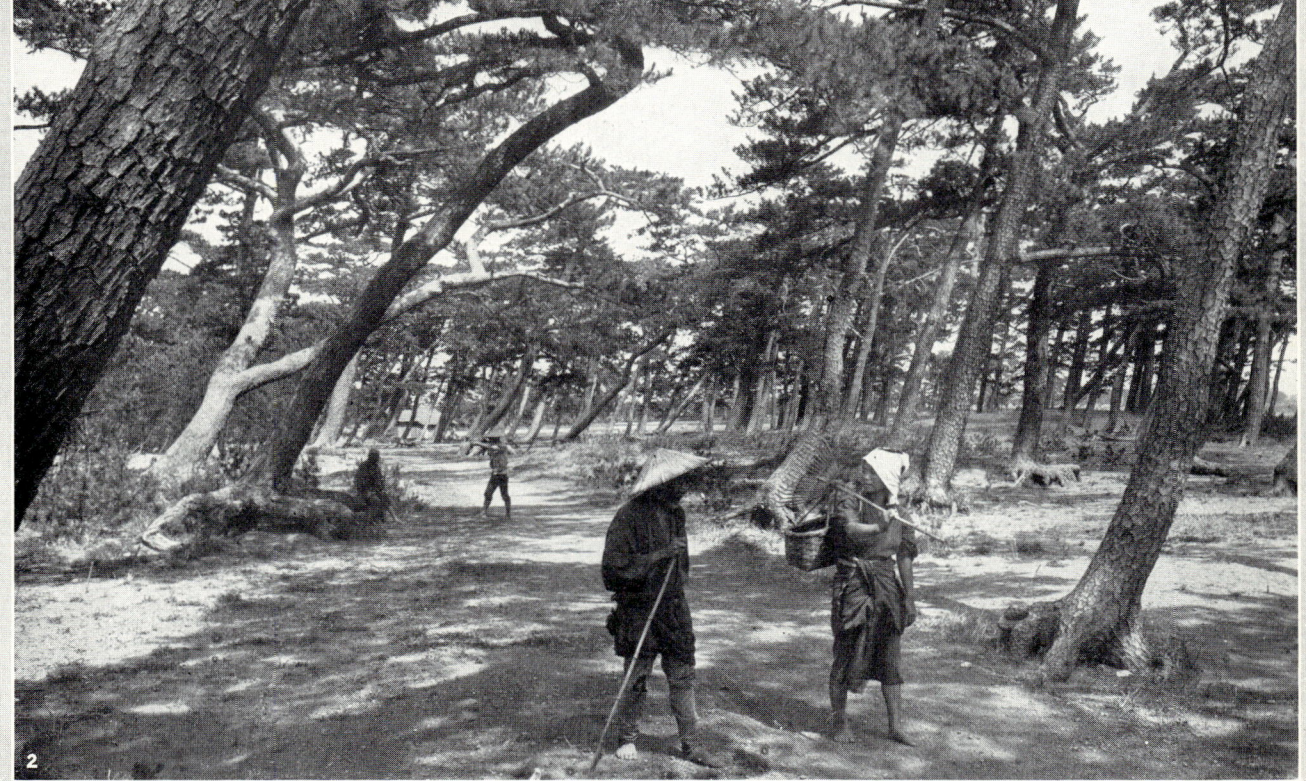

THE GROUNDS OF TWO JAPANESE TEMPLES

1. Wistaria garden in Kameido (in the environs of Tokyo). The gardens are part of the grounds of a Shinto temple dedicated to Sugawarano-Michizano, a court minister who died in A.D. 903. The photograph shows the Taikobashi or "drum bridge" in front of the temple.
2. The pine-clad sands of the peninsula Mio-no-Matsubara, near Shizuoka, where the Shrine of Mio stands

PLATE II JAPAN

BY COURTESY OF HERBERT G. PONTING, F.R.P.S.

ASPECTS OF JAPANESE LIFE

1. **A tea-bearing hillside and a plain chequered with rice fields.** About two-thirds of the tea-crop of Japan is consumed in the country. Rice is cultivated extensively on irrigable ground

2. **Japanese ladies travelling in 'Kago.'** The bearers' wide straw hats are typical of Japanese dress as are the sandals, held by a cord between the great and second toe

had to surrender in 1590. The Daimyōs of the north also tendered their submission. This time Hideyoshi treated his vanquished enemies with unusual severity. The Hōjōs were ordered to commit suicide and their provinces were given to Iyeyasu who was recognized as ruler of the Kwantō. Hideyoshi's return to Kyōto was a veritable triumph. Custom would not allow him to become Shōgun, for the office was restricted by tradition to those of Minamoto lineage, but in 1591 he received at his own request the title of Taikō by which he is generally known. This title, which had fallen out of use, had formerly been used by the Fujiwara, when they retired from the office of Kwampaku. Hideyoshi was now master of the whole country and has been called the Napoleon of Japan. There is some truth in this name, for he began to show signs of overweening ambition.

Korean War.—Hitherto his objects had been eminently reasonable—for who can doubt that Japan needed unification?—but he now aimed at the conquest not merely of Korea, but of China. His motives are unknown. The Jesuits assert that his prime object was to acquire land outside Japan where he could settle all the Christian nobles and Samurai, and keep them out of mischief. But though he sent 20,000 Christian troops to Korea, and may have thought it a good plan to leave them there, this is not likely to have been his chief reason for embarking on so great and dangerous an enterprise. Remarks attributed to him earlier in his career suggest that he had long cherished the scheme: he was undoubtedly impressed with the value of foreign commerce, and acquaintance with the Spaniards and Portuguese may have opened his eyes to the advantage of foreign conquests. Also he probably found it easier to subdue Japan than to rule it in peace. Though he had broken the power of the ancient great houses so completely that only five of them were left, the country was full of new military leaders who were ready enough to follow him in any profitable adventure but who, he may have felt, were likely to grow restless in peace and quiet. At any rate as early as 1587 he complained to the Korean court of their failure to send embassies to Kyōto. The diplomatic correspondence which ensued was not altogether amicable and it is noticeable that in writing to the king of Korea (as also to the Spanish governors of the Indies and Philippines) Hideyoshi expressed himself as if he were sovereign of Japan and made no allusion to the emperor. Finally he informed the king of his intention to invade China and called for his co-operation. The king of Korea refused and is said to have remarked that the idea of conquering China was like "a bee trying to sting a tortoise through its armour." However, an army of some 300,000 men was prepared and despatched against Korea in May, 1592, from Nagoya in Hizen where Hideyoshi spent more than a year superintending the preparations. He did not go to Korea himself and Ukida Hideiye was named commander-in-chief. Transport was, of course, the great difficulty but every feudatory was ordered to furnish ships in proportion to his revenue. The plan of campaign was to divide the invading force into three parts. The van, consisting of three army corps, was to land at Fusan and advance at once on Seoul by three routes, eastern, central and western. Then four more corps together with the troops under the direct orders of the commander-in-chief were to cross and effectually subdue the regions through which the van had passed. Finally two more corps were to be sent by sea up the western coast to Phyong-Yang (Heijo) and there join the van, which by that time would be preparing to march into China across the Yalu river. The first part of this programme was duly executed. Before autumn the first and second parts of the expedition occupied Seoul and Phyong-Yang, but disasters at sea prevented the third portion from reinforcing the troops which were to advance into China. At this period the Japanese had nothing which could be called men-of-war, but merely open transports propelled by rowing. The Koreans, however, who had been taught by experience in fighting pirates, had "turtle-shell" ships, which, being covered and protected, gave them a great advantage. The Japanese flotilla was practically destroyed and thus the troops already in Korea were isolated from their base. In October the Chinese awoke to the fact that their territory was threatened with invasion, but with their usual self-confidence thought it sufficient to send 5,000 men across the Yalu. The Japanese had no difficulty in routing this small force, but then the tide turned. The Government of Peking at last realized the danger and despatched a considerable army. The Japanese troops had to evacuate Phyong-Yang and fall back on Seoul and to evacuate that city in turn in May 1593. Though after this the Chinese gained no more victories, and though the war continued until 1598 not wholly unsuccessfully for the Japanese, yet from this point onwards it ceased to be an attempt at conquest. The Japanese held a line of forts along the southern coasts of Korea and took the fortress of Chinju with a terrific slaughter of Koreans but Hideyoshi devoted his attention chiefly to obtaining honourable terms of peace. The negotiations were slow, for though the Chinese seem to have been willing to make terms, the Koreans were not. At last, in 1596, a Chinese embassy was received by Hideyoshi at Osaka, but when the envoys handed him a patronizing missive from the Ming emperor recognizing him as king of Japan he flew into a passion and sent them back. Large reinforcements were despatched to Korea next year and this time the Japanese were successful in a naval engagement, which secured their communications. The Chinese also sent reinforcements and the struggle recommenced. In October 1598 the Satsuma detachment of Japanese troops gained a victory of which a gruesome memorial still survives in the Mimizuka or Ear mound at Kyōto. It is said that 38,000 of the enemy fell. Their ears were cut off, packed in barrels and sent to the capital where they were buried under this tumulus. This was followed by a brilliant Japanese victory at Junten, but meanwhile, though it was not known in Korea at the time, Hideyoshi had died on September 16th. It is said that before his death he requested Iyeyasu to arrange for the immediate termination of hostilities. At any rate, a general withdrawal of troops from the peninsula was at once begun, though not without difficulty, since, in spite of the armistice, the Chinese and Koreans attacked the transports. The exact date when diplomatic relations were resumed is uncertain but it was soon after 1600.

Iyeyasu and Hideyori.—The question of Hideyoshi's successor now became all important. His son had died and in 1598 he handed over the office of Kwampaku to his nephew Hidetsugu, a man of some ability but of an extremely cruel isposition, whom he intended to make his heir. But in the same year one of his wives bore him another son who received the name of Hideyori. Hideyoshi then quarrelled with his nephew, who was finally ordered to commit suicide, and the infant Hideyori was recognized as heir apparent. At the time of Hideyoshi's death Iyeyasu was the most important Daimyō in Japan. He ruled the Kwantō and his new fortress town of Yedo was rapidly growing. The dying Taikō asked him to become the guardian of his son. Iyeyasu was unwilling to do this, but by the Taikō's last instructions he was installed as chief of a board of five regents and Hideyori with his mother resided in the great castle which his father had built at Osaka. The board of five ministers appointed in 1585 was retained to administer the country under the direction of the five regents who collectively acted as Taikō, yet another board, called middle counsellors, being appointed to arrange all difficulties which might arise between the two bodies. But this complicated arrangement did not work well, and the divergences of opinion between the two boards gradually took the form of a more personal quarrel between Iyeyasu and Ishida Mitsunari, a man of great ability who had been easily first among the ministers and now found himself overshadowed by the regents. He formed a powerful combination against Iyeyasu, charged him with disobeying the Taikō's last instructions and practically declared war. Iyeyasu, however, showed even greater ability in forming a counter-combination and in inducing Ishida's confederates not to give him effective support. The issue was decided at the great battle of Sekigahara in the province of Mino on Oct. 21, 1600, one of the most important dates in Japanese history as it practically inaugurated the Tokugawa régime. Iyeyasu, however, for the moment took no steps against Hideyori but absolved him and his mother of all complicity and proceeded to consolidate his own power. As the Tokugawa family were a branch of the Minamoto, he was eligible as Shōgun and he obtained this title from the emperor. Strictly speaking, it had been in abeyance for only six years, as the last of the Ashikagas lived on in obscurity until 1597, and Iyeyasu himself held it for only two years for, following the inveterate Japanese habit of abdicating while retaining the real power, he ceded the title to his son Hidetada in 1605. He fixed his residence at Shizuoka and for some time kept on friendly terms with the young Hideyori, who was encouraged (perhaps in order to get rid of some of his great wealth), to re-erect the temple of Hokoji in Kyōto and a colossal image which had been set up by his father but destroyed in the earthquake of 1596. When the building was ready, Iyeyasu objected to the inscription placed on a bell and forbade the dedication ceremony. Subsequent explanations did not remove the misunderstanding—if indeed there really was one—and a breach became inevitable. Hideyori and his advisers invited to Osaka all who had suffered by the general redistribution of fiefs which took place after the battle of Sekigahara and finally Iyeyasu besieged the castle at the end of 1614. The resistance was stubborn and in Jan. 1615 a peace was arranged, one of the terms being that the moats should be filled in and the outer ramparts demolished. This considerably reduced the strength of the defences and Iyeyasu found a pretext to renew the siege in May. The fortress was stormed at last. Hideyori committed suicide: his cause collapsed and Iyeyasu's rule was undisputed.

THE TOKUGAWA PERIOD

The Dutch.—It was at this time that the Dutch first landed in Japan. In 1600 the "Liefde" was towed into the harbour of Funai in Bungo after a terrible voyage. On board was the "pilot major" of the expedition, an Englishman, Will Adams of Kent, whom Iyeyasu summoned to Osaka and honoured with his confidence. Adams was made master ship-builder to the Yedo Government, was employed as adviser and diplomatic agent in dealing with foreigners and received a substantial estate. He died in Japan in 1620. In 1605 the Shōgun gave the Dutch a licence to trade and four years later the Dutch East India Company established a factory in Hirado.

Adams, Saris and Cocks.—In 1613 an English factory was established there by Capt. John Saris of the "Clove." Saris received from Iyeyasu a most liberal charter which stated that "ground in Yedo in the place which they may desire shall be given to the English and they may erect houses and reside and trade there." Adams, who entered the service of the company, strongly advised that Uraga in the neighbourhood of Yedo was a better site than Hirado, but Saris would not listen. The enterprise was not successful, possibly because Iyeyasu's wish that Yedo should be its headquarters was disregarded. Saris departed in 1613 leaving Richard Cocks behind him as chief merchant. Cocks kept a diary which contains interesting information, but he was apparently not a good man of business: the "English House" came to an end after a troubled existence of ten years and was dissolved with a loss.

Christianity.—Iyeyasu seems, like Hideyoshi, to have started with no prejudice against Christianity but, like him, to have come to the conclusion that the Church as administered by Spanish and Portuguese priests was a dangerous political machine. Will Adams explained to him the difference between Roman Catholics and Protestants and how in Europe Catholic priests had been expelled from Protestant countries. The Portuguese Jesuits did all they could to calumniate the Spanish Franciscans and urged the Government to expel them. More than once the Spaniards advised the expulsion of the Dutch, and in 1611 an envoy sent by the viceroy of New Spain actually proposed to send Spanish men-of-war to burn all Dutch ships found in Japanese ports. Some incidents in Japan also roused Iyeyasu's suspicions. The Christian Prince of Arima endeavoured to obtain some disputed territory by means of forged documents and was most severely punished. All Christians holding offices at court were at the same time dismissed. The Spaniards had obtained permission to survey the Japanese coast, the Government seeing no harm in what was then a novel request, but when a Franciscan friar called Sotelo hastened to take an active part in the survey, suspicions were aroused. Although Hideyoshi's edict of 1593 was in force, Sotelo opened an oratory in Yedo and held services. He himself was merely imprisoned for a short time but his converts were executed. Some Christians were also executed in Nagasaki, and Iyeyasu was much annoyed because their remains were worshipped as relics. On Jan. 27, 1614, a proclamation was issued suppressing Christianity. It directed that all foreign priests should be collected at Nagasaki and then removed: that all churches should be destroyed and that Japanese converts should be compelled to renounce their faith. As on previous occasions the priests refused to comply and either hid in Japan or returned after a short absence. The siege of Osaka distracted Iyeyasu's attention but did not mollify his severity, for there were many Christians on Hideyori's side.

A somewhat perplexing incident of this period is the despatch of an embassy to the pope and the king of Spain by Date Masamune, Daimyō of Sendai. He was a patron of art and literature as well as a most successful warrior and may well have been in favour of foreign trade and interested in Christianity. But it is not clear why he should have thus taken the initiative in approaching European powers. Perhaps at this moment Iyeyasu, who was cognizant of the whole business, may have been glad to have more information about Europe and have thought it a good thing to send a mission which could not be represented as coming from the Japanese Government if its credentials were seriously examined. Date obtained the release of the Father Sotelo mentioned above and despatched him in 1613 with one of his retainers called Hasekura and 60 persons to Mexico and thence to Spain and Rome. Hasekura was solemnly baptized in the presence of Philip III. and received with great pomp by the pope. When the mission returned in 1620, Date's views on religion and foreign policy had apparently changed. Its members were ordered to renounce Christianity, but Hasekura refused to do so and was not persecuted. Sotelo was less fortunate. On his way back he was detained two years in Manila and when he at last reached Japan he was imprisoned and ultimately burned.

Iyeyasu.—Iyeyasu died in 1616 and next year his remains were transferred with great pomp to Nikko. A well-known caricature represents Nobunaga as grinding flour, Hideyoshi as baking, and Iyeyasu as eating the cake. It may, perhaps, be said that he snatched it from Hideyoshi's heir and certainly statesman-like—a non-moral adjective—is the gentlest term that can be used to describe the proceedings by which he removed Hideyori. But it is hardly doubtful that the removal was for the good of Japan, for had Hideyori remained, Japan seemed likely to relapse into its previous woeful condition of internecine war. Iyeyasu had not perhaps the genius of Hideyoshi. On the other hand he avoided such perilous ventures as the Korean war and with admirable sagacity so consolidated and organized the system of Government that it remained almost unchanged in the hands of his descendants for two centuries and a half. Although he inaugurated the Tokugawa era, yet he was not responsible for the best known feature of it, namely, the seclusion of Japan and the almost complete expulsion of foreigners. Had he lived longer he might, like his grandson, have found this policy necessary, but up to the end of his life he drew a distinction between foreign trade and missionary enterprise. The former he wished to encourage: the latter he considered a political danger as preparing the way for foreign aggression and tending to draw Japanese away from their natural allegiance. But under his rule there were no executions of foreign missionaries. Before describing the conditions of Japan in the Tokugawa period it will be well to recount how in the next few decades the comparatively liberal principles of Iyeyasu gave way to the exclusion policy of Iyemitsu.

Exclusion Policy.—In 1616 Iyeyasu was succeeded by his son Hidetada who had already been nominal Shōgun for 11 years. A few months after his father's death he issued an edict against Christianity severer than any which had preceded it, although its enforcement was postponed until the next year on account of the obsequies of Iyeyasu. It again ordered the expulsion of all foreign Christian priests, and for the first time it was now declared a capital offence for any Japanese to become a Christian or have any connection with Christian missionaries, the punishment being death by burning and confiscation of property. Moreover, Daimyōs were forbidden to keep Christians in their service or on their estates.

The Government probably thought that Christianity could be stamped out without much bloodshed, for in many districts Japanese had been forcibly converted wholesale by order of their feudal lords. But, as on previous occasions, the missionaries refused to leave. Japanese Christians, too, who, apart from religious convictions, had learnt from feudal warfare that loyalty to a cause is the first of human duties, showed extraordinary fortitude. There seem to be no accurate statistics of the number of native victims but it must have been very large. Japanese records speak of 200,000 persons being "punished," but this does not mean executed. The Jesuit Father Cardim gives a list of between 1,400 and 1,500 martyrs. Several foreigners perished. Two priests, de l'Assumpcion and Machado, who had been deported returned in 1617 and were decapitated. Instead of inspiring terror their execution gave new courage: thousands flocked to their tomb, which was believed to work miracles, and the two vice-provincials of Augustinians and Dominicans came out of hiding and started open propaganda. They were beheaded secretly. After some isolated executions of foreigners, there occurred in 1622 what was known as "the great martyrdom of Nagasaki," when 25 persons (including nine foreign priests) were burnt alive and 30 others were beheaded.

Iyemitsu.—Hidetada nominally abdicated in 1623 in favour of his son Iyemitsu and died in 1632. On becoming Shōgun Iyemitsu reissued the existing anti-Christian decrees, and 300 persons were executed in the immediate domains of the Tokugawa family, where hitherto there had not been much persecution. But it now continued uninterruptedly throughout Japan, being most violent in Kyushu because there were more Christians in that island than elsewhere, and the governors of Nagasaki were exceptionally rigorous.

Shimabara.—The last act of this tragedy is known as the Shimabara revolt. This district is a peninsula to the east of Nagasaki and opposite to it is the large island of Amakusa. In both Christianity had taken root earlier and more thoroughly than anywhere else in Japan and both had been the scene of severe persecutions. At the end of 1637 they rose in open rebellion. The old Dutch and Portuguese historians are disposed to regard this rising as mainly an agrarian revolt due to economic causes, especially over-taxation, whereas Japanese authorities treat it as a religious and political insurrection. Both causes were probably operative but it seems certain that for a long time the most stubborn and militant Christians had been collecting in this district, prepared to make a last stand. At the beginning of 1638 the insurgents withdrew from the island and fortified the ruined castle of Hara, where they defended themselves—some 37,000 men, women and children—for about three months against the forces sent to subdue them. Dutch ships assisted the Shōgun's troops in the siege and fired on the castle. When it was at last stormed an appalling massacre took place. Only 105 prisoners were taken and Christianity in Japan was practically suppressed. After this we hear of comparatively few martyrs. In Nagasaki and the neighbourhood the practice of Efumi, that is, trampling on pictures of Christ or the Virgin and Child, was enforced in the first month of each year. All the inhabitants, even children, were required to perform this ceremony to show that they did not belong to what was called the "wicked sect." The assertion that the Dutch complied with this regulation in order to ingratiate themselves with the authorities, though often made, seems not to be proved. The ceremony was not officially abolished until 1856. Yet it is said that Christianity was not entirely exterminated and that when the country was thrown open to foreigners in 1858, Roman Catholic priests found some of their co-religionists in Kyushu and Sado who had maintained their worship in secret.

Anti-foreign Legislation.—But the political consequences of the insurrection were most important. It is clear that the Tokugawa court were obsessed with the idea that foreigners were planning some sort of aggressive action. Hidetada had already got rid of the Spaniards, being moved chiefly by the reports of an investigator, Ibi Masayoshi, whom he had sent to make confidential enquiries in Europe. Whereas his father had sent envoys to Manila, he refused to receive a Philippine embassy in 1624, and an edict was published ordering all Spaniards to be deported. Thus intercourse between the Japanese and Spaniards came to an end after lasting 32 years (1592–1624) but the Portuguese were allowed to trade at Nagasaki for 15 years longer. In this period the Tokugawa government clearly became more and more anti-foreign. In 1636 it was enacted that no Japanese vessel and no Japanese subject should go abroad under pain of death; that all descendants of Spaniards should be expelled; and that no ships large enough to cross the ocean should be constructed. At the same time many restrictions were placed on the Portuguese and in Nagasaki the artificial island of Deshima was constructed for their reception in front of the former Portuguese factory. In 1638 an edict was issued saying that since the Portuguese had continued to bring missionaries into Japan in spite of previous edicts, and since they had instigated the Shimabara rebellion, from that time onwards every Portuguese ship coming to Japan should be burnt with all her cargo and that all on board her should be executed. The Portuguese were most unwilling to abandon their profitable commerce. Four elderly and respected citizens of Macao were sent to Nagasaki on a special vessel carrying presents but no cargo, with instructions to explain that the Portuguese had no connection with the late rebellion and that the cessation of trade would injure Japan as much as Portugal. Their reception showed that the Japanese were in earnest. By order of the Shōgun to whom their arrival was reported the envoys and 57 of their companions were beheaded, 13 being sent back to Macao to tell the tale with a message which bade the Portuguese "think no more of us just as if we were no longer in the world." In spite of this very decided answer the Portuguese made one more attempt. For some years they had been subject to Spain. When they recovered their independence, Don Gonzalo di Siqueira was sent in 1647 with two vessels to explain that Portugal was now actually at war with Spain, and to urge that commercial relations with Japan should be reopened. But the reception was not much better than before. There was, indeed, no bloodshed but the Portuguese were surrounded by armed men and were glad to escape with their lives.

Now came the turn of the Dutch. Though they lost no opportunity of explaining to the Japanese that they did not belong to the same religion as the Spaniards and Portuguese and though they showed their animosity to Catholicism on many occasions, notably at the siege of Hara mentioned above, they did not escape suspicion and evidently there was a strong party against them at the Shōgun's court. Their factory was at Hirado and, apart from foreign politics, the authorities of Yedo were not disposed to see the Daimyōs of Kyushu, always ready to become semi-independent, strengthened by overseas trade. The governor of Ft. Zelandia in Formosa was badly received when he visited Yedo in 1627 and he subsequently quarrelled with a Japanese vessel in his own territory. As a result the Dutch factory at Hirado was suspended for four years and when it re-opened irksome restrictions on the sale of goods were imposed and there was much vexatious interference. The governor of Batavia sent an envoy to remonstrate and appeal to Iyeyasu's charter. But he was merely informed that the Japanese Government attached no importance to foreign trade and that the Dutch might remain only on condition of leaving Hirado and living in Nagasaki.

Dutch at Deshima.—Here their residence was restricted to Deshima, the artificial island which had been constructed for the reception of the Portuguese. It was not more than 300 paces in any direction and lay close to the shore with which it was connected by a bridge. Within these narrow limits and under almost intolerable conditions, the Dutch factory existed for more than two centuries. Communication with the shore and even domestic life on the island were subject to rigorous police surveillance and, though as time went on this severity was somewhat relaxed, the existence of the Dutch merchants was always humiliating. Their only outing was an annual mission to Yedo to offer presents to the Shōgun and his court. We have a picture of one of these missions and of the life at Deshima from the pen of Kaempfer, a Westphalian who entered the service of the Dutch East India Company and arriving in Japan in 1690 spent two years there. According to his account the mission was on the whole well treated though subjected to disagreeable espionage, and he gives a strange description of how they appeared before the Shōgun and were obliged to dance, jump, pretend to be drunk, and perform other antics supposed to be illustrative of European life.

The question of allowing the British to trade in Japan never arose, because the British factory in Hirado, not being a financial success, was voluntarily closed in 1623 before serious friction between the Japanese Government and foreigners had begun. In 1673 the English East India Company attempted to reopen its trade and sent to Nagasaki a ship called the "Return" with a copy of the privileges granted to the former factory at Hirado, asking for their renewal. The vessel was not roughly treated but the crew were not allowed to land and the only reply vouchsafed was "that since our King (Charles II.) was married with the daughter of Portugal, their enemy, they could not admit us to have any trade and for no other reason." The seclusion of Japan was thus complete.

No Japanese might go abroad and no foreigner might come to Japan except a limited number of Dutch under special conditions as described. This state of things continued until American ships under Commodore Perry arrived in 1853.

Tokugawa Social System.—Iyemitsu, the third Shōgun, who ruled without abdicating until his death in 1631, is justly regarded as the chief author of the singular social system which prevailed in the Tokugawa period. But though he was of a haughty and imperious disposition, it is clear that his counsellors and the general opinion of the country saw no objection to his institutions. Japan of this time is well described in a document called the Legacy of Iyeyasu, which may contain some principles of its reputed author but was certainly not completed in its present form until the reign of Iyemitsu. But, though it may be called a forgery, it is a purely Japanese production and good evidence of custom and sentiment in the middle of the 17th century. In a hundred short sections it describes the constitution of society and the proper working of government. The Japanese were familiar with the division of society into three classes, the court nobles (*Kuge*), the military class (*Buke* or *Samurai*) and the common people (*Heimin*). This division was maintained theoretically by the Tokugawas but they also sanctioned the change which had gradually grown up in the period of internal war, namely the practical pre-eminence of the great feudal houses. The *Kuge* of Kyōto, of whom 138 houses survive, all claimed descent from ancient emperors or from deities. They ranked high above the military class and had a hereditary right to many great offices of state. Practically, having lost their estates and being reduced to poverty, they merely filled court sinecures in Kyōto and spent most of their time in artistic pursuits. The emperor, strictly guarded by the Shōgun's troops, was invisible and unapproachable for all except his court and high officials, his duty being not to govern but to mediate between his heavenly ancestors and his subjects. An exceedingly curious passage of the Legacy (sections XXIX. and XXX.) describes how an imperial prince is to be installed as chief abbot of the Toyeizan temple at Tokyo, and that in the event of the emperor at Kyōto being "assailed by inimical barbarians" this princely abbot is to be elevated to the throne and receive the armed support of the Shōgun. In other words, if the emperor is so unwise as to make friends with the enemies of the Shōgun, the latter may depose him and has ready at hand a substitute whom he can immediately appoint in his place. There was actually an attempt to put this procedure in force in 1868 when the opponents of the emperor Meiji carried off the princely abbot to the north and proclaimed him as emperor there. Under the Hōjō and Ashikaga Shōguns great estates frequently changed hands according to the fortunes of war, but under the Tokugawas, though redistributions of fiefs occurred, a nobility grew up, each Daimyō enjoying considerable independence, provided that he conformed strictly to the general principles of government as laid down at Yedo. The extraordinary ability of Iyeyasu is shown by the way in which he consolidated and arranged his conquests. The estates of those whom he vanquished formed an immense territory which passed into his hands and was so redistributed that all important strategic positions were held by nobles of undoubted loyalty, while every feudatory who was open to suspicion had for his near neighbours partisans of the Tokugawa family. Moreover, great Daimyōs were not allowed to remain too long on their estates, lest they might become too important as local potentates and independent of the central administration. They were obliged to have mansions in Yedo where their wives and children under age resided permanently, while they themselves had to visit the capital in alternate years.

No Daimyō might intermarry with the court nobility without the consent of the Shōgun or make any application to the emperor or build a new castle on his own estate. The Daimyōs were divided into two classes: *Fudai* or hereditary vassals of the Tokugawa, defined in the Legacy as those who followed Iyeyasu and proffered their fealty before the siege of Osaka, and *Tozama*, or outside lords, those who submitted after its downfall. The *Fudai* were more directly dependent on the good-will of the Shōgun than the others, for he could alter their revenues or transfer them from one fief to another, but they only (with rare and late exceptions) were eligible as members of the *Gorōjū*, or Shōgun's council of State, and as governors of the great castles of Osaka, Fushimi and the Nijō in Kyōto. The last was practically charged with the custody of the emperor. Owing to their position the *Tozama* Daimyōs of the north and west enjoyed considerable independence. The Shōguns, for instance, were exceedingly cautious in interfering in the affairs of Satsuma.

The wealth of a Daimyō was estimated in terms of *Koku* of rice, the value of one *Koku* being about £1. About half the amount went to the Daimyō himself, the other half to the tillers of the soil. The richest was Mayeda of Kaga, who had more than a million *Koku*. The Tokugawa family itself was divided into the three houses of Mito, Kii and Owari (the fiefs bestowed by Iyeyasu on three of his sons), and in event of the Shōgun having no direct issue it was from these that the heir was chosen. The general body of Samurai or retainers lived frugally on stipends calculated in terms of *Koku*. In theory they paid no taxes, but in practice the presents which they were obliged to present to their superiors at stated intervals were a heavy impost. Comparatively few owned land, which was usually bestowed as a reward of conspicuous merit. An important class of small landowners was formed by the Hatamoto (under the flag) who were supposed to be immediate retainers of the Shōgun and ranked immediately after the Daimyōs. The Rōnin (wavemen), who play some part in history and a greater one in Japanese romance, were homeless and lordless Samurai, who had left their master's service for some reason, it may be for misconduct or it may be because they proposed to do something—*e.g.*, to take revenge—which, though regarded as a moral duty, might bring their master's house into trouble if performed by his retainers. In Yedo there were two distinct classes of population between whom little love was lost, the townsmen subject to the civil magistrates, and the Samurai under the direction of their feudal chiefs, who were guided by the *Buke Shohatto*, or regulations for the military class, supposed to be issued at the beginning of each Shōgun's reign. The feudal chiefs resided in mansions called Yashikis near the palace, often with grounds of considerable extent and surrounded by a labyrinth of tortuous streets and small dwellings assigned to their retainers.

The Heimin, or commoners, were divided into three classes, husbandmen, artisans and traders. Of these the first were the most respected, and a farmer on his own land might wear one sword, but never two, that being the privilege of the Samurai. Artisans were also esteemed, particularly as they were often artists in our sense of the word and were in the permanent service of feudal lords from whom they received fixed salaries. But throughout the Tokugawa period traders were regarded with disdain and stood lowest in the social scale, though still more contemptible were the outcasts, *Eta* and *Hinin* who were regarded as being outside the community and performed such disagreeable duties as slaughtering animals and executing criminals. The Eta lived in separate villages and could not eat or intermarry with others. In spite of many hypotheses, no certain account can be given of their origin. They were officially enfranchised in 1871, but the popular prejudice against them is still strong and gives rise to occasional riots.

The Government of Yedo, like the Chinese, had a great dislike of litigation: every attempt was made to discourage it and to settle disputes by arbitration or conciliation. The various classes of magistrates had also other functions such as municipal duties and the collection of revenue. It was some time before a Supreme Court was evolved and even then it was not quite independent of the administration, for members of the council of State could be present unseen and supervise its proceedings behind a curtain.

Iyetsuna.—Iyemitsu died rather suddenly in 1651 and was succeeded by his young son Iyetsuna, whose guardianship he entrusted to Hoshina of Aizu. The situation was not without danger but was saved by the heads of the houses of Kii and Mito, who were younger sons of Iyeyasu and supported the new Shōgun. In the same year there was a formidable conspiracy of Rōnin, led by Yui and Marubashi. The former was the son of a dyer who had formed the dangerous ambition of emulating Hideyoshi: the latter was the son of the dispossessed Daimyō of Tosa who had fought against Iyeyasu at Osaka. The plot was discovered. Yui had time to commit suicide, but his partner and accomplice with many of their wives and children were either crucified or beheaded. It was part of the conspirators' design to set fire to Yedo, and the events of 1657 showed what awful proportions such a conflagration might assume and how easy it would have been for a band of desperadoes with their plans prepared to take possession of the city. In that year a fire broke out during a hurricane: Yedo was almost literally reduced to a heap of ashes and the loss of life was appalling. Waegener, who was there at the head of the annual Dutch mission, estimated it at 100,000. Fortunately the Government granaries were defended by thick mud walls which withstood the flames and, as in 1923, the administration dealt ably and energetically with the work of relief and reconstruction.

In 1669–70 occurred what is called the Great Ainu Revolt, a last attempt of the aborigines to assert their independence. It had important consequences, for Mutsu and Dewa, the distant provinces of the north, were now utilized as granaries of the empire. The legislation of 1635 had made it illegal to build sea-going vessels, but this drastic legislation was now modified and a regular service of rice-transports was organized to provision Yedo and Osaka. Under the rule of Iyetsuna an attempt was also made to render the laws of Japan more humane. Cruel punishments were somewhat mitigated and the relatives of criminals were less severely treated, *Junshi*, the suicide of retainers in order to follow their master in death, was forbidden and accessories were punished. Iyemitsu had actually ordered some of his counsellors and attendants to "follow him on the dark path," and how deeply rooted this idea is in Japan may be seen by the fact that Gen. Nogi and his wife killed themselves on the occasion of the emperor Meiji's funeral in 1912, and for having done so are held up as an example to the youth of Japan and almost deified.

Iyetsuna, who had never taken an active part in the business of government, became an invalid in 1675 and left everything in the hands of Sakai Tadakiyo, who filled the office of Tairo. Five years later he died without issue. Sakai proposed to revert to the practice of the old Kamakura administration and to appoint an imperial prince as Shōgun, remaining regent himself. But the council refused to accept this proposal. Sakai had to retire and Iyemitsu's fourth son Tsunayoshi (1680–1709) succeeded.

Tsunayoshi.—He became known to the populace by the nickname of the Shōgun of dogs. Though he was an ardent student of Confucian literature, he was also a devout Buddhist and carried to an extreme length the beautiful Buddhist precepts forbidding cruelty to animals. He made it a crime not only to kill but even to maim animals, and by his orders a page was beheaded for having accidentally killed a bird. The first of these decrees was published in 1687 and from that time to Tsunayoshi's death hardly a year passed without the issue of edicts re-affirming or supplementing this unusual legislation. It is interesting to see that the Shōgun's position was so strong that he was able to make his subjects submit to what most of them must have regarded as a craze, for though the eating of meat was not common at this period, the Samurais' code attached little value to the life of men, let alone animals. The chief reason for this obedience was no doubt the extreme efficiency of the Tokugawa despotic system. Even if a Daimyō was not in Yedo himself his family were obliged to be in his mansion there and could be made answerable for any act of disobedience on his part.

Tsunayoshi had also a passion for the *Nō* drama and appeared on the stage himself, for it was a peculiarity of these plays that the aristocratic amateurs could take part in them without losing caste, whereas other kinds of acting were considered disgraceful. Theatres of all kinds flourished in Yedo, and life was not only gay but artistic. The products of the Genroku epoch (1688–1704) are of remarkable excellence, especially the lacquer. The provinces were impoverished because the Daimyōs were continually imposing new taxes on the cultivators to pay for their own town amusements, but there was plenty of money in the capital. The coinage was depreciated but as the Samurai received their stipends mostly in kind and had more rice than they required for their household needs, they sold the surplus and cash was abundant. Ultimately the money squandered on actors and geishas passed into the pockets of the mercantile class, for none of it went abroad. Though they were still theoretically the lowest grade of the social scale, merchants amassed such large fortunes that it was impossible to ignore them. Many of the commercial magnates of modern Japan, such as the Mitsui and Sumitomo, were already flourishing at this time. Another side of life is illustrated by the story of the Forty-Seven Rōnin, the most celebrated of Japanese romances. A certain nobleman was insulted in the Shōgun's palace in the year 1701 and drew his sword within the sacred precincts. For this unpardonable outrage he was obliged to commit *harakiri* at once, his family was declared extinct and his retainers were disbanded. They accepted their position without hesitation: the code of military honour obliged them to slay the man who had insulted their master, although the Civil Code threatened them with capital punishment for doing so. They spent two years in every kind of adventure, and having at last surprised and killed their adversary, they deposited his head on their lord's grave amidst the applause of admiring crowds, and all disembowelled themselves. The temple in Tokyo where they are buried is still a resort for popular pilgrimages and incense is kept continually burning before their tombs. In 1703 and 1708 the life of Yedo was disturbed by disastrous earthquakes and there was also an eruption of Mount Fuji. As he grew older, the Shōgun devoted himself more and more to art and literature and let his favourite Yanagisawa manage all public business. After the death of his mother in 1705 he secluded himself entirely under plea of mourning. Four years later he died somewhat mysteriously but apparently the story that he was murdered by his wife does not merit credence. He was succeeded by his nephew Iyenobu, who promised to be a competent ruler but unfortunately died in 1712 three years after his accession. The people went into voluntary mourning for him, a compliment which had been paid to no previous Tokugawa. He was succeeded by his infant son, Iyetsugu, who also held the nominal office for only three years. No events of much importance occurred in this interval, but an interesting description of the life of the period has been preserved in the works of Arai, the tutor and afterwards the adviser of Iyenobu. He relates among other things how he examined the Italian priest Sidotti, who came to Japan on a missionary enterprise and died in prison. With the death of the infant Iyetsugu the line of Hidetada, the second Tokugawa Shōgun, became extinct, and an heir had to be found in one of the three Tokugawa houses descended from Iyeyasu. Iyenobu, foreseeing that his own son was not likely to live long, had designated as heir Yoshimune of the house of Kii.

Yoshimune.—Yoshimune was perhaps the best of the Tokugawa Shōguns and illustrated the excellence of paternal government when exercised by a capable and unselfish sovereign. His long rule (1716-1744) offers few exciting incidents but is a continuous record of reform and beneficial legislation, much of it obviously directed against the dangers threatening a capital and military class entirely given over to luxury. He did his best to make the court ceremonial simpler and more rational. Whereas previous Shōguns had received the Dutch envoys unseen and sitting behind a curtain, he met them face to face and conversed with them. Similarly, he made a practice of receiving ordinary Samurai in audience, if they had in any way distinguished themselves. In order to know more of the opinions and grievances of simple citizens he revived the ancient institution of a "Complaint (or suggestion) Box," which was set up outside the Supreme Court. He kept the key himself and any properly signed communication received due attention. Yoshimune spent his leisure in hunting and hawking whence, in contrast to his predecessor Tsunayoshi, he was called the Hawk Shōgun or Bird-catching Shōgun. Believing outdoor sports to be a good corrective of the luxurious life of Yedo, he encouraged the Samurai to accompany him and devised for them such strenuous forms of exercise as the unexpected swimming of a river. In 1726 he organized a great hunting expedition in which 60,000 men took part and were put through evolutions like an army in the field. There was, it appears, no code of law at this time, but Yoshimune made a beginning by himself supervising the preparation of the Hundred Articles of Kwampō, which became the basis of the criminal law. These articles were issued in 1742, but it is interesting to note that it was not thought necessary to bring them to the notice of the public, but merely to distribute copies among the judges and other officers concerned. Ōoka Tadasuke, a sort of Japanese Solomon, was city magistrate of Yedo in this period and his sagacious and often amusing decisions are among the best known stories even now.

Yoshimune was strongly in favour of primogeniture as a principle for settling disputed succession and thus avoiding the dissensions from which almost every great family suffered. Unfortunately his own family showed that the principle has disadvantages, for his eldest son Iyeshige was a debauchee and of no ability, whereas his second son seemed a most desirable successor and his advisers suggested that he might be named heir apparent. But Yoshimune was unwilling. He retired nominally in 1744, his eldest son being declared Shōgun and his grandson Iyeharu heir apparent. His intention was to supervise Iyeshige and, if he proved incorrigible, to make him retire when Iyeharu attained his majority, but he died himself before that happened. He also established his two younger sons as heads of new Tokugawa houses and later his grandson, the second son of Iyeshige, received the same honour. The three houses thus formed were those of Tayasu, Hitotsubashi and Shimizu and, in the event of direct heirs to the Shōgunate failing, had a right to the succession. Iyeshige (1744-1760) proved a deplorably bad ruler, especially after his father's death in 1751. He is not charged with specially heinous acts of tyranny but at this time the personal power of the Shōgun was so great that if he was dissolute himself he was bound to injure the whole administration. For instance, if he required money for his pleasures, the Daimyōs were informed that (contrary to the practice in Yoshimune's time) the gifts which it was the custom for them to present on ceremonial occasions ought to be of real value. Great officials imitated the Shōgun and naturally givers of presents recouped themselves at the expense of their dependents. Favouritism, extortion and corruption became rampant and risings of the peasantry occurred. The management of affairs passed into the hands of chamberlains and secretaries. Nevertheless, no great disaster occurred under Iyeshige's rule. He died in 1761 having abdicated the year before in favour of his son Iyeharu, then aged 23. Iyeharu was a youth of good parts and began his rule with some legal reforms. But though he was not a profligate like his father and inherited his grandfather's love of open air sport, he had also a dangerous love of display and magnificence and let himself be ruled by favourites, the chief of whom was Tanuma, who is said to have amassed a colossal fortune. The dissipation and extravagance of Yedo increased and spread to the surrounding districts, for it was the custom to hire servants for the Daimyōs' mansions by the year, after which many of them returned to the country with their morals not improved. But still, contemporary testimony states that in south-western Japan and in the great fief of the Uyesugi family, whose capital was at Yonezawa, the local administration was good. A little later an interesting light is thrown on the condition of the rural districts by the career of Ninomiya (1787-1856) who founded in the Kwantō and neighbouring provinces a system of credit associations to which farmers subscribed and from which they obtained loans in case of need. The later years of Iyeharu were darkened by a series of terrible natural calamities. Earthquakes and eruptions were followed by a drought known as the famine of Temmei (the period 1781-1789), and after this came equally destructive floods. More than a million persons are said to have perished in these various disasters and the measures proposed by the Government to relieve the distress proved totally inadequate.

Iyenari.—Iyeharu died in 1786. His two sons had predeceased him and he had adopted as his heir Iyenari of the house of Hitotsubashi, according to the arrangement mentioned above. The young prince did not attain his majority until 1793, and during this period the Government was administered by Matsudaira Sadanobu, who really belonged to the Tasuya house and was a grandson of Yoshimune, although he had been adopted into the Matsudaira family. Tanuma, the late Shōgun's favourite, had to retire, his son having been assassinated two years before. According to Titsingh, the head of the Dutch factory at Deshima to whom we owe an interesting account of this period, this son was "of a truly enlightened and imposing character" and would have opened Japan to foreigners, but Japanese accounts state that the family were hated for their rapacity and corruption. The populace stoned the funeral cortège of the victim, and the assassin, though he had to commit suicide, became an object of public veneration.

Matsudaira Sadanobu's administration (1786-93) was one of the periods of reform and retrenchment which occurred periodically in the history of the Tokugawa Shōgunate. There was, indeed, something self-contradictory in the principles of that Government. Soldiers were recognized as the highest class and yet there was no place for the soldier's occupation—fighting. Japan had no dealings with foreign nations and consequently no foreign wars: even defence against foreign aggression was not a practical necessity. Internal wars between the great feudal houses were obviously harmful to the country. The result was that most Samurai, especially in Yedo, tended to drift, not towards insurrection (for the extraordinarily efficient discipline averted this danger), but towards dissipation and effeminacy. The regent set himself to correct public morals and with considerable success. The system of requiring presents was abolished; favouritism and corruption were greatly diminished and the administration of justice, which had grown very bad, became prompt and efficient. But he found the military class so hopelessly in debt that they could not pay if they lived by honest means, and therefore he had recourse to the old device of a cancellation of debts. All debts of more than six years' standing incurred by Hatamotos were nullified and more recent ones were payable at reduced interest. These ordinances were accompanied by unusually severe sumptuary legislation. The use of gold and silver for ornament was practically interdicted and there were rigorous regulations about dolls and sweetmeats. Sadanobu's reforms seem to have done real good for a time but in some other ways he was less judicious and under his rule we see faint signs of the movements which were destined to overthrow the Shōgunate and restore the authority of the emperor. Hitherto the Shōguns had been on good terms with the court of Kyōto and had kept it in obscurity while treating it with great respect. But in the interests of economy Sadanobu requested them to despatch less frequent missions to Yedo, which was taken amiss and he had a misunderstanding with the Emperor Kokaku about the imperial right to confer titles. For the moment nothing of great importance happened, but several enthusiasts, notably Gamō, Hayashi and Takayama travelled about the country preaching the duty of paying more respect to the emperor. Takayama committed *harakiri* as a public protest against the neglect of loyalty and Hayashi was imprisoned for seeming to exalt the emperor to the prejudice of the Shōgun, but in the Meiji era he received posthumous rank as a reward for his services to the imperial house. Sadanobu retired from the regency in 1793 and the young Shōgun assumed control of the Government which he continued to exercise for 48 years, for though he abdicated in favour of his son in 1837 he continued to rule until his death in 1841. Though not devoid of talent, Iyenari cannot be ranked among the ablest men of his house, and he was somewhat under the influence of his friends and especially of his numerous seraglio. For the first 13 years of his rule he was also strongly influenced by his father, who considered he had been slighted by Sadamaru and disliked the latter's reforms. Accordingly the old tendency to magnificence and luxury set in again. Iyenari married a daughter of Shimazu of Satsuma who had been adopted into the Konoye family, one of the branches of the Fujiwara house. He was thus brought into intimate relations with the court nobility and the great but very distant house of Kyushu, and this tended to give the Fudai—or vassals of the Tokugawa house—less power than they had previously enjoyed.

The influence of the Rōjū or council of State also declined. Iyenari paid most respectful attention to the emperor who showed his appreciation by conferring on him several titles which added nothing to his real power, but so great is the importance attached to ceremony that the Shōgunate seemed to have reached the acme of its magnificence. After the death of Iyenari's father Mizuno Tadashige became chief adviser and favourite, and when he died in 1835 he was succeeded by another Mizuno, Tadakuni, who became well known as the author of another set of sumptuary laws which were not very successful. He also seems to have been in favour of foreign intercourse.

About this time there was a famine, and popular indignation was aroused against the guilds of merchants, who were accused of buying up necessaries and selling them only at outrageous prices. A serious outbreak occurred at Osaka where one Oshio designed to kill the magistrates, seize the castle and force the merchants to distribute their stores. Though the plot was betrayed and frustrated, there was serious fighting and a great part of the city was burnt. Mizuno dealt drastically with the guilds and practically suppressed them for some years, but it was found necessary to revive them and his ordinances against luxury were not more permanent. Apparently they were so worded as to bear heavily on the ordinary townsfolk, whereas earlier legislation of the same kind had chiefly affected the upper classes. Mizuno was suddenly dismissed in 1843, restored to his office next year but dismissed again and banished for good in 1845. Meanwhile, Iyenari had died in 1841 and his son Iyeyoshi, who was already titular Shōgun, had to govern without his assistance. Though Iyeyoshi was 45 years of age he had no will of his own and counted for nothing during his rule which lasted till 1853, the year of Commodore Perry's arrival.

Shinto Movement.—Under the long rule of Iyenari various movements which conspired to bring about the surprising transformation of Japan in the latter part of the 19th century began to make themselves felt. One of these was a movement in favour of pure Shinto, as distinct from Chinese Confucianism and Buddhism, the two systems most favoured by the Tokugawa régime. Yet the origin of the movement may be traced to the literary activity of Mitsukuri (1628–1700), head of the Mito branch of the Tokugawa family, who, with the help of a band of scholars composed the Dai Nihonshi, a general history of Japan down to 1413, which is still a standard book. The practical bearings of his studies are shown by the fact that he destroyed 1,000 Buddhist temples on his estates. In the next century followed such distinguished exponents of Shinto as Mabuchi (1697–1769), Motoori (1730–1801) and Hirata, his even more influential pupil (1778–1843). Though this movement seems to be literary and philosophic, it had a most important political bearing. It was intensely Japanese and anti-Chinese. But in exalting everything that was purely Japanese it had to fall back on the Kojiki and Nihongi and other ancient lore which dealt with the imperial house of divine descent. Here it naturally found itself in conflict with the doctrines which were acceptable at Yedo, for all its teachings tended to glorify the emperor and had no place for the Shōgun. A work of Hirata's which had won the admiration of the court at Kyoto was suppressed and he was banished to his native town in 1840.

COURTESY OF THE PRESBYTERIAN BOARD OF FOREIGN MISSIONS
SHINTO PRIEST IN PAPER CEREMONIAL ROBES

Dutch Learning.—Another intellectual movement, small in numbers but of great importance, was the furtive pursuit of Dutch learning. The Japanese are the most inquisitive people in the world and the terror of European aggression did not prevent the few who had any opportunity from learning all they could about Europe, especially its science and inventions. It has been truly observed that the adventures of these pioneer students were often as interesting as the most thrilling romances published in Yedo. A physician called Sugita Fusai (c. 1780) has left an autobiography in which he describes his difficulties and troubles in learning Dutch and practical anatomy, which latter he studied on the execution ground. He wrote a book on the human body and was allowed to present a copy to the Shōgun. In this he was more fortunate than his predecessors, for a little while before, a work published by a naturalist called Gotō had been suppressed, simply because it contained the Dutch alphabet. Though the Government discouraged the study of Dutch, the Shōgun Yoshimune himself had Dutch books translated for his own benefit, and Titsingh tells us that several "persons of quality" diligently studied the language and that the Prince of Satsuma (the father-in-law of the Shōgun Iyenari) used the Roman alphabet in his letters when he wished to write secrets. When Siebold was in Japan (1823–29) his house was frequented by pupils from every part of the empire, but they got into trouble and he himself had difficulties. A little later clubs for the study of Dutch were established. There was strenuous opposition, but on the other hand medical opinion insisted on the importance of the study and made itself heard. The Government decided that only physicians might learn Dutch and a medical school was established in Osaka in 1838. The result was that everyone who wished to learn Dutch professed to be a medical student and 3,000 pupils are said to have passed through the school in 24 years. In 1795 an edict required all candidates for official posts to subscribe to the doctrines called Teishu, that is, the particular interpretation of Confucian philosophy which was taught in Government schools, though many learned men favoured other interpretations. Though these persistent efforts to suppress foreign learning and freedom of thought affected comparatively few, they contributed to the unpopularity of the Shōgunate. It had not many disinterested friends when the great upheaval came after 1854.

Intercourse with Europe and America.—Though the opening of Japan came quite suddenly and though the Shōgun's Government enforced the prohibition of intercourse with all foreigners except the Dutch with extraordinary rigour and efficiency until the last, yet naturally, from stress of weather or other causes, foreign vessels occasionally touched at Japanese ports. They were generally driven away, sometimes by gunfire even when their object was benevolent, such as the repatriation of Japanese who had strayed abroad. In 1808 when Great Britain and Holland were at war a sensation was created by the brief apparition at Nagasaki of H.M.S. "Phaëton" in pursuit of Dutch ships. The Japanese saw in this a sign of European aggression and the Dutch, wishing to preserve a monopoly of foreign trade, worked on these fears. The first attempts at establishing relations with Japan were made by the Russians in connection with the fur trade. A Russian envoy appeared at Nagasaki in 1804, but only to receive a flat refusal. Collisions followed between Japanese and Russians in Sakhalin and the Kurile islands, but renewed Russian attempts to find some basis of amicable intercourse failed. The whaling industry began to grow at this period and ships often sent boats to the Japanese coast to obtain supplies. In 1824 the crew of an English vessel who landed in this way near Kagoshima slaughtered cattle and used other violence. This aroused strong ill-feeling and next year the Government published an expulsion decree, ordering the local authorities to drive away all foreign vessels attempting to put into port and to arrest or execute any foreigners who might land. Somewhat later the Japanese became impressed with the growing power of England in the Far East, as shown by the cession of Hongkong and the opening of various Chinese ports and Mizuno Tadakuni, who was then at the head of affairs, issued in 1843 modified instructions to local authorities saying that though foreigners were on no account to be allowed to land, yet foreign ships were not to be driven away but were allowed to receive provisions and fuel. At the same time he requested the Dutch at Deshima to supply him with models of European machines and copies of illustrated books and newspapers. Even the Dutch now began to recommend the opening up of Japan, and the king of Holland sent an envoy with a despatch advising the Shōgun to abandon the policy of isolation. The envoy was not allowed to proceed beyond Nagasaki and when a reply was at last sent in 1845 (after the fall of Mizuno) it simply stated the law of Japan as it stood, adding, "Henceforth pray cease correspondence."

Owing to the increase of whaling enterprise of trade with China, American ships were beginning to frequent the Far East but their occasional visits to Japanese ports had left a disagreeable impression, the "Morrison" having been fired on in 1837. In 1845 a resolution was introduced in Congress recommending that "commercial arrangements" should be made with Japan and for this purpose Commodore Biddle was sent with two ships next year. He stayed nine days at Uraga but his attempts to negotiate a treaty met with a flat refusal and he was roughly handled himself but, as his instructions ordered him to do nothing that could excite hostility, he accepted the apologies offered and returned to the United States.

Commodore Perry.—The Government of Washington, however, determined not to drop the matter and on July 8, 1853, Commodore Perry entered Uraga harbour with four ships and 560 men. He bore a letter from the President requesting the conclusion of a commercial treaty but abstained from any attempt to coerce or threaten. He presented his letter, distributed many presents consisting chiefly of mechanical toys and instruments, and after staying ten days sailed away to China, saying that he would return in the spring. The Japanese, who, since the days of the Mongol invasion, had not seen more than a couple of foreign ships together, were panic-stricken at the appearance of the American squadron. The emperor at Kyōto was solemnly informed of the awful event, and his majesty ordered that prayers for the destruction of the barbarians should be offered at the seven principal shrines. At first the Government of Yedo seems to have thought of resistance. The prohibition against building sea-going ships was removed and feudal chiefs were ordered to build and arm large vessels; the Dutch at Deshima were asked to furnish a man-of-war and modern military appliances and the army was prepared for action. But the conviction soon prevailed that effective resistance was impossible, and on Dec. 2 instructions were issued that if the Americans returned, they were to be given a pacific reception. Perry did return in the February of the next year (1854) with a still more formidable force of ten ships and 2,000 men and after six weeks of negotiation obtained a treaty of peace and friendship which stipulated that the ports of Shimoda in Izu and Hakodate should be opened to American ships and that Americans be allowed to frequent them within definite limits: that American consuls or agents might reside in Shimoda: that shipwrecked sailors should be relieved and that ships might obtain fuel and provisions in Japanese territory.

Perry remained in Japan till June and then went to Canton. His visit had been short and successful, but the last entry in the *Journal* of Wells Williams, his interpreter, is "Thus ends my expedition to Japan, for which praise God."

Meanwhile Japan was in a ferment. The Shōgun died in 1853 and was succeeded by two nonentities, Iyesada (1853–1858) and Iyemochi (1858–1866). It may be mentioned that the name Tycoon commonly used by foreigners at this time is the Japanese Taikun or great prince. The title had been used in negotiations with Korea in the 16th century and was now resumed in dealing with western powers, with the object of enhancing the dignity of the Shōgun since that word means simply generalissimo. This was explained in a despatch addressed to Townsend Harris in November 1857.

The emperor was Kōmei (1847–1867) the father of Meiji, a man of more character than his immediate predecessors and of strongly conservative, that is anti-foreign, principles. From 1853 to 1860 the chief power was in the hands of Ii Naosuke, who was Tairō or First Minister, during the last two years of his life. He was a man of great intelligence and courage who, seeing that Japan had no chance of successfully withstanding foreign insistence, assumed the responsibility of signing the treaties. His policy had many prominent opponents, especially Tokugawa Nariaki of Mito, and the quarrel was complicated by this latter's desire to make his own son Shōgun. This son (who eventually became the last Shōgun under the name of Keiki or Yoshinobu, had been adopted as heir of the house of Hitotsubashi and hence was eligible for succession, but Ii successfully supported the claims of Iyemochi of the house of Kii. Ii was assassinated by Rōnin of Mito in 1860—a victim to anti-foreign sentiment and clan intrigues. However, it was not possible to refuse to other powers the concession already granted to America. Russia, Holland and England soon secured for themselves similar treaties. But these instruments were in reality mere grants of privileges and not commercial treaties such as are usual among friendly nations. America again led the way. Townsend Harris, the first consul general of the United States, arrived at Shimoda in 1856 and in the next year signed a convention which gave American citizens the rights of permanent residence at Shimoda and Hakodate and opened Nagasaki to American ships. But Harris was not satisfied with this and pressed for permission to proceed to Yedo and negotiate directly with the Shōgun. After ten months he succeeded and was received in audience. In 1859 a treaty was signed providing that the port of Yokohama should be opened from July 4, and that commerce between Japan and the United States should be freely carried on there. The Shōgun's ministers signed this document without receiving the imperial sanction and were well aware of the danger they were incurring in acting contrary to public opinion, but they were also greatly impressed by the news communicated to them by Harris, of the suppression of the Indian Mutiny, the capture of the Taku forts, the Treaty of Tientsin and the impending arrival of British and French plenipotentiaries with squadrons to enforce their demands. They therefore thought it better to sign at once a moderate treaty with America which they could offer to other powers and perhaps prevent them from asking for more. A few weeks after the signature of this treaty Lord Elgin, British commissioner to China and Japan, arrived at Shimoda, and on Aug. 20 concluded a treaty with Japan on the basis of the American treaty and in the following October Baron Gros did the same thing for the French. In Feb. 1860, the Japanese despatched their first foreign envoys to Washington. Their time of absence was strictly limited and they remained only six weeks in America. A second mission was despatched in 1862, this time to all the European courts in succession, and it returned after spending a year in making this round of visits.

The Emperor and the Shōgun.—Meanwhile the position of the Shōgun himself was becoming very difficult. Quite apart from the question of foreign intercourse, there had arisen a party whose watchword was the sanctity of the imperial house. When foreigners insisted on landing, the sentiment of the people was at first hostile. The Government of the Shōgun, having to face the practical work of negotiation and the possibility of a bombardment, was comparatively liberal in its attitude, whereas the emperor, disturbed by no disagreeable contact with the outside world, remained severely aloof and naturally came to be regarded as the guardian of Japan's sacred soil which his servant the Shōgun could not or would not protect from barbarian invasion. The cry Son-o jo-i, "revere the Sovereign": "expel barbarians," which was heard everywhere, began to be interpreted as meaning revere the emperor not the Shōgun, and the incidents of the protracted crisis naturally made intelligent citizens feel the evils of a dual and not always harmonious Government. The Tokugawa statesmen did their best to bring about some form of union. A marriage was arranged between the young Shōgun and the emperor's sister and took place at Yedo in 1862. The year after, the Shōgun was summoned to Kyōto which no Shōgun had visited since 1634. He remained there three months, showing the utmost deference to the emperor and finally agreed to the issue of orders directing Daimyōs to muster troops and prepare to assist the court in the task of "sweeping out barbarians." When such a temper prevailed, it is not surprising if murderous attacks were made on foreigners. In 1862 two sentries had been killed in an attack on the British legation and an Englishman called Richardson had been cut down on the road between Yedo and Yokohama, because he got in the way of the retinue of the prince of Satsuma. The British Government demanded an indemnity and punishment of the murderers, but Prince Shimazu refused to comply and as he was the most independent of all the feudal chiefs, the Government of the Shōgun could not have compelled him to give satisfaction even had they desired it.

Bombardment of Satsuma and Chōshū.—Accordingly in Aug. 1863, Kagoshima, the capital of Satsuma, was bombarded and partially destroyed by a British fleet. In the same year the Daimyō of Chōshū, the extreme western province of the main island, whose batteries commanded the Straits of Shimonoseki, fired on Dutch, French and American vessels. As a reprisal for this an allied fleet of nine British, four Dutch and three French warships bombarded Shimonoseki in 1864 and an indemnity of $3,000,000 was demanded. This indemnity was not completely paid until 1875, and the conduct of the Powers in using it as an instrument of diplomatic pressure and in exacting payment from the Meiji Government, which certainly was not responsible for the outrage, occasioned much rancour. As a matter of fact the Daimyō of Chōshū was in rebellion, for shortly before firing on the foreign ships, he had done the same to a vessel which was carrying a mission from the Shōgun to Kyūshū and had killed two officials. The effect produced by these bombardments was wonderful. The emperor had to withdraw his instructions for the expulsion of foreigners, for it was plain not only that foreigners were vastly superior in all mechanical arts connected with warfare, but that they were acting in combination against Japan. Henceforward the real question was not how to get rid of them but how to imitate the useful features of their civilization. This new attitude was particularly noticeable in Satsuma: the population had already shown themselves willing to use such small opportunities of foreign intercourse as they had, and the murder of Richardson and the refusal to give satisfaction had been due to their traditional arrogance and independence rather than to hatred of Europeans. They showed no resentment after the bombardment, but were eager to establish friendship with the British for whose naval efficiency they felt the greatest admiration. Much the same sentiments prevailed in Chōshū and the two clans agreed to co-operate, though subsequently their rivalry became a feature in Japanese politics. In 1865 Sir Harry Parkes arrived as British minister. His chief objects were to obtain from the emperor a ratification of the existing treaties, which had not yet been vouchsafed, to reduce the duty on imports from 15 to 5% ad valorem, to secure the immediate opening of Osaka and Hyōgo (Kobe) and to receive payment of the Chōshū indemnity. He was a man of somewhat peremptory methods and arranged with his colleagues to proceed with a fleet of British, Dutch and French vessels to Hyōgo, the place appointed for the negotiations. The recent memory of the bombardments of Kagoshima and Shimonoseki and the mere idea that such proceedings might be repeated in the neighbourhood of the sacred city of Kyōto sufficed to make the court yield and the emperor gave his consent on Nov. 22, 1865, in a brief order addressed to the Shōgun directing him to make the necessary arrangements. In the next year the treaties were supplemented by a new tariff convention.

These proceedings may seem to be a victory for the Government of Yedo, but they were not, and the Shōgunate was now tottering. To begin with, the idea of abolishing the emperor was unthinkable to any Japanese. If the administration was to be simplified, it was clear to everyone that it was the Shōgun who had to go. And for practical purposes it was no doubt better that the impending work of reconstruction should be undertaken by a power which, though ancient and sacrosanct, emerged from its retirement like something new, than by a worn out feudal administration hampered by numerous quarrels with its vassals. In consenting to the treaties in 1865 the emperor was far from indicating that he yielded to the views of the Yedo Government. On the contrary he dismissed and punished the negotiators—a step without precedent and tantamount to withdrawing the administrative commission given to the Tokugawa family in the time of Iyeyasu. On this the Shōgun presented his resignation, but at the same time handed in a memorial showing that the opening of the country was inevitable. For the moment the resignation was not accepted.

Parkes showed good judgment in getting into touch with the distant but powerful clans who were about to play a great part in the making of new Japan. In 1865 he went to Shimonoseki, where the authorities expressed satisfaction with the new treaty and next year he visited Kagoshima, where Prince Shimazu entertained him with the utmost cordiality, and Shikoku. Satsuma purchased steamers and manufactured breach-loaders, and a batch of Satsuma youths were smuggled on board ship and sent for a course of instruction to England. Chōshū continued to be in rebellion and the Government of Yedo at last persuaded the unwilling emperor to begin an active campaign against it in the summer of 1866, but a few months afterwards the Shōgun died at the age of 20, leaving no issue. Hereupon the emperor ordered the suspensions of the operations against Chōshū which had not been proceeding very satisfactorily. After some months Hitotsubashi, who had been put forward as a candidate for the Shōgunate in 1858, most reluctantly consented to accept it now and took the name of Keiki. He made it a condition that the emperor should listen to his advice and that the Daimyōs should promise him their support. He was invested with his dignity at Kyōto and never visited Yedo as Shōgun, a significant sign of the change which had taken place. Part of his programme was the punishment of the rebellious Chōshū clan, but three weeks after his investiture the emperor Kōmei suddenly died of smallpox on Feb. 3, 1867, and in view of the court mourning and the accession of a new emperor the Shōgun agreed to order the disbandment of the troops on both sides.

MEIJI PERIOD

Kōmei was succeeded by his son Mutsuhito, aged 15, who under the title of Meiji (meaning Enlightened Government) became the best known name in modern Japan. The new Shōgun Keiki was a man of ability and mature intellect who had been convinced by events that it was impossible for Japan to continue in seclusion. He gave proof of his convictions by attempting to remodel the army and navy on European lines and by sending his brother to see the Paris exhibition. But there was a strong party against him in which the Daimyōs of Satsuma, Tosa and Chōshū were prominent. In Oct. 1867 Yōdō, the chief of Tosa, presented to him a memorial setting forth the difficulties of the present position and suggesting that the administration should be restored to the emperor. Keiki at once summoned a conference of heads of clans in Kyōto and informed them that he approved of the suggestion and intended to surrender his authority to the throne. The proposal was accepted without discussion, and the resignation was formally tendered and accepted. Thus ended the system of government which had been established by Iyeyasu in 1603.

Keiki left Kyōto secretly and retired to his castle at Osaka, but the clan of Tokugawa were not so ready as their lord to give up their privileges. Their enemies also, the clans of Satsuma and Chōshū, were not satisfied and, suspecting Keiki of an intention to come back, induced the court to take measures against his followers which were, perhaps, needlessly irritating. All officials connected with the Tokugawa were deprived of the offices they held in Kyōto and the Shōgun's troops were removed from the palace gates which it was their ancient privilege to guard. Keiki could not restrain the indignation of his followers, and at last reluctantly allowed them to march against Kyōto. The attempt was a failure and they were beaten back. Keiki fled to Yedo and made unconditional submission, but in the north the struggle was not over till August 1869. The Matsudairas of Aizu resisted with especial stubbornness until their stronghold of Wakamatsu was taken and, as mentioned above in speaking of Iyeyasu's institutions, an attempt was actually made to proclaim the princely Abbot of Ueno as emperor. This prince's life is an instance of the extraordinary careers which Japanese can have. Ordained in his youth, he was head of the temples of Nikko and Ueno. At the age of 19 he was carried off to the north and proclaimed emperor. When his partisans were defeated, he was unfrocked and sent to study in Europe, where he spent seven years. On his return he commanded in Formosa, under the name of Prince Kitashirakawa, and a Shinto temple dedicated to him is one of the principal sights of the capital of that island. Yenomoto, an officer in the Shōgun's navy, who had recently returned from a stay of six years in Europe, fled with several ships to the island of Yezo (Hokkaido), which was then an almost unknown country, and established himself in Hakodate with the intention of founding an independent state. Hopeless as was their cause, he and his followers showed the greatest courage and skill and for six months kept at bay all the forces sent against them. When their fortress was at last captured their lives were spared and Yenomoto and others eventually held important posts under Meiji.

In 1868 two unfortunate attacks on European officials were made near Hyogo. But adequate reparation was offered and the Japanese officers held responsible were ordered to commit suicide in the presence of foreign witnesses. In his *Tales of Old Japan*, Lord Redesdale (Mitford) has given a most impressive account of the terrible rite of *harakiri* at which he was officially present.

In considering the extraordinary changes effected in the Meiji era, it must be remembered that only the nobles and the military class, about one-sixteenth of the population, were concerned in them. The mass of the people were amenable to discipline, but had few anti-foreign prejudices. They were, of course, alarmed when they were told that Japan was going to be overrun by barbarians and there were misunderstandings with individual foreigners. But from early times they had always been ready to assimilate when opportunity offered. In the 7th century they eagerly adopted Chinese usages: in the 16th, considering the small number of missionaries, the number of converts to Christianity was surprising. Kaempfer observed that the Japanese "have so much sense and innate curiosity that if they were not absolutely denied free and open conversation and correspondence with foreigners they would receive them with the utmost kindness and pleasure," and in the 19th century Europeans often noted the contrast between the cordial hospitality which they received from the ordinary folk and the fierce antipathy shown by officials and Samurai. But even in the upper classes it is clear that there was a strong movement of curiosity and acquisitiveness. As far back as the time of Hideyoshi there was a craze for wearing Portuguese clothes, and Iyeyasu was anxious to import such inventions as he considered useful. But his successors formed the deliberate conviction that intercourse with Catholic Europe was a national danger, and had their knowledge been wider, had they known the history of Goa and Ceylon, of Mexico and Peru, can we suppose that they would have changed their conviction? The fear that Japan might become a European dependency was by no means absurd. The closing of the country to foreigners was the work of a few individuals and so was its re-opening. But it is clear that both in the 17th and 19th centuries what was done by the few was not disapproved by the many.

The collapse of the Yedo Government was not unnatural: it had lasted longer than the rule of the Ashikagas and Hōjōs, and in its later phases it showed the same feature of a want of really able men. The grouping of the clans about 1865 indicates that the great south-western fiefs, which had always been quasi-independent, wished to contest the supremacy of the Tokugawas. It was a chieftain of Tosa who suggested the abolition of the Shōgunate, and probably many in Satsuma desired to secure some sort of pre-eminence for their own house. Besides this, the movement in favour of Shintō had created a wide feeling that the emperor was not allowed to exercise the power which was his by right. But what is truly surprising is the manner in which not only individuals like the last Shōgun but, later on, whole classes like the Daimyō and Samurai surrendered their privileges in what they believed to be the interests of their country. Considering everything, the opposition offered to the astonishing changes which took place between 1867 and 1878 was very slight.

Another remarkable feature is that, whereas in previous critical epochs the ultimate settlement and reconstruction were the work of some man of genius such as Yoritomo, or Iyeyasu, no such figure appeared now and no individual or noble house reaped the harvest of the change. The prime movers were Samurai like Kido, Ito, Inouye, Matsukata, Okuma and Yamagata who won great distinction, but merely aspired to posts attained by any successful public man in Europe. The emperor, indeed, found himself in a new and much higher position, but obviously the change was not due to the ability or ambition of Kōmei or his young son Meiji. The latter, however, at once began to act (on the initiative of his council of course) as the sovereign of Japan in a way unknown to his predecessors. In Feb. 1868, he informed the foreign representatives that he had assumed the supreme executive authority and that his title should be substituted for that of the Shōgun in existing treaties. An imperial rescript was also published notifying his subjects that "intercourse with foreign countries shall in future be carried on in accordance with the public laws of the whole world." His Majesty also appeared out of doors, received diplomatists and summoned the nobles to the palace, where he took in their presence what was called the charter oath. Like many Far Eastern documents, this charter seems to consist of moral maxims rather than of definite legal statements, but it promises that a deliberative assembly shall be summoned, that all classes shall have a share in the government and that justice, not ancient custom shall in future be the guiding principle of the administration. As a further sign of the change which was being made the emperor and his court removed to Yedo, which henceforth bore the name of Tokyo, or the eastern capital, as distinguished from Kyōto. The abolition of the Shōgunate and the accession of Meiji are generally called by Japanese the Restoration (Isshin), the idea being that the rightful powers of the emperor were now restored to him.

The Abolition of Feudalism.—In the early days of the Restoration it had probably not been realized that the unification of the nation, which was one of the watchwords, implied the abolition of feudalism. Yet it became clear that this was necessary. As things stood every feudal chief collected and spent the revenues of his fief, and was an autocrat within his own territory. There was no homogeneous system of law operative throughout the empire. It is not easy to see how unification and uniformity could have been achieved by imperial edicts or any form of compulsion, but such was the spirit of the times that the change was made spontaneously and without any difficulty. In 1869 the chiefs of the four great western clans of Satsuma, Tosa, Chōshū and Hizen publicly surrendered their fiefs to the emperor begging him to re-organize them and bring them under the same system of law. The idea is said to have originated with Okubo Toshimichi of Satsuma and the example of the four clans was quickly imitated. In making this remarkable surrender the Daimyōs followed the advice of their leading clansmen, who doubtless thought that they might find better opportunities for a brilliant career under the new régime, but still men like the chiefs of Satsuma

JAPAN   PLATE III

BY COURTESY OF (1, 3) CANADIAN PACIFIC STEAMSHIPS, (2) HENRY MILLER, (4, 6) HERBERT G. PONTING, F.R.P.S., (5) THE NATIONAL BOARD OF THE Y.W.C.A.

ASPECTS OF LIFE IN JAPAN

1. Fisherman with a newly-caught octopus. Note characteristic loose robes
2. Memorial service for victims torpedoed on a transport in the Russo-Japanese War
3. Women (near Shizuoka) picking tea
4. Abbot of Buddhist temple at Ikegami, where the Buddhist Saint, Nichiren, died
5. The bow, a ceremony requiring long training
6. An avenue of torii (gateways) at a Temple

PLATE IV

JAPAN

NATURAL SCENERY IN JAPAN

1. Amanohashidate or "The Bridge of Heaven," a sand bar nearly two miles in length, covered with pine trees, at the mouth of Maidzura Bay on the west coast of Japan. It is one of the "Scenic Trio of Japan," the others being Matshushima and Miyajima (fig. 9). 2. Tomonaura, a small fishing port of Seto Island on the Inland Sea. 3. The shore of Setonaikai, the Inland sea of Japan, near the city of Tomonutsu. A shrine or small temple is situated at the edge of the cliff. 4. Poling the rapids on the Kiso River. 5. Fujiyama, 600 ft. deep. The last recorded eruption was in the latter part of 18th century. It is regarded as a sacred mountain, and many pilgrims make the ascent each year. 6. Ranzan, near Kyoto, as it appears in spring time with cherry trees in full bl┬om (background). 7. Herds of tame deer in the temple park at Nara, near Osaka. 8. Hakone Lake, a resort near Yokohama, famous for its hot springs. 9. Shrine Island on the Inland Sea (see fig. 3). The pavilions, in which dancing festivals are held, are built at the level of high tide, so that they seem to be floating on surface of the water.

BY COURTESY OF THE CONSULATE GENERAL OF JAPAN, NEW YORK

and Tosa must have been inspired by a rare patriotism, for they gave up an almost regal position without any return. The emperor acknowledged the sacrifice in a laconic rescript, but it was decided to proceed with caution. The feudal chiefs were appointed as governors of the districts in which they had ruled and the Samurai retained their salaries and positions. At the same time the distinction between the court nobles and the Daimyōs or feudal chiefs, who had previously ranked below them, was abolished. But the system of local autonomy thus introduced was clearly transitional, and in 1871 a second edict was issued by which territorial nobles ceased to be governors and a system of local autonomy was abolished; taxes were to be paid into the Treasury and all officials were to be appointed by the central Government. At the same time the chiefs of Satsuma, Tosa and Chōshū accepted ministerial office in Tokyo and sent contingents of troops to form the nucleus of a national army. But the Samurai still remained a great difficulty. They were the essence of the feudal system, but now that it was abolished their existence had no meaning and their stipends practically became pensions. There were about four hundred thousand men in receipt of incomes mostly hereditary which had been granted them in consideration of their devoting themselves to military service. In 1873 a decree announced that the Government was ready to commute these pensions at the rate of six years purchase for hereditary and four years for life pensions, one half of the commutation to be in cash and one half in bonds bearing interest at the rate of 8 per cent. The Samurai were allowed to give up their swords and to engage in other occupations. Contempt for money was part of their code and they showed their loyalty to it by the fortitude and resignation with which they accepted these disadvantageous conditions. Only in Saga was there a small rebellion. At first the commutation was voluntary but further legislation followed. A conscription law made every adult male liable to military service without regard to his social standing, and in 1876 commutation was made compulsory and the wearing of two swords, the ancient badge of the warrior, was forbidden. This overtaxed the already sorely tried temper of the Samurai. It was not the financial loss which wounded them but the ruthless destruction of their old ideals and customs. Before a generation accustomed to another outlook and new occupations had time to arise, the incomes, traditions, rights and status of the gentry were all swept away: military service became a necessary part of everyone's life instead of a special career, and all this was done by a Government which when it first started could not have lasted a day without the support of the Samurai. Feelings like this played a great part in bringing about the Satsuma rebellion.

The Satsuma Rebellion.—This was the only serious reactionary movement with which the Restoration had to contend and the wonder is that there were not more. The immediate cause was a dissension in the cabinet respecting the question of declaring war on the Koreans. They had treated Japan with discourtesy and when the change of administration was notified, had sent a contemptuous reply which the Japanese Government thought it prudent to conceal for the time. In 1875 they fired on a Japanese gunboat which was surveying the coast. The gunboat replied and got very much the best of the fighting which followed. The majority of the cabinet thought that war was most undesirable at this juncture, but some members who were in favour of it resigned. The principal of these was Saigō Takamori, who retired to his native district of Satsuma. He had played a brilliant part in the Restoration and was a man of commanding character and presence; his ambitious character also doubtless influenced his conduct at this time. Satsuma was in many ways an exceptional province and the natives had a strong individuality. It had rendered little more than nominal obedience to the Shōguns: its chief had contributed more than anyone else to the establishment of the new Government by setting the example of surrendering his fief, and the people were disposed to welcome European inventions. But they remained a clan of fighting men and disliked the recent social changes. Saigō settled down in a country seething with discontent and established there schools of arms in which young Samurai were trained in the old traditions, and also in gunnery and other branches of modern military science. He soon had an efficient and devoted army of 40,000 men and in 1877, shortly after the publication of the edicts finally abolishing the status of the Samurai, he declared war, not of course against the emperor but against his majesty's evil counsellors. The struggle lasted eight months and Saigō's defeat was apparently due to his having made the mistake of turning aside to invest the castle of Kumamoto and wasting men and time in a long siege. If he had advanced to the main island, he would certainly have found the Government unprepared to oppose him, and it is impossible to say what the issue might have been. As it was, Saigō and a band of devoted followers were all killed or committed suicide in a last battle fought outside Kagoshima. The result of this rebellion was most important, for it demonstrated to the people that the new army created by the Government was not to be despised. They had put 65,000 men into the field and had proved that military virtue was common to all Japanese and not the exclusive property of the Samurai class. It is remarkable, too, that not one of the Satsuma men in the service of the Government, military or civil, forsook it during the rebellion, not even Saigō's younger brother, who was himself a distinguished soldier. Yet Saigō did not suffer in the public esteem: he had been stripped of his honours as a rebel during his lifetime, but the court restored them posthumously in 1890, his son was made a marquis and a statue was erected in his honour at the entrance of Ueno park.

Reforms.—In the years following 1868 all manner of reforms were introduced. All the restrictions on Japanese going abroad were removed: Christianity was permitted, vaccination, posts and telegraphs, and steamships were introduced. The press became a power. The first railway (between Tokyo and Yokohama) was built with the assistance of English engineers and opened in 1872. Torture was abolished and European dress was prescribed for officials. European and American advisers were freely employed and the indiscriminate imitation of everything European was in danger of leading to vandalism and stupid blindness to the many beauties and merits of Japanese culture.

Though the general tendency was to adopt European institutions indiscriminately and too rapidly, the administration showed some circumspection in introducing parliamentary government. In the charter oath the emperor was made to say that all things must be determined by public discussion. But the first deliberative assembly was composed of nobles and Samurai only. It had no legislative powers and was dissolved after two sessions. In 1874 arrangements were made for annual meetings of provincial governors and the first was convened in Tokyo. These officials also had no legislative powers and being appointed by the cabinet could not be said to be in any way representative of the people. Their function was simply to keep the central administration informed of events and public feeling in their district. The foundations of a legislative assembly were indeed laid in the next year when a senate (Genrō-in) was appointed by imperial decree. Its duty was to discuss and revise all laws prior to their promulgation. Though this senate was abolished in 1889, yet Genrō or elder statesmen continued to play an important part in politics and were frequently consulted by the emperor. Even at the present day (1928) it is often announced that Prince Saionji, the only surviving Genrō, had been so consulted, for instance, about the formation of a new ministry.

The Government seemed disposed to let the question of representative institutions drop, but one of the leaders of the Restoration, Itagaki Taisuke, insisted on keeping it before their notice. He resigned his post in the cabinet, like Saigō, because he was in favour of war with Korea and retired to his home in Tosa, where he began a campaign in favour of representative government, and was joined by discontented Samurai and by many ambitious young men who had visited Europe or America, and found on their return that they could not obtain the posts that they desired. When the Satsuma rebellion broke out Itagaki took advantage of it to present a memorial in which he charged the administration with restraining public opinion by oppressive methods, and demanded the creation of a legislative assembly. But still the Tosa Liberals were not really demanding popular government in the European sense, and it is on record that Itagaki would have been satisfied with an assembly consisting half of officials and half of non-official Samurai. Having mastered the Satsuma rebellion, the Government felt emboldened to refuse even this, but they had a disagreeable surprise when next year, 1878, Ōkubo Toshimichi, who had been prominent as an opponent of Saigō, was assassinated by sympathisers of the latter who came not from Satsuma but from Kaga. They gave themselves up to justice and stated that one of their motives was to call attention to the Government's failure to grant representative institutions. Two months after the assassination an edict was issued ordering the establishment of elective assemblies in various prefectures and cities. A property qualification was prescribed for the electors and members. The duties of the assemblies were to levy and spend local taxes, subject to the approval of the Home Office, and they were authorized to address the central Government. On the whole they worked well, but, though they were a good school for future parliamentarians, they did not at all satisfy the ambition of Itagaki and his friends. He redoubled his agitation and was helped by the growing power of the Press. He founded the first political organization in Japan under the name of Jiyūtō or Liberal party. As its members indulged in great freedom of speech, their meetings were frequently broken up by the police, which attracted both attention and sympathy. In 1881 another political party was founded by Okuma Shigenobu who seceded from the ranks of the Administration. It was called the Shimpōto or party of progress. It might be supposed that this party would have united with the existing Liberal party, but they did not combine and indeed were rather hostile to one another. In studying recent Japanese politics, one must remember a feature which even now has hardly disappeared. A party is a body of men who follow a certain leader to whom they owe loyalty and from whom they expect reward. It is in fact the ancient clan reappearing in another sphere. The party may advocate certain principles, but its essence does not consist in any programme or platform, and identity of principles does not mean identity of party. Also the House of Peers has parties of its own which may from time to time support parties in the lower house but are not identical with them.

The Constitution.—The Administration felt the gravity of the popular demand but still would not allow itself to be hurried. An edict was issued in Oct. 1881, declaring that a National Parliament was to be established in 1890 in order that the imperial purpose of gradually creating a constitutional form of government might be accomplished. In the interval of nine years which remained, the Government made preparations for the coming change. At the Restoration in 1868, the mediaeval form of the executive had been revived, but in 1885 it was replaced by a cabinet on the European model, at the head of which was a minister-president. Itō was the first to fill the post. The senate was abolished and a privy council (Sumitsu-in) composed of persons who had won distinction in the public service was appointed.

The laws were reformed and codified. A criminal code, modelled on that of France, was brought into practice in 1882, but was subsequently modified in 1890 and 1908. Civil and commercial codes were not drawn up until 1899, and followed in the main the principles of German law. It was agreed that the future legislature should consist of two houses, peers and commons, but it was necessary to define the peers, and in 1884 an imperial rescript established five orders of nobility rendered in English as: princes, marquises, counts, viscounts and barons. In 1887 the court ceremonial and the imperial household were reorganized on the German model.

Financial questions were also taken in hand, for the national treasury was in a bad way. The Satsuma rebellion had greatly increased the already heavy liabilities of the Government and there had been a large issue of inconvertible paper currency, which had fallen 60% as compared with specie. In 1879 the Yokohama Specie bank was founded, and in 1882 the Bank of Japan to which was reserved the privilege of issuing notes, other banks being deprived of this right which they had previously enjoyed. This issue of convertible silver notes brought paper back to par and it remained so for ten years. The railway, postal and telegraphic services were steadily extended: harbour works were constructed and the foundations of a strong mercantile marine were laid: numerous students were sent at the public expense to complete their studies in Europe or America, and the system of competitive examinations was introduced. The Government, however, did not receive in all quarters the credit which it deserved. The Opposition, while waiting for the Constitution, became more violent in its methods, not even shrinking from assassination. A class of political bullies called Sōshi came into existence who, like the ancient Rōnin, but without their romance, often terrorized the capital. The ministers had not yet assimilated European usages sufficiently to think of arguing or defending themselves in public speeches, but they gave extraordinary powers to the police. Meetings, associations and newspapers were frequently suppressed and many Sōshi were summarily banished or imprisoned. The Constitution was at last solemnly promulgated in 1889. It had been drafted by Marquis Itō who had visited Europe and America in order to study on the spot various systems of parliamentary government. According to its provisions two chambers were created, the House of Peers and the House of Representatives, with the rights of legislating, imposing taxes and petitioning the emperor. The upper house consisted of not more than 300 members, including (a) all princes and marquises, (b) one-fifth of the remaining peers, elected by themselves, (c) citizen delegates elected by the fifteen richest men of each district, (d) men of learning and ability nominated by the emperor. The House of Representatives consisted of 300 members, the electorate consisting of persons who paid at least fifteen yen in direct taxes.

His majesty opened both chambers in Nov. 1890. Prince Yamagata was induced to act as prime minister but handed over the office to Matsukata, the minister of finance, in 1891, and the career of the new parliament was at first far from peaceful. One of the great objects of Itagaki and his followers had been to abolish the clan system, but they found to their regret that it flourished under parliamentary institutions even better than before. The Sat-chō, as the two great clans were compendiously termed, managed to get the running of the whole machine into their hands, Satsuma controlled the navy, finance and industries; Chōshū the army, civil service and education. Also the cabinet's tenure of office depended solely on the emperor, and his ministers took their mandates from him and not from parliament. Hence it was impossible to turn a ministry out by a mere vote: it could be made to fall only by obstruction which rendered legislation and finance impossible and, as many of the Opposition had suffered imprisonment or fines during the recent period of agitation, the virulence of their attacks knew no bounds. Had not the House of Peers been consistent in its support of the Government the necessary routine of administration might have become difficult. But a great change occurred in the attitude of the Opposition when war with China broke out in 1894. There has never been any doubt about the patriotism of any Japanese party, and when once the interests of the country were at stake all combined to assist the administration.

Treaty Revision.—Before passing on to the wars of modern Japan, it will be well to say a few words about a question which exercised the minds of both Japanese and foreigners during many years, namely the revision of the treaties made with foreign Powers. In 1882 when the first conference met in Tokyo to consider the possibility of settling this question, the situation was as follows. Since the signature of the first treaty by Commodore Perry, a number of others had been made with foreign Powers and as they all contained a most favoured nation clause all were practically identical. The principal provisions were (a) Kanagawa and five other ports were opened to foreign trade and foreigners were allowed to reside within a radius of about 24 miles round each, called treaty limits. (b) Foreigners enjoyed extra-territoriality; that is to say, they were exempt from the jurisdiction of

Japanese law courts and were justiciable only to their own consular courts. (c) A very low rate of import duties was fixed, mostly 5% *ad valorem*. In the days of their early ignorance the Japanese found these arrangements quite convenient, for extra-territoriality saved much trouble. But when they began to go abroad they soon perceived that the situation had another aspect which was most galling to their national pride. It meant that they were not really treated as the equals of other nations and were regarded as people who could not be trusted to administer justice or impose reasonable duties, although all the Western Powers trusted one another to this extent. As hostility towards foreigners soon died out, no objection was felt to giving them freedom of residence if Japan could obtain judicial and tariff autonomy. As early as 1876 a treaty which gave the Japanese most of what they desired was concluded with the United States, but it was of little use, except as an admission of principles, for it contained a clause saying that it would come into force only when the other Powers made similar agreements. Meanwhile the laws were revised with the assistance of French and German experts. The negotiations which began in 1883 lasted no less than eleven years and the delay was not entirely due to the hesitation of foreigners. Mexico, Russia and Germany signed agreements, when suddenly Japanese opinion seemed to change. It was proposed that for a few years four foreign judges should assist the Japanese courts in trying cases in which foreigners were concerned and this was bitterly denounced as derogatory to the national dignity. The patriots of the Opposition began to talk of the danger of Japan being swamped by a foreign invasion and a bomb was thrown at Count Okuma, the minister of foreign affairs, which blew off his leg. Naturally the Japanese Government thought it well to proceed with caution and public opinion began to change again. Negotiations recommenced and a new watchword, probably inspired by the Government, "Treaty revision and equal rights" became popular. Great Britain, which had hitherto shown little disposition to make concessions, now came to the front and in 1894 consented to a new treaty which abolished extra-territoriality and gave Japan the right to fix her own import duties and a monopoly of the coasting trade. Similar treaties with other Powers were soon concluded and the emperor issued an edict declaring in unequivocal terms that it was his desire to abolish all distinctions between natives and foreigners. 1899 was the date fixed for bringing the treaties into force and it was duly observed. Complete tariff autonomy, however, was not obtained till 1911.

In the period following the institution of parliamentary government, Japan undertook two considerable wars, one with China (1894-5) and one with Russia (1904-5). She also took part in the expedition to Peking (1900) and made an alliance with Great Britain. Looking back, one can see that this military activity was well timed. During the period of metamorphosis external entanglements had been avoided: coming when it did, military and naval success consolidated the nation. The severest critics of the new régime had to admit that it had made of Japan a State which was accepted by the world as one of the Great Powers, capable of competing with the others in peace or war. As early as 1874 an incident occurred which might have led to a breach with China, if not carefully handled. A ship from the Ryū-kyū islands was wrecked on the coast of Formosa, then nominally Chinese territory, and its crew were barbarously treated by the natives. Representations at Peking had no result, so the Japanese sent a punitive expedition to the island. The Chinese Government protested, and the matter was arranged by the intervention of the British minister at Peking, Japan agreeing to withdraw her troops and China to indemnify her for the expenses of the expedition. The political status of the Ryū-kyū islands was obscure and complicated. They had a king of their own: for about two centuries they had been rather fitfully administered by the Daimyō of Satsuma, and they paid occasional tribute to both China and Japan. In 1875 Japan boldly made them into a prefecture, probably knowing that no serious trouble would occur. China protested and discussions ensued, but Japan kept the islands. The king received a pension and subsequently was made a marquis.

In dealing with the question of Sakhalin at this period the Japanese showed themselves eminently pacific. Some Japanese had settled there as early as 1620, but Russians arrived in 1847 and under the Shōgunate there were negotiations for the partition of the island, which led to no result. Apparently both parties came to the conclusion that the territory was not worth much. At one time the Russians seemed not unwilling to sell the whole, but the Japanese withdrew from the bargain and in 1875 agreed to an arrangement by which they recognized Russia's title to the whole of Sakhalin, while Russia recognized Japan's title to the Kurile islands.

The Chinese War.—At first, Japan's attitude towards Korean questions was similarly pacific. As related above, the majority of the cabinet refused to declare war in 1875, though Korea had offered provocation, and some of the ministers resigned. Japan proceeded to treat Korea in the same way as she had herself been treated by Commodore Perry. A considerable fleet was sent to demand a treaty of amity and commerce. This was signed in 1876 and three Korean ports were opened to foreign trade. When one remembers the ambitions of Hideyoshi in the 16th century and likewise the ultimate fate of Korea, it is hard not to think that Japanese statesmen were already meditating the conquest of the peninsula, but their avowed policy was perfectly pacific and reasonable. They claimed the right of trade and residence, just as western countries had claimed it in Japan, and they wished to introduce reforms, fearing that the state of Korea might become so bad that other Powers might have an excuse for intervening to restore order and for establishing themselves in a position inconveniently near to Japan. But continual difficulties were created by the Government of Peking, which adhered to the ancient doctrine of tributary states. It was the immemorial policy of China to surround herself with petty states which might act as buffers to break the shock of foreign contact: if any other Power interfered with these states she protested, but if they misbehaved themselves, she admitted no responsibility. Such a relationship had worked well in the middle ages, but it was clearly not practicable in the new era of international intercourse which had already begun. On the one hand, China seemed to recognize the independence of Korea by permitting the conclusion of treaties with Japan and subsequently with other countries: on the other, a Chinese resident, who practically directed all important affairs, was stationed at Seoul. The members of the Min family to which the queen belonged were allowed to monopolize office and misgovern the country and, whenever there was a rising, Chinese troops were despatched to suppress it. On two occasions, in 1882 and 1884, the Japanese legation was burnt in the course of outbreaks, partly, it would seem, owing to the Korean hatred of Japanese immigrants, many of whom were low-class adventurers. After the attack in 1882, Japan was allowed to have troops in Seoul for the protection of the legation, and in 1885 a convention was concluded with China by which each Power undertook not to send troops without notifying the other.

In the following years some reforms were introduced in Korea: the customs service was reorganized and foreign settlements were opened, but the Japanese continually had reason to complain that they were prevented from enjoying the commercial rights guaranteed to them by treaty and that the Chinese resident prevented them from obtaining redress. In 1894 another rising against the Korean Government broke out. The Chinese sent a force of 2,500 men to suppress it and conformably to the convention notified the Japanese, describing Korea at the same time as a tributary state. The Japanese Government replied by sending 8,000 men and stated that they would not be withdrawn "without some understanding which would guarantee the peace and good order of Korea." As the rebellion, which had been the pretext for China's intervention, had meanwhile died a natural death, the Japanese further stated that the dispatch of any more Chinese troops would be regarded as an act of hostility. In spite of this the Chinese sent by sea 1,200 troops which encountered the Japanese cruiser "Naniwa." There is some discrepancy in the accounts of what occurred, but it is generally stated that the Chinese fired first. At any rate, their ships were sunk and the troops perished. War was declared by both nations a few days later on Aug. 1. The campaign which followed was a succession of triumphs for Japan. The Chinese entrenched themselves at Phyong-Yang (the same town which had figured in Hideyoshi's campaigns) and made leisurely preparations for defence. The Japanese took some time to arrive, but when their columns converged on Phyong-Yang they carried all the positions in a day, with great loss to the Chinese and little to themselves. On the very next day, Sept. 17, they won a brilliant naval victory at the mouth of the Yalu river. They then took Port Arthur and Talien-wan with little difficulty, but had a stubborn fight with the remainder of the Chinese fleet at Wei-hai-wei. But there, also, the Chinese were obliged to surrender and the war was at an end, having lasted seven months and a half. The Chinese sent Li Hung-Chang to negotiate terms and he signed a treaty of peace with Itō, the prime minister, on April 17, 1895, at Shimonoseki. It recognized the independence of Korea and ceded to Japan Formosa and the Pescadores islands, as well as the southern part of Manchuria: China was to pay an indemnity of 200,000,000 taels and to give new facilities to foreign trade. Japan had now a disagreeable experience of European diplomacy. Russia, Germany and France presented a joint note recommending that the territory ceded on the mainland should not be occupied permanently, and it was understood that they were ready to enforce this advice by an appeal to arms if necessary. The Japanese Government grasped the position and yielded at once, but the incident long rankled in the memories of both ministers and people.

In the years between the Chinese and Russian wars there were no fewer than six ministries, but these vicissitudes were signs of the rise and fall of various cliques rather than of any serious change in policy. The two important struggles which went on all the time and continued until quite recently were, first, the contest between the oligarchs of the great clans and the more radical elements and, second, the contest between civil and military authorities for the upper hand. A significant event in parliamentary history was the foundation of the Seiyukai party by Prince Itō in 1900. It corresponded to some extent to a liberal party in Europe, but the sentiments enunciated in its original manifesto are so vague and non-committal that one might suppose all Japanese would accept them. But Prince Itō's action implied that a cabinet ought to represent a party, a principle which had not been admitted by any one of his eminence before. The position of Prince Yamagata, then prime minister, became untenable and for the fourth time Prince Itō formed a ministry, but held office for less than a year.

The Japanese emerged from the Chinese war with the island of Formosa and a free hand in Korea. They took possession of the former without much trouble, although the Chinese population rose in what was known as the Black Flag rebellion. In 1896 a Japanese administration was introduced into the island and it was duly divided into departments and prefectures. But, considering the length of time it has been in Japanese hands, the process of introducing peace and order has not been so rapid as might have been expected, for even now the unruly tribes of the north-eastern portion are imperfectly subdued and still practice head hunting.

Korea.—In Korea, too, there were many difficulties. Chinese obstruction being now removed, the Japanese tried to introduce reforms which they hoped might lead to the establishment of order and the increase of trade. Count Inouye was sent to Seoul for this purpose, but seems to have erred by excess of zeal. His successor, Gen. Miura, was even less successful and came into collision with the queen, who was a woman of most masterful character. A conspiracy was formed in which Japanese were implicated and in Oct. 1896, the palace was surprised and the queen was killed with all her suite. As the Japanese legation was accused of being privy to this conspiracy, the minister and his staff were at once recalled and put on their trial at Tokyo, but were acquitted. The results of the whole incident in Korea were disastrous. The king took refuge in the Russian legation and remained there for two years, during which time he did his best to nullify all the reforms extorted under Japanese pressure and gave valuable concessions to the Russians, including the right to cut timber in the valley of the Yalu river. In 1898 the Germans occupied Kiao-Chiao in Shantung as an indemnity for the murder of two missionaries. Immediately afterwards Russia received from China a lease of the Liaotung peninsula, although three years before she objected to the cession of the same region to Japan, and permission to construct a branch of the Trans-Siberian railway through Manchuria from north to south. Soon after this, in 1900, came the Boxer rising and the siege of the legations at Peking. Japan acted throughout in concert with the Powers of Europe and, being the nearest country geographically, was the first to send a force to relieve not only her compatriots but the Europeans and Americans who were beleaguered in Peking and Tientsin. The conduct and results of this expedition were most gratifying to the Japanese: their troops co-operated with Europeans on an equal footing: practical comparison showed that they were inferior to none in efficiency and discipline and their behaviour was good, better in fact than the behaviour of some of the European troops. All this was eminently satisfactory to the authorities at Tokyo, but at the same time the action of Russia caused them the gravest anxiety. One result of the Boxer troubles was that Russia remained in military occupation of Manchuria and this, combined with strong pro-Russian feeling in the official circles and also among the populace of Seoul, created a position most dangerous for Japan's interests. Japan undoubtedly desired peace and while realizing that war might be inevitable did her best to avoid or postpone it. She acted in concert with Great Britain and the United States, and Russia was induced to sign a treaty pledging herself to withdraw her troops from Manchuria in three instalments.

Anglo-Japanese Treaty.—The position of Japan was further strengthened by the Anglo-Japanese Treaty (the precursor of the Anglo-Japanese alliance) which was signed on Jan. 30, 1902. It recognized "the independence of China and Korea, the special interests of Great Britain in China and of Japan both in China and in a peculiar degree, politically as well as commercially and industrially, in Korea, and the rights of both parties to take such measures as may be indispensable to safeguard those interests either against the aggressive action of any other Power or in the case of disturbances in either country." In the event of either party becoming involved in war with a third Power, the other party was to remain neutral unless "any other Power or Powers should join in hostilities against that ally, when the other high contracting party will come to its assistance and will conduct the war in common and make peace in mutual agreement with it."

The Russian War.—Russia did not withdraw her troops from Manchuria at the dates fixed, and the Japanese Government opened direct negotiations at St. Petersburg (Leningrad). They proposed that Russia and Japan should each recognize the other's status in Manchuria and Korea respectively: that both Powers should respect the territorial integrity of China and Korea and be parties to an engagement that all nations should have equal commercial and industrial opportunities in Korea and Manchuria. The negotiations lasted for five and a half months, but Russia proved unyielding and unconciliatory. The representations made in St. Petersburg were received with a silence that seemed discourteous. As the position became intolerable, the Japanese severed diplomatic relations on Feb. 6, 1904. The war which followed contained many striking incidents, especially the capture of Port Arthur and the annihilation of the Russian fleet by Admiral Tōgō. The details are given in a separate article (see RUSSO-JAPANESE WAR).

Brilliant as had been the victories of Japan, it was doubtful if she could continue the contest. In Russia the war had never been popular with the nation and the inglorious struggle had been most depressing. When, therefore, in June 1905 the President of the United States made an offer of mediation it was gladly accepted. The plenipotentiaries of both countries met at Portsmouth in New Hampshire, and on Aug. 29, 1905, the treaty of peace was signed. It recognized Japan's "paramount political military and economic interests" in Korea: provided for the evacuation of Manchuria by both parties: transferred to Japan Russia's lease of the Liaotung peninsula, together with the southern section of the Manchurian railway from Port Arthur to Kwang-cheng-tse and all collateral privileges, mining or other: and ceded to Japan the southern half of Sakhalin. It was agreed that Japan should receive £4,000,000 on account of moneys spent in maintaining Russian prisoners. But, with this trifling exception, Russia refused to pay any indemnity and the Japanese plenipotentiaries did not dare to imperil the negotiations by insisting. But the Japanese public were indignant at the terms. The war had cost 170 millions sterling and 230,000 men killed or wounded, and the material gain in return for this expenditure seemed totally inadequate, however great might be the increase in prestige. Angry riots broke out at Tokyo, and the police buildings were burnt, but no better terms were obtainable. The prime minister, Prince Katsura, resigned, feeling that he could not face the diet. He made it, however, a condition that his successor, Prince Saionji, should carry through a measure which he had prepared for the nationalization of the railways of the empire and this was duly done in 1906. Katsura returned to power in 1908 and it was pretty plain that an arrangement had been made to enable him to retire until the nation's anger at not receiving an indemnity had subsided.

The Anglo-Japanese Alliance.—His services had indeed been considerable for just before the Treaty of Portsmouth was signed, he had concluded a new treaty of alliance with Great Britain. Unlike the agreement of 1902 it did not deal with the independence and integrity of Korea, but it bound the contracting parties to come to each other's assistance and conduct war in common, if "by reason of unprovoked attack or aggressive action wherever arising on the part of any other Power or Powers either party should be involved in war in defence of its territorial rights or special interests." These were defined as (a) the maintenance of peace in Eastern Asia and India, (b) the independence and integrity of China and the principle of equal opportunities for the commerce and industry of all nations there, (c) the maintenance of the territorial rights of both Powers and the defence of their special interests in Eastern Asia and India. In the same year a third treaty was signed with China confirming the transfer to Japan of Russia's rights in Manchuria. Two other agreements concluded with France and with Russia in 1907 further consolidated Japan's international position.

In view of the Treaty of Portsmouth the Powers withdrew their legations from Seoul and replaced them by consulates, and the Japanese sent Prince Itō as resident-general. A comprehensive scheme of reforms was introduced embracing law, police, education, taxation and currency. At first the Korean Government was asked to effect the necessary changes by employing Japanese advisers. But no attention was paid to the advice of these officials and a new arrangement was made in 1907 by which the resident-general practically became a governor with legislative and executive powers, including authority to appoint and remove officials and to employ Japanese in the administration. Prince Itō also found it necessary to disband the standing army, as being inefficient and a useless expense. The soldiers resisted vehemently, and many of them formed the nucleus of an insurrection which lasted two years. Though the proposed reforms seemed excellent in conception, they were perhaps enforced somewhat drastically and were most distasteful to the natives. While Prince Itō was on a visit to Harbin in 1909 he was assassinated by a young Korean, who claimed that he was avenging the wrongs of his country. Naturally the attitude of the Japanese Government became more severe: the insurrectionary movement of the disbanded soldiers was repressed with considerable loss of life, and it was shortly decided that the country must be annexed to the Japanese empire. This was done by an imperial rescript in 1910.

The Russian war had been costly but the Japanese were not afraid of spending money to secure military efficiency. Six divisions were added to the army and a new law of conscription was introduced, the general result of which was to provide within 10 years a fully trained army of 1,500,000 men and half a million recruits who could be used for reinforcement. New ships, arsenals and dockyards were built. Of course the financial burdens of the nation increased. The national debt rose from 56 millions sterling in 1904 to 227 in 1908, and taxation became very much heavier. It is indeed surprising that there was no serious financial embarrassment, but the development of trade and industry, improved economic conditions, and the good international status of Japan combined to prevent any crisis.

Japanese Immigration into America.—Although the relations of Japan and the United States had hitherto been excellent, a question now began to arise which is still troublesome and from time to time creates difficulties. This is Japanese immigration into American territory, especially California. To a less extent the same question affects British Columbia. Experience shows that the Japanese do not settle willingly in new countries where the climate and standard of comfort are not what they are accustomed to, such as their own territories of Formosa and even Hokkaido, but that they gladly migrate, at least temporarily, to regions like the Pacific Coast of North America where the pioneer work of colonization has already been done and conditions are to their liking. In 1908 it was stated that there were more than sixty thousand Japanese in California who did not intend to become American citizens but to make money and return to their homes. They were objectionable to other classes of the population, partly on account of the difference in their customs, but chiefly because they were ready to work for longer hours and less wages than labourers of European descent. The State legislature of California made certain enactments designed to restrict the entry and residence of Japanese, and this produced intense popular indignation in Japan. In order to understand the attitude of the Japanese Government and people in this matter, which is still far from settled, it must be remembered that the recurring cause for irritation is not so much the actual inconvenience which may be occasioned by restrictive enactments, as the implication which seems to be contained in them that the Japanese are not really the equals of Europeans and Americans, but belong to an inferior race. President Roosevelt attempted to calm the anti-Japanese agitation in California without much success, but in 1911 the Japanese Government made an agreement (originally concluded with Canada, but subsequently extended to the United States) by which without surrendering any of their treaty rights they voluntarily undertook to limit the immigration of their subjects. This was known as the "Gentleman's Agreement" and though it by no means closed the question, it was admitted that the Government of Tokyo were sincere in their efforts to execute it.

It also became apparent that there was a divergence between American and Japanese views as to Manchuria, for in 1910 Mr. Knox, the Secretary of State, made an unexpected proposal that all railways in that district should be neutralized. This suggestion was not to the taste of Russia, China or Japan and fell through, but it had the result of bringing Russia and Japan together. They signed an agreement by which they pledged themselves to maintain the *status quo* in Manchuria and to abstain from any unfriendly competition in developing that region. In the same year a modification was made in the Anglo-Japanese alliance. A general treaty of arbitration between Great Britain and the United States was then under discussion, whereas the treaty with Japan, without mentioning any names, provided for the possibility that Great Britain might be her ally in the event of a war with the United States. It was now stipulated that nothing in the treaty should entail on either contracting Power the obligation to go to war with any third Power with whom a treaty of general arbitration might be in force. This new treaty was for ten years and after that period was to continue automatically unless denounced by either party.

Death of the Emperor Meiji.—In 1911, Marquis Katsura, who had been premier for nearly five years and had accomplished various financial reforms as well as the annexation of Korea, resigned and was succeeded by Prince Saionji, the leader of the Seiyukai party. Next year the Emperor Mutsuhito, better known as Meiji, died and the period called by the same name came to an end. His decease caused profound regret and was an event of unusual importance for the nation. It cannot be said that he initiated or was responsible for the amazing changes which occurred in the Meiji era and even under his "enlightened Government" the sovereign was hidden by a veil which makes it hard to tell how great was the part which he personally played. But all accounts agree that he was a man of strong and even obstinate character and that after he attained manhood no important steps were taken without his knowledge and consent. It is known that he interfered in national crises and apparently he was never on the wrong side. During the 45 years that he was emperor he witnessed and took part in a succession of extraordinary changes such as can hardly have occurred in any other one reign in any other country of the world and, unlike most revolutionary changes, they were not to the detriment of the monarchy. Though he delegated his authority, he did not impair it and he retained until his death the veneration and devotion of his people.

He was succeeded by his son Yoshihito, born in 1879, who adopted as the title of his reign *Taishō* or Great Righteousness. Soon after his accession the Saionji cabinet fell, because the military party insisted on having two army divisions in Korea, to which the other ministers were opposed on grounds of economy. Other short and confused ministries followed.

Prince Katsura returned to political life, but found the lower house intractable. He then resigned and started in 1913 a political party called Rikken Doshikai, the Constitutional Comrades association. It attracted a large membership but unfortunately its founder died almost immediately. The Yamamoto cabinet which followed (1913) was also short lived owing to a naval scandal and the trial of high officers on the charge of having accepted bribes from a foreign company in connection with the building of a Japanese warship.

JAPAN AND THE WORLD WAR

The Siege of Tsingtao.—In April 1914 Count Okuma, who of recent years had been devoting all his energies to the foundation and development of the Waseda university in Tokyo, undertook to form a cabinet. It lasted only two years but is memorable because under this administration Japan joined the Allies in the World War and, since the Germans were in occupation of Kiao-Chiao, was called upon to take action at once. On Aug. 14, an ultimatum was sent to Berlin demanding the immediate withdrawal of German warships from Chinese and Japanese waters and the surrender of Kiao-Chiao to China before Sept. 15. As no answer was returned to this communication, Japan declared war against Germany on Aug. 23 and Tsingtao, the principal town in the German leased territory was invested. It fell on Nov. 7, and Japan assumed the administration of the territory. (For an account of the operations and capture of the city by the Anglo-Japanese forces *see* the article TSINGTAO, SIEGE OF.)

Admiral von Spee's ships were now seriously menacing commerce in the South Seas. Japanese squadrons were sent to the China sea and Pacific ocean and two cruisers co-operated with British vessels in patrolling the western coast of America. Towards the end of 1914, as a result of these concerted operations, von Spee's squadron was chased in the direction of Cape Horn and was ultimately sunk off the Falkland islands. The Marshall, Pelew, Caroline and Marianne islands were captured. The Japanese did not send any troops to Europe, but Admiral Saito proceeded to the Mediterranean and assumed the duty of convoying Allied vessels from port to port and protecting them against the attacks of German submarines. It is said that in all they successfully escorted 788 ships.

In 1918, Japan joined Great Britain, France and the United States in sending an expedition to Siberia and landed a considerable force at Vladivostok and in October Czechoslovak troops from the interior made their way through to the coast. An anti-Bolshevik government under Admiral Kolchak was established at Omsk and an expedition into European Russia was contemplated, but was rendered unnecessary by the Armistice of Nov. 11. Japanese troops did not advance farther inland than Chita and Irkutsk.

Okuma retired from ill-health in 1916 and Terauchi, of the party called Seiyukai, was appointed to succeed him, although the majority in the diet belonged to the Kenseikai (Constitutionalists), a party which was an amalgamation of the Doshikai with some smaller associations and led by Kato. This appointment created considerable hostility and was considered to be due to the influence of the Genrō. The diet proved so unmanageable that Parliament was dissolved and a general election took place in 1917. It resulted in a striking victory for the Government party or Seiyukai, the Kenseikai losing heavily. This may seem a strange result considering the popular clamour which led to the election, but until quite recently the Government under whose auspices an election is held and which is in charge of the necessary police arrangements has never lost an election in Japan. In view of the war Terauchi was desirous of obtaining unanimity in foreign policy. For this purpose he created the temporary Diplomatic Investigation council, on which all political parties were represented. But in spite of its victory at the polls in 1917, his cabinet had continual trouble, complicated by rice riots and strikes, and he resigned in 1918. Hara, leader of the Seiyukai in succession to Saionji, was selected as the new premier. He was remarkable as being the first commoner to hold office and also his cabinet, as representing a party professing certain principles, approximated more nearly to European political institutions than any of its predecessors. In March 1918 the Government had been obliged by popular demand to bring forward an Electoral Reform Bill by which the property qualification for voters was reduced from a payment of ten yen in taxes to three yen. But a decided democratic movement began to show itself. This extension of the vote was not regarded as satisfactory: there was a clamour for universal suffrage and a bill providing for it was introduced by the Opposition in Feb. 1920. The Government, however, contended that as no election on the basis of the extended suffrage had yet taken place, it was premature to make a further suffrage reform without consulting the country. The diet was accordingly dissolved and at the election which took place immediately afterwards the Government party, that is the Seiyukai, as usual obtained a large majority. The position was somewhat curious for the Seiyukai, who were supposed to be the liberal party, were against universal suffrage and the Kenseikai were supporting it for political reasons, though it was distasteful to many of them.

Peace Conference.—At the Peace conference held in Paris in 1919, Japan brought forward a proposal, most dear to Japanese sentiment, that the principle of racial equality should be admitted. The Powers were invited to accord as soon as possible to all nationals of the States members of the League equal and just treatment in every respect, making no distinction either in law or in fact on account of their race or nationality. In making this proposal Count Makino explained that the clause did not demand the immediate realization of racial equality: it enunciated the principle only and left the methods of applying it in the hands of the Governments concerned. In the course of discussion the wording was somewhat modified in the hope of meeting objections, but even so the proposal obtained only 11 votes out of 17 and it was ruled that unanimity was essential. Japan accepted the decision, reserving the right to raise the question again at an opportune moment, but no doubt this refusal to recognize racial equality created a very unfortunate feeling. In other respects the main results of the peace for Japan were two in number. First, the former German islands in the Pacific lying north of the Equator which had been under Japanese occupation since 1914 were now allocated to Japanese administration under mandate. Secondly, in spite of the objections of China, it was finally decided to give Kiao-Chiao to Japan, but on the understanding that she would not retain it but would restore it to China as a mark of goodwill and friendship. Both these transfers of territory created a good deal of discussion, which was continued at the Washington Conference summoned at the end of 1921. One of the islands transferred under mandate was Yap in the Caroline group, which had a special importance as being a centre of the cable system in the Pacific. The United States took exception to Yap becoming an integral part of Japanese territory on the ground that it vitally affected the world's communications. The question was eventually settled: an agreement was signed in which the United States admitted the authority of Japan as the mandatory power in Yap, while Japan accorded to the United States full rights and facilities in respect of cables.

The question of the rendition of Kiao-Chiao was complicated by the relations which had arisen between China and Japan during the war. In 1915 the Powers of Europe were engaged in a conflict the issue of which was by no means certain; should Germany prove victorious Japan's prospects in China were not at all favourable. The internal condition of China was equally uncertain and no one could say what form of government might eventually be established there. Japanese troops were in occupation of Tsingtao and a portion of Shantung. In these circumstances the statesmen of Tokyo thought it wise to make use of the opportunity and strengthen the position of their country.

The Twenty-one Demands.—Baron Kato, the minister of foreign affairs, presented to the Government of Peking what became known as "the Twenty-one Demands," ranged in five groups dealing with (*a*) Shantung, (*b*) Manchuria, and Eastern Mongolia, (*c*) the Hanyehping Company, (*d*) an engagement that China would not cede any harbour to a third Power. The fifth group was not at first made public but was presented confidentially as "wishes." It included the appointment of Japanese as advisers in political, financial and military matters: the priority of Japanese capital in railways, harbours and mines in the province of Fukien opposite to the Japanese island of Formosa: and other important points. The demands were presented in January and for some time no reply was received, but in May the Japanese Government pressed for a definite answer within a time limit and China accepted within the month. Two treaties were concluded, one dealing with Shantung and the other with Mongolia and Manchuria.

The Washington Conference.—By the latter the leases of Port Arthur and Dairen as well as of the South Manchurian railway and the Antung-Mukden railway were extended to 99 years and Japanese were accorded various privileges, residential, commercial, agricultural and industrial. The question of these treaties did not come up at the Washington Conference officially but, since it stood in the way of a good understanding, informal discussion between the Chinese and Japanese delegates was arranged. The restoration of the former German leased territory to China was agreed upon. The Japanese delegates also stated that in view of the changes which had taken place since 1915 they were ready to withdraw many of the demands then made and granted; *e.g.*, the preferential rights regarding Japanese advisers. The most important part of the treaty of 1915 still remaining in force is the agreement respecting the Kwangtung peninsula (another name for the Dairen territory), South Manchuria and Eastern Mongolia. In virtue of it the leases of that peninsula, of the South Manchurian railway and the Antung-Mukden railway remain extended for 99 years, that is till 1977, 2002 and 2007 respectively. The administration of the former German leased territory in Shantung was actually transferred to China in Dec. 1922.

The Japanese troops remained in Siberia longer than those of other Powers, but a promise was made at the Washington Conference to withdraw them as soon as the situation permitted. Japan, as a near neighbour, was affected by the fact that Siberia, since the death of Kolchak, was in Bolshevik hands and a most unfortunate incident had occurred in March 1920 when 700 Japanese were massacred at Nikolaievsk by a Bolshevik guerrilla gang. On this the Japanese occupied northern Sakhalin. The troops on the mainland were withdrawn in 1923 and in the same year negotiations were started for the recognition of the Soviet Government. These negotiations were at first informal but were subsequently conducted by the Japanese and Soviet representatives at Peking and resulted in a convention signed in Jan. 1925. By its terms Japan recognized the Soviet Government which tendered "an expression of sincere regret" for the massacre of Nikolaievsk. Japan undertook to withdraw her troops from northern Sakhalin immediately, special arrangements being made for the working of oilfields in this region by Japanese firms. There were further stipulations as to granting other concessions and fishing rights. It is significant that whereas in 1915 the Japanese Government seemed inclined to adopt a forward policy on the mainland, their subsequent attitude became most unassuming. They withdrew from Shantung and Siberia and did not even attempt to retain the northern portion of Sakhalin.

For the various agreements respecting the limitation of naval armaments and other matters at the Washington Conference, *see* that article. Of special importance was the agreement by which the Anglo-Japanese alliance was brought to an end and replaced by a Four-Power Treaty between France, Great Britain, Japan and the United States.

In 1921 the Crown Prince Hirohito made a tour in Europe and was received in Great Britain with the greatest cordiality by both the court and the public. This was the first time that a prince in the direct line of succession had left the sacred soil of Japan. In 1922 the Prince of Wales returned the visit and was received with equal cordiality.

The health of the emperor had never been robust. From the beginning of 1920 he ceased to appear in public and on Nov. 25, 1922, the Crown Prince was appointed regent. In 1924, H.I.H. married the daughter of Prince Kuni, head of one of the collateral princely houses.

THE GREAT EARTHQUAKE

The Hara cabinet continued in power until Nov. 1921. From a Japanese point of view, it was only moderately successful in foreign politics and many accusations of corruption in domestic matters were brought against it. Nevertheless the sudden assassination of Mr. Hara on Nov. 4 appeared to be the act of a crazy youth rather than a sign of popular resentment. Takahashi, minister of finance, succeeded Hara both as prime minister and head of the Seiyukai party but, finding the cabinet not amenable to his leadership, resigned after six months and Admiral Tomosaburo Kato, minister of marine and chief delegate to the Washington Conference, became prime minister in June 1922. Though he had no party affiliations he was promised the unconditional support of the Seiyukai. His first act was to abolish the temporary Diplomatic Investigation Council established in 1917. He endeavoured to cope with the growing social unrest and with the very serious commercial depression which was beginning to set in as a reaction after the abnormally favourable conditions which had prevailed at the end of the war. Unfortunately his health was bad and he died after little more than a year of office. Count Yamamoto, who had lived in retirement since the collapse of his cabinet in 1914, was commanded by the throne to form a ministry and while he was engaged on the task there occurred the terrible earthquake of Sept. 1, 1923 (*see* EARTHQUAKE). This stupendous disaster relegated ordinary political affairs to a secondary place for some time.

The Government took prompt action for the relief of the afflicted population, but the question of reconstruction created great divergences of opinion and the projects of Viscount Goto, minister of the interior, and the officials principally concerned created much discussion. On Dec. 27 another crazy youth made an attempt on the Prince Regent's life and the cabinet, regarding it as a disgrace to their administration, resigned. This action was entirely in accordance with Japanese political etiquette, but it was probably also a not unwelcome escape from a difficult position. Viscount Kiyoura was summoned to form a ministry. His cabinet was non-party and consisted almost entirely of bureaucrats and, as it showed no marked ability in dealing with the pressing problems created by the earthquake, discontent became general. The Seiyukai split into two sections, the seceding party being called the Seiyuhontō. A general election was held in May, 1924, at which the Kenseikai party obtained 162 seats, the Seiyukai 137, and the Seiyuhontō 94. Viscount Kato Takaaki, former minister of foreign affairs and ambassador at London, formed a coalition cabinet and in March, 1925, carried through the Universal Suffrage Bill, by which all males above 25 received the vote. But divisions began to appear in the coalition cabinet and some important members resigned. Gen. Giichi Tanaka became head of the Seiyukai and there was much talk of this party reuniting with the Seiyuhontō. In July the cabinet could not agree upon a scheme proposed for the reduction of taxation and Kato resigned. He was ordered, however, to continue as prime minister and accordingly formed a new and homogeneous cabinet, consisting entirely of Kenseikai members but, unfortunately, he died suddenly in the following January. The minister of home affairs, Wakatsuki, succeeded him. Difficulties connected with immigration into America increased. In 1921 California and the other Western States made it illegal for a Japanese to own or lease land or even act as guardian for his own children born in America (who are by law American citizens) if they held land. On May 15, 1924, Congress passed an immigration law excluding Asiatics, which was regarded as equivalent to a declaration that Japanese were inadmissible as immigrants. This discrimination aroused resentment in Japan and the Government protested.

The Emperor Taisho died on Christmas Day 1926 and was succeeded by his son the prince regent, who adopted Showa as the title of his reign.

In November and December 1928 the new Emperor performed all the ceremonies prescribed by tradition, and made several pronouncements declaring the policy of the Showa era. A new ministry was formed by Yuko Hamaguchi, July 2, 1929.

BIBLIOGRAPHY.—Wenckstern's *Bibliography of the Japanese Empire* contains the names of all important books about Japan, both ancient and modern. Vol. ii., published in 1907, deals with literature which appeared from 1894–1906. The most important recent work on Japanese history is Murdoch, *A History of Japan*, 3 vols. Other recent works are Sir E. Satow, *A Diplomat in Japan* (1922); J. H. Gubbins, *The Making of New Japan;* J. L. Longford, "Japan" in the series, *Nations of To-day* (1923). (C. EL.)

PERIODS OF ART. An art period is that duration of time within which the main arts, both fine and applied, show a general recognizable trend or group of characteristics. These characteristics which the reader will find described under the various articles listed at the end of this article, like those of the human beings who created them, are usually complex and difficult to describe, often being wholly unrecognizable until the observer has equipped himself with a considerable experience in the identification, comparison and classification of various works of art and, even when he is so equipped, these characteristics are sometimes found to be the basis of irreconcilable discussion so far as details are concerned, by the greatest of experts. That there are, however, specific characteristics upon which the majority of authorities agree and which clearly indicate the time and geographical location on the earth's surface, wherein some certain work of art was conceived and made, cannot be denied. It is on such expert classification quite as much as upon the deductions of archaeological research that the whole fabric of the history of art, as well as our understanding of the extent and characteristics of the various cultural periods, is based.

As was pointed out in the notes under the first chart in the reference to the period between 500 B.C. and 350 B.C., there seems to occur at times a nearly world-wide stimulus or depression in the field of art. From A.D. 1400 to A.D. 1500 that great movement called the Renaissance prevailed through southern Europe; at the same time the Gothic movement in northern Europe was still productive; western Asia saw perhaps its highest pinnacle in painting, pottery making, rug weaving and the other arts; and in the Far East the great Ming Dynasty (1368 to 1644) was at its height. It seems strange that though the individual causes seem to differ, the results were nevertheless equally worthy.

Yet when we study that small part of the history of man of which we have records we find that the development of civilization has extended over only a comparatively brief period of time and that it has in the various parts of the earth been parallel and consistent. Thus, though we of the western world may look down upon the civilization of the Far East, it is evident on closer study that the Chinese are very much like the Westerners. They understood and used bronze at about the same time and, though they have never taken the same interest in iron and steel, it was their invention of the lens and gunpowder which made possible these modern battleships.

Not only were there a number of cultures which originated at about the same time, but it must be kept in mind that from 2,000 years ago (at just the time these cultures began to take on marked individual characteristics) travel, inspired by commerce and war, commenced to bind together the races of man with an ever stronger bond. It is therefore not so surprising that at certain given times man's development in the various parts of the world should produce simultaneously great artistic achievements.

The tremendous wars which the Mongols waged under Jenghis Khan and which influenced the East and West alike may have dammed the flood of production until it rose to the irresistible pressure which found expression in the courts of the Ming Dynasty as well as in those so similar ones of Renaissance Italy. The religious fervor which made Gothic art possible was not dissimilar to that felt in Western Asia and China and both were probably the result of the oppressions of war and at the same time reactions against a too materialistic wealth.

This consideration leads us to question what now seems to be the world trend. What can be hoped for the immediate future? To a remarkable degree the improved methods of travel and communication are bringing together the various peoples. National characteristics are being so blended as to show signs of a loss of identification. The Japanese artist is like the French, influenced by Cézanne, and there are American sky-scrapers in China. Undoubtedly this is going to prove a happy thing for all art as well as for civilization though just now the process is a discouraging one. There is bound, however, to emerge a functional art with a world-wide appeal.

A much more threatening element is that easily perceived interest on man's part in the new toys provided him by a bountiful science. The publics of all countries are becoming so interested in the moving pictures that there is little time to spare for looking at paintings. Similarly, the radio, the automobile and a thousand other inventions bid for man's amusement and time, and compete with all artists. How long it will take the world to adjust itself to this melting down of various characteristics, and to the building up of wider and more profound characteristics; how long it will take artists to adjust themselves to the new competitive demands and learn to make use of the inventions of science rather than combat them or have them make use of art, is a question that cannot yet be answered, but it is certain that until these two obstacles are overcome there can never be great art such as there has been in the past.

Thus we must get out of the habit of thinking that the last art is the best art. There is more loss than gain to be seen when the earlier arts such as those of Egypt or China or Greece are weighed in the scale against the modern, in spite of (or perhaps because of) all the new means available to artists of to-day which these earlier civilizations did not know. (W. E. Cx.)

ART. Far Eastern Methods. The art of the Far East aims to depict the spirit, rather than the semblance, of a thing. So the mission of an oriental artist is not necessarily to represent, but to interpret, the inner meaning of his subject. Vain, indeed, is an attempt to reproduce with paint a phenomenon of Nature. A picture of a wild flower, for example, may be true to form and colour, but where are the inherent purity and the fragrance of the blossom? Realizing the utter impossibility of imitation, the eastern painter seeks, instead, to express the impression which he has gained through admiration of nature or to give form to an ideal, by means of his brush, even as the poet expresses himself in words. The mood of the artist, then, is one of self-forgetfulness, since he is merely an interpreter of the beautiful and the mysterious in nature.

It has been said that "art is a tryst," for in the joy of it maker and beholder meet. In the West, this epigram is explained as the reproduction, on the part of the beholder, of the artist's mood at the time of his conception of a work of art. But this dual process, when applied to the art of the Far East, assumes a deeper significance; for in the East art becomes a whole only when the beholder's imagination co-operates with the suggestion conveyed by the artist in his work. The aesthetic nature of the oriental first

ART

PLATE I

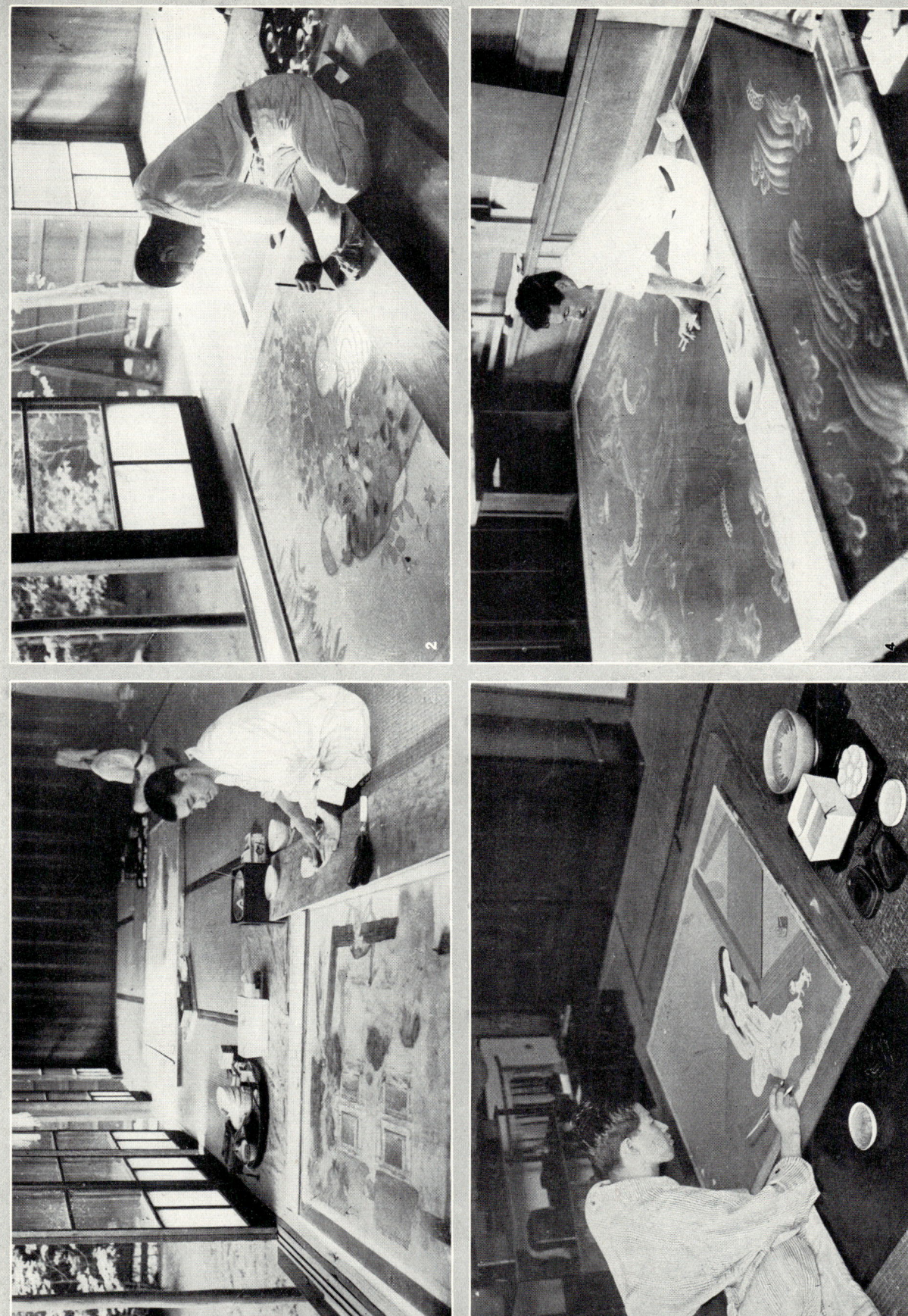

JAPANESE ARTISTS AT WORK

1. Kaoru Asuno at work in his studio
2. Fumio Noda at work in his studio
3. Gakuryo Nakamura, a member of the Bijutsuin Art Association
4. Professor Ryushi Kawabata at work in his studio

PLATE II

ART

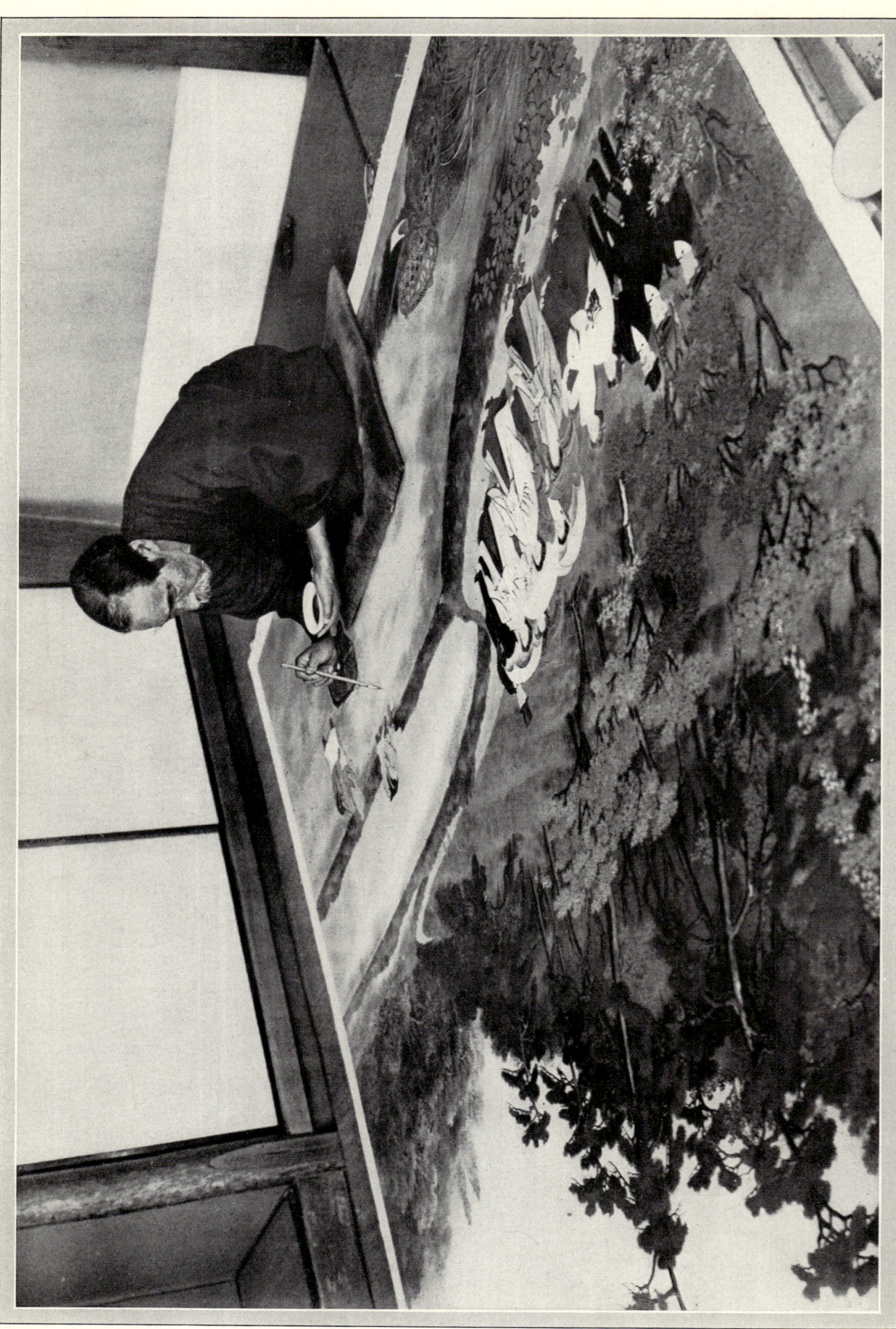

A JAPANESE WATER-COLOUR ARTIST AT WORK

PHOTOGRAPH, SPORT AND GENERAL PRESS AGENCY, LTD.

PERIODS OF ART

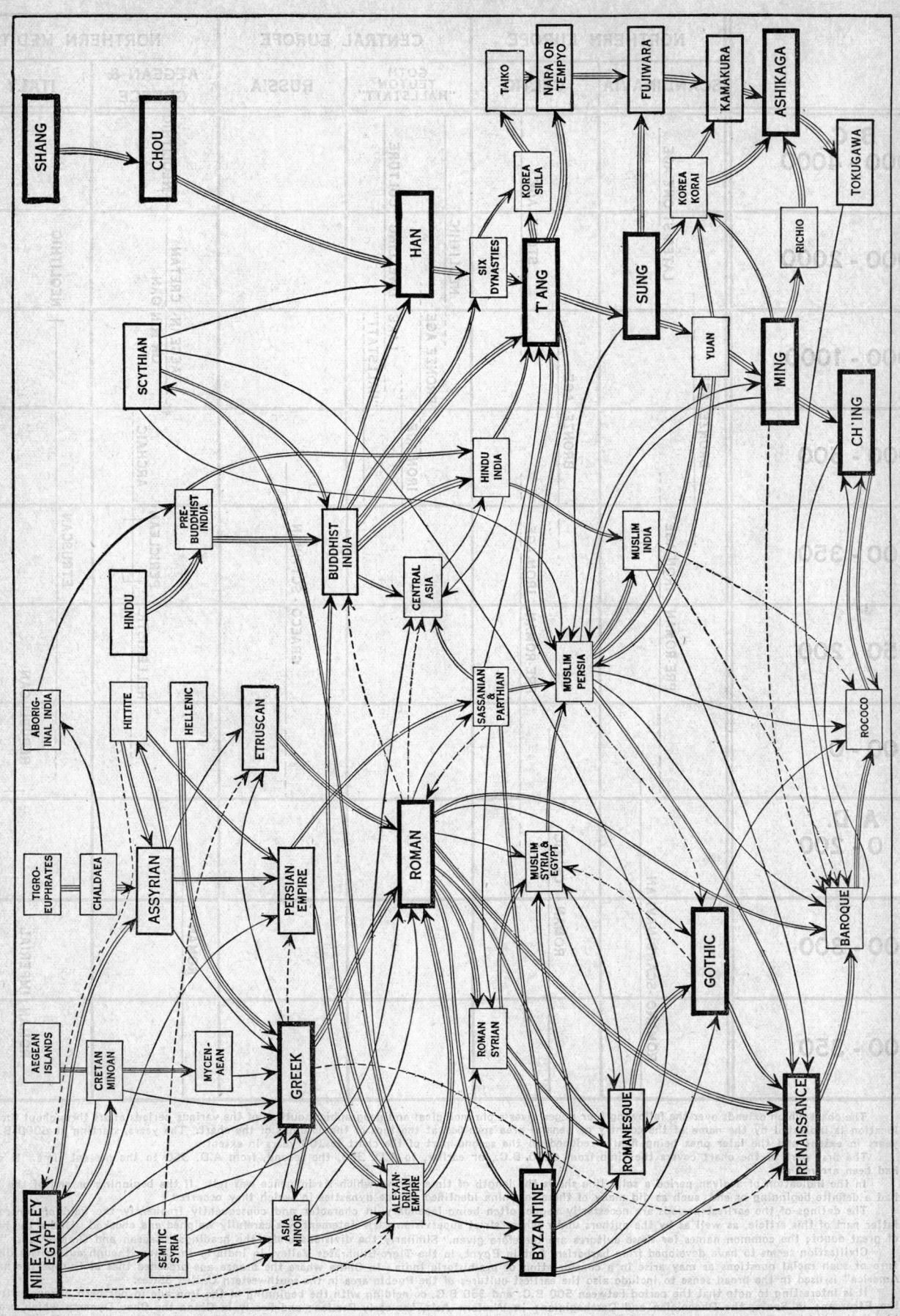

A dotted arrow indicates traces; a single arrow, definite but slight influence; a double arrow strong; and a triple arrow such influence as to be a dominant factor in the period. Arrows running both ways indicate reciprocal influences such as those between Muslim Persia, and T'ang China. In general the terms used are in their broadest interpretations; thus, "Romanesque" covers Carolingian, as well.

This chart is not designed to show chronological relationships though the earlier civilizations are near the top and the more recent arranged below (for chronological comparisons the charts on the preceding four pages should be consulted)—neither is there any attempt to arrange the countries in which the periods occurred geographically, the primary intention being simply to show those influences which were brought to bear upon the various most important periods, omitting all question of the original genius of each nation which received, amalgamated and translated these influences as well as added their own contributions. The importance of the period is indicated by the weight of the outline. It will be seen that there are three classifications.

PERIODS OF ART

	NORTHERN EUROPE		CENTRAL EUROPE		NORTHERN MEDITER-	
	SCANDINAVIA	CELTIC	GOTH TEUTON "HALLSTATT"	RUSSIA	AEGEAN & GREECE	ITALY
B.C. 6000-4000	LATER STONE AGE	STONE AGE	NEOLITHIC / LAKE DWELLING CULTURE		NEOLITHIC	
4000-2000	LATER STONE AGE / BRONZE AGE	STONE AGE / BRONZE AGE	NEOLITHIC / LAKE DWELLING CULTURE / BRONZE AGE		AEGEAN-CRETAN OR MINOAN	NEOLITHIC
2000-1000	BRONZE AGE	BRONZE AGE	BRONZE AGE / "HALLSTATT" / IRON AGE		AEGEAN-CRETAN OR MINOAN	
1000-500	BRONZE AGE	BRONZE AGE	IRON AGE		ARCHAIC	
500-350	PRE-ROMAN IRON AGE	PRE-ROMAN IRON AGE		GRAECO-SCYTHIAN	PERICLEAN	ETRUSCAN
350-200	PRE-ROMAN IRON AGE	PRE-ROMAN IRON AGE		GRAECO-SCYTHIAN	HELLENISTIC	REPUBLICAN
200-0					HELLENISTIC	REPUBLICAN
A.D. 0-200		ROMAN-CELTIC				
200-300	ROMANO-SCANDINAVIAN	ROMAN-CELTIC			ROMAN	ROMAN IMPERIAL
300-350	ROMANO-SCANDINAVIAN					ROMAN IMPERIAL

The chart which extends over the following four pages gives a chronological and geographical outline of the various periods of art throughout the world location is indicated by the name of the country or general area specified at the tops of the columns of the chart. The years, starting at 6000 B.C., or years in extent and the later ones being finally reduced on the second part of the chart to 100 years in extent.

The first part of the chart covers the time from 6000 B.C., or earlier, to A.D. 350, the second, from A.D. 350 to the present time. It should had been arrived at.

In the indication of a given period a solid line shows the length of time during which its influence was felt. If the beginning or end of the line is had a definite beginning or end, such as did many of those in China identified by the dynasties in which they occurred.

The datings of the earliest periods are necessarily vague, often being legendary in character and consequently frequently the field of controversy. latter part of this article, as well as by the authors under whose strict supervision each statement was carefully weighed and checked. Under the heading of great doubt; the common names for these cultures are therefore given. Similarly the divisions under the headings "Aegean and Greece" and "Italy"

Civilization seems to have developed from barbarism first in Egypt, in the Tigro-Euphrates Valley, in India or in China, though authorities differ as ture or such racial questions as may arise in a consideration of pre-historic India. In China where the bronze age preceded that of Europe the more or America" is used in the broad sense to include also the earliest cultures of the Pueblo area in the southwestern United States.

It is interesting to note that the period between 500 B.C. and 350 B.C. coinciding with the beginning of the iron age in northern Europe, witnessed the Etruscan; in Spain, the Phoenician and Carthaginian; in Western Asia, the early Persian; and finally in China the Chou Dynasty which produced his studies and keep in mind the relative growth and decline of the arts of various arts of the earth, in a way that would be very difficult otherwise

PERIODS OF ART

RANEAN / SPAIN	WESTERN ASIA	EGYPT	INDIA	CHINA	JAPAN	SOUTH AMERICA	CENTRAL AMERICA	
	CHALDAEAN / SUMERIAN	PRE-DYNASTIC	NEOLITHIC & CHALCO-LITHIC	PALAEO-LITHIC				
		PYRAMIDS	EARLY INDUS VALLEY CULTURE	HSIA	PRE-LEGENDARY		MAYA	MEXICO / PUEBLO AREA IN SOUTHWEST U.S.
	BABYLONIAN / HITTITE	18TH DYNASTY	INDUS VALLEY CULTURE / EARLY VEDIC	SHANG				BASKET MAKER I
	PHOENICIAN / ASSYRIAN	DECLINE / FOREIGN DOMINATION	LATE VEDIC				ARCHAIC	BASKET MAKER II
PHOENICIAN AND CARTHAGINIAN	PERSIAN		PRE-MAURYA	CHOU				BASKET MAKER III
PHOENICIAN	HELLENISTIC	PTOLEMAIC	MAURYA	TS'IN				PUEBLO I
	ROMAN	ROMAN	SUNGA		PREHISTORIC	SHELL-HEAPS	ARCHAIC BEGINNINGS	
	PARTHIAN		ANDHRA	HAN		ARCHAIC	FIRST MAYA EMPIRE	ARCHAIC
ROMAN	ROMAN	COPTIC	INDO-HELLENISTIC	WEI / SHUH HAN / WU / SIX DYNASTIES				PUEBLO II
SASSANIAN			GUPTA					

so that a clear understanding of the time of occurrence, the duration and the relationship of these periods can be gained at a glance. The geographical
earlier, are grouped into sections indicated at the left hand side, and it will be noticed that these sections are not constant, the earlier ones being 2000

be noted that the geographical divisions of the second section differ from those of the first, owing to the fact that more definite demarcations politically

dotted it shows a gradual development or decline. If there is an abrupt beginning or end terminated by a small cross-line this shows that the period

But this compilation represents the consensus of the best founded opinions and has been carefully brought together by the authorities enumerated in the
"Goth, Teuton, Hallstatt" are included a number of European cultural expressions irrespective of their actual racial origins which are still a matter
are called by their cultural names without consideration of any of the existing racial differences or similarities.
to which culture came earlier. It was not thought advisable to attempt to indicate the differing racial elements that created Chaldean and Sumerian cul-
less legendary dynasties of Hsia and Shang have been indicated in accordance with the dating of the Chinese chronicles while the heading "Central

the excellence of the Greco-Scythian period in the territory now known as Russia, while in Greece the Periclean culture was at its height; in Italy,
some of the most beautiful bronzes known to the collectors of to-day. Thus, the reader will find it possible, through the use of this chart, to organize
to bring together from various sources of information.

PERIODS OF ART

A.D.	SCANDINAVIA	GERMANY	FRANCE	ENGLAND	GREECE	ITALY	SPAIN	NORTH AFRICA
350-500	ROMANO-SCANDINAVIAN	ROMAN	ROMAN	ROMAN		ROMAN / EARLY CHRISTIAN	ROMAN	ROMAN / COPTIC
500-750	ROMANO-SCANDINAVIAN	CAROLINGIAN	CAROLINGIAN	ANGLO-SAXON		EARLY CHRISTIAN		COPTIC
750-1000	VIKING AGE	CAROLINGIAN	CAROLINGIAN	ANGLO-SAXON	BYZANTINE		VISIGOTHIC	
1000-1100	SCANDINAVIAN ROMANESQUE	ROMANESQUE	ROMANESQUE			ROMANESQUE	ROMANESQUE	EARLY MUSLIM (EGYPT)
1100-1200	SCANDINAVIAN ROMANESQUE	ROMANESQUE	EARLY AND RAYONNANT GOTHIC	NORMAN ROMANESQUE		ROMANESQUE	ROMANESQUE	EARLY MUSLIM (EGYPT) / HISPANO-MOORISH
1200-1300			EARLY AND RAYONNANT GOTHIC	EARLY ENGLISH GOTHIC		GOTHIC	HISPANO-MOORISH	
1300-1400	GOTHIC	GOTHIC		DECORATED GOTHIC	DOMINANCE	GOTHIC / EARLY RENAISSANCE		MOORISH
1400-1500		FLAMBOYANT GOTHIC	FLAMBOYANT	PERPENDICULAR GOTHIC		EARLY RENAISSANCE / PLATERESQUE		TURKISH MUSLIM
1500-1600	RENAISSANCE	EARLY RENAISSANCE	FRANCIS I / HENRY II / HENRY IV	TUDOR AND JACOBEAN	TURKISH	HIGH RENAISSANCE	CLASSIC REN. / PLATERESQUE	
1600-1700	RENAISSANCE	DEVELOPED BAROQUE RENAISSANCE	LOUIS XIV / HENRY XIII	PALLADIAN (I. JONES)		BAROQUE	BAROQUE	
1700-1800	ROCOCO	ROCOCO	LOUIS XV / LOUIS XVI	ADAM / CLASSIC REN (WREN)		CLASSIC REVIVAL		
1800-1900	RENAISSANCE REVIVAL / GOTHIC REVIVAL	EMPIRE / NEO-GREC / GOTHIC REVIVAL / CLASSIC REVIVAL	GREEK REVIVAL / GOTHIC REVIVAL		GREEK REVIVAL	NEO-BAROQUE		
1900-	RENAISSANCE REVIVAL / MODERNIST	MODERNIST / RENAISSANCE REVIVAL	MODERNIST / RENAISSANCE REVIVAL	MODERNIST		MODERNIST		

It was found necessary in the above second section of the chart on the periods of art, not only to make smaller subdivisions of time ranging from 250 geographical subdivisions because of the altered, more numerous and more definite national demarcations. The countries of Europe separated, and though partly distinct from, but parallel with, the continent. Korea and Japan, though closely bound to China, found their own expression, and finally North new culture in this area. Many authorities include Carolingian and Romanesque under the general title of Romanesque Art and the line between early Syrian under "Western Asia" are sometimes considered variant forms of the Byzantine; even the widely divergent Armenian style is occasionally called shores of the Adriatic.

A new use for these charts is illustrated in this second one: that of the study of one single period of art, such as the Gothic and its development "Early and Rayonnant" style in France followed almost immediately by its rise in Germany, Spain and England, later in Scandinavia, and still later characteristics that made the Baroque so appealing, at a later date, Gothic art soon became flamboyant as indeed it immediately afterwards became in there was a revival in Gothic art between A.D. 1800 and A.D. 1900 not only in Germany, France, and England, but in America where the original in the various countries and the approximate dates easily fixed in mind.

PERIODS OF ART

WESTERN ASIA	PERSIA	INDIA	CHINA	KOREA	JAPAN	SOUTH AMERICA	CENTRAL AMERICA	NORTH AMERICA
SYRIAN	SASSANIAN	GUPTA	SIX DYNASTIES	PREHISTORIC				PUEBLO II
		PALLAVA / CHALUKYA	T'ANG	SILLA	SUIKO		FIRST MAYA EMPIRE	
		RASHTRAKUTA	FIVE DYNASTIES		NARA OR TEMPYO	QUIMBAYA (COLOMBIA)		
BYZANTINE / ARMENIAN		PALA / RAJPUT / CHOLA / KHMER				PROTO-ICA (PERU)		
		HOYSALA	SUNG	KORAI	HEIAN / FUJIWARA	MANABI (EQUADOR) / ICA (PERU)	SECOND MAYA EMPIRE / ZAPOTEC (S. MEXICO)	PUEBLO III
		PANDYA			MILITARY EPOCH	NASCA (PERU)	TOTONAC / CHOROTEGA	FLORESCENCE
	PERSIAN MUSLIM		YUAN		KAMAKURA / HOJO	TIAHUANACO	TOLTEC (NORTHERN YUCATAN)	PUEBLO IV
	MOHAMMEDAN / VIJAYANAGAR		MING		ASHIKAGA	INCA (PERU)	TOLTEC	
TURKISH		MOGUL / RAJPUT PAINTING		RICHIO	MOMOYAMA	CHIBCHA (COLOMBIA)	AZTEC	PUEBLO V
		BRITISH / KANDYAN	CHING		TOKUGAWA	SPANISH BAROQUE	SPANISH BAROQUE	EARLY COLONIAL
								DEVELOPED COLONIAL / SPANISH COLONIAL
					MEIJI		ROMAN REV. / GREEK REV. / GOTHIC REV. / RENAISSANCE REV.	ADAM TYPE
							FUNCTIONALISM	

years to 100 years owing to the continually increasing speed in the development of art periods throughout the world, but to alter and add to the
there was a strong mutual influence, each began a more or less individual national development. England, starting with the Roman period, developed
America which had known only Pueblo culture until the 17th Century became inhabited by Europeans who brought to it and developed an entirely
Christian work and certain work of the Italian Romanesque styles is quite impossible to fix definitely. Both the Coptic under "North Africa" and the
Byzantine. The word Byzantine as used on the chart is confined to that art produced under the direct influence of Constantinople, in Greece and on both

in the various countries which felt its influence. With this section it may be seen that Gothic art started between A.D. 1100 and A.D. 1200 in the
in Italy where its influence lasted for only a comparatively short time, giving way to the Renaissance. In Germany perhaps because of the same national
France while in England it was, after the original introduction, first the "decorated" style and later the "perpendicular" style. It may also be seen that
period had never existed. In the same way, the influence of the Roman, the Carolingian and Romanesque, as well as many other periods, can be traced

seeks intrinsic beauty and then evolves extrinsic completeness. The function of a picture, therefore, is not to display but to suggest; the beautiful is present but it is concealed. After all, a painted twig is important in that it invites one to reconstruct, by exercise of the imagination, a towering tree through which the joy of life flows, and a painted figure is interesting if it depicts the inner nature with its striving for the highest. Hence, the suggestive quality of the art of China and Japan is a vital factor; the more emphatic the suggestion on the part of the artist, the more profound the appeal to the beholder.

It is true that in the pictorial art of the Far East there are various schools or styles, as in the art of the West: idealistic, impressionistic, romantic, realistic, etc.; then, too, the subjects treated by eastern artists include all things religious and secular, animate and inanimate. Yet, taken as a whole, one may note that oriental paintings are distinct, not only in aesthetic expression, but also in technical achievement. In creating a picture, the Far Eastern artist, before all else, grasps the spirit of his subject, then conveys this mood to the brush. He paints, not what he sees, but what he feels. This does not mean an occult treatment of the theme, for in presenting it an intelligible delineation of the subject is demanded. Broadly speaking, the external form is but a mask under which reality hides and this reality the artist attempts to reveal. The importance of the embodiment of soul in a picture was mentioned in China as early as the 4th century; emphasis on this point, however, may be said to date from the 5th century when Hsieh Ho laid down his celebrated "Six Canons of Painting," which have been the basis of art criticism in the Far East throughout the subsequent centuries. The canons, translated freely, are (1) life-motion engendered by spiritual harmony; (2) use of the brush in rendering bone-structure; (3) delineation of forms in conformity with the objects; (4) application of colours appropriate to the kinds; (5) spacing based on proper planning; (6) copying of classic pictures, thereby preserving tradition. A masterpiece should exemplify all six points. It is to be noted that spiritual expression, or life-quality, in art is the prime requisite of the canons. Turning to the remaining five canons, all of which refer to technique, it will be seen that the use of the brush is placed before imitative accuracy in form and colour, composition or tradition; for "brush-strokes" are considered in the light of the bodily structure of that which encases the spirit, while "form" and "colour" are but the flesh and the skin. The term "spacing" means embellishment of the design, and "copying" refers to the transfusion of principles established by past masters. But brush-strokes are more than bone-structure; they are the nerve system as well, for they suggest force, in that they invoke living motion. Motion being durative in nature is best conveyed in uninterrupted lines made by a feeling hand. The strokes, therefore, are more than mere outlines or spots indicating shapes or areas; by their very vigour, they express the life-quality of the subject pictured. Brush-strokes at the same time are an index to the character of the individual who made them, the more inspired the artist, the more spontaneous their response. If the painter is noble-minded, the spiritual expression in his handwork is abundant, and if the spiritual expression is abundant, the picture causes life-motion; otherwise, mere dexterity in brush-manipulation is but the skill of an artisan.

Use of Brush and Ink-tones.—The Far Eastern artist, accordingly, is trained to perceive and to feel that which is beautiful and interesting in nature and to put his conception into execution. His early training is devoted to copying repeatedly model works by his master, consisting of simple drawings effected in broad and vigorous strokes. He begins by grinding "China ink" on an ink-slab, and with a large brush he draws on paper with a view to reproducing the exact order and strength of each stroke of the model. The brush is held perpendicular to the paper, almost at right angles to the hand and is firmly grasped, at a considerable distance from the point, by the thumb, index and middle fingers. During the process of drawing, the fingers remain almost immobile, for the work is done by the arm unsupported, with barely the point of the hair touching the paper. Constant practice in manipulation of the brush in this manner makes the arm alert and flexible, so that lines of even and continuous strength, some swift and some gentle, may be produced through proper control of the nerves of the arm. Only when drawing extremely delicate lines does the hand make use of the wrist as a support.

Ordinarily an oriental artist does not use an easel when painting or drawing, since he works seated with paper or silk spread before him. As he paints, his head is bent down, the shoulders supported by the left arm, of which the hand rests on the table or floor. By long and unceasing practice in handling the brush, he becomes efficient in producing strokes thin or heavy, light in touch or abrupt in force. The brush-strokes in a painting are often compared to those employed in the calligraphy of China and Japan. In fact, in the matter of the use of the brush there exists but little distinction between the two arts. That much attention has been paid to brush-strokes in the Far East is evidenced by careful studies of various types of brush-marks which have been made by great and old masters. There are collections of strokes used in delineating figures, rocks, water, trees, etc., which are referred to as either "wrinkles" or "touches." For drawing and painting the manifold contours of mountains and rocks, there are 16 (or 18) kinds of strokes, each of which is known by a fancy name such as rain-drops, scattered brushwood, alum crystals, demon skin, large axe, horse's teeth, folded belt, hemp fibres, lotus leaf veins, unravelled rope, bullock hair, eddying water, etc. Again, in drawing figures, especially their draperies, there are "touches" known as "harp string," "moving cloud and flowing water," "rat-tail," "willow leaf," etc. These have always been useful guides to painters, and have served to deter beginners from attempting crude and meaningless styles. It must be understood, however, that over-emphasis on classification of this sort and strict adherence to it is detrimental to initiative.

Having acquired a certain amount of facility in manipulation of the brush, the student is next taught the value of ink-tones. The ink used in Far Eastern painting is a mixture of lampblack or pine soot with glue, moulded into cake form. Upon a slate-like slab with a depression at one end to hold a small amount of liquid, the cake of ink is rubbed, with an admixture of water, until the latter becomes a solid black. This process takes place just before painting. When light shades of black are desired, the liquid ink is mixed with water by means of the brush, in a white porcelain saucer, according to the requirement. The much-valued lustre of the ink when dry on paper or silk depends largely upon the quality of the ink itself, as well as upon the stone employed for grinding. It is said that an artist who thoroughly understands the proper use of ink is able to ascertain the shade immediately upon dipping his brush without testing it on the white saucer or on paper.

Like the quality of the brush-strokes themselves, the quality of the ink-tones differs according to the painter, and determines his artistic ability. It is important that a good painting in ink should show proper relation of light and dark tones varying from lustrous black to delicate grey. Satisfactory results demand that various shades be applied in harmonious order, so that there may be no violent break in gradual tone-scales. Indeed, a correct use of ink produces a sense of natural colours, and atmospheric perspective, colours being after all but intermediaries between black and white, and differences in distance but degree of visibility. It must be pointed out that dark ink does not necessarily suggest strength, nor light ink weakness, nor does a heavy stroke always indicate vitality or a thin stroke lack of it. A proper combination of brush-power and ink-tone creates life-motion in a picture. The duration of an inspired mood is but temporary; hence the transference of this mood into ink with the brush must be relatively spontaneous.

There are, roughly, two types of brush-strokes—one broad and often massive, which in itself forms a component part of a picture; the other thin and crisp which is used in the nature of an outline. On both alike, the technical demand of expressiveness is imposed. The brushes used naturally differ in size, but because all except the flat varieties, are so made, of the hair of a deer, goat, fox, badger or rabbit, as to possess needle-like points when wet, and because generally the tips only touch the surface for painting, a small drawing may be made with a comparatively large brush. It may be remarked in passing that painters of certain schools use almost the entire length of the hair when it is desired to reproduce an effect of light and shadow in a single stroke. First the brush is allowed to absorb a light shade of ink; then, after touching the tip of the hair to the thick black, a leaf, for example, is immediately painted, the brush being used sidewise and a little pressure being exerted as the drawing is made. The running of the dark ink into the light automatically results in gradation producing in a single stroke the effect of chiaroscuro. A variety of paper which absorbs ink very quickly is used in practising manipulation of the brush, which includes making strokes and producing ink-tones. Because of the bibulous nature of this paper and of the ink used, blurring is likely to occur, unless the amount of ink held on the brush is carefully gauged and the brush-marks made swiftly. The paper admits of no erasing or retouching, thus compelling the pupil to be certain of his every movement prior to actual execution of a picture. Having been instructed in proper use of the brush and in quality of ink-tones, the pupil is allowed to study and sketch from nature.

Sketching and Colouring.—Generally speaking, in the art of the Far East sketching from actual objects does not mean working from a model so much as training an artist in the observation of that which is real. According to the Chinese idea, the spirit of all phenomena originated in Heaven and was formed into shape on earth; every phenomenon is endowed with spirit and is a worthy subject for a picture; each is an inspiration for a painter who, by searching inquiry into its peculiar nature, may succeed in grasping its very spirit. Thus an artist is urged to examine every significant feature of his subject and to imagine himself to be it before delineating it. By this means and this alone may he be able to express its spirit. So a sketch-book of an artist may be a jumble of unrelated and incomplete parts of all kinds of plants, landscapes, figures, etc. Useful though these actual sketches are, their importance is insignificant in comparison to the deep mental notes which he has made. For example, a bamboo under different atmospheric conditions, in wind or in rain, in sunlight or in moonlight—how preserve the impression except by mental notes? A great master, in painting a bamboo leaf, though it hang downward, would still indicate its longing to point to the sky; and a story is told of a Chinese painter who, finding that his sketch of caged insects did not adequately picture them, freed the insects in their natural haunts, and himself lying on the ground for purposes of close observation, succeeded in catching the spirit of his subject. Indeed, orientals doubt the desirability of employing, for the sake of anatomical correctness, an ordinary man as a model for a picture of a king. For painting a horse trotting, a study of an animal in a stall is of little value; accordingly, the artist of the Far East tries to delineate his impression of the appearance the horse presented when in motion. It is said that a good picture must needs be truthful, but in reality an attempt at faithful reproduction in paint and with brush is futile; so a painter's aim should be to create a picture which will make on the beholder a deeper impression than the original itself.

The same observations apply to the use of colour. It is true that all visible phenomena have shape and colour, but in making pictures of them, a painter is not concerned with the idea of reproduction. If he were, a sculpture in the round with appropriate colouring would be the ideal medium for his purpose. For this reason, the art of the Far East considers colour but an accessory which adds a certain decorative value to a picture. In introducing colours the artist merely intends to approximate the colour-aspect of the object depicted. Some Eastern connoisseurs argue that since "China ink" correctly used creates a sense of chromatic beauty and the presence of pigments in a painting suggests artificiality, the latter are therefore detractive to the minds of those who love purity. In any case, the palette of the eastern artists is limited, the colouring materials being drawn chiefly from mineral, earth and vegetable substances compounded with fine glue. The medium is water, which fact contributes toward the free movement of the brush, a rigid requirement in order to illustrate motion at the sacrifice of realism.

Conception and Composition.—In their pictures, the artists of the Far East attempt to present a certain space and time within a comparatively small area. Oriental painters seek first to grasp the essential attributes of their subjects and then to depict them with the utmost economy of brush-strokes. Landscapes provide the subjects most often treated. The artist feels that a landscape shows Nature with her manifold mysteries and that therefore it is worthy to be his pictorial theme. He considers it his mission, as well as his privilege, to interpret and present this large subject in a small space, so that both he and the beholder may enjoy and admire nature in her varied forms. Majestic mountain peaks, rambling brooks, gnarled trees shrouded in mists, a solitary hermit —all may be brought to one's home by the artist. In order to represent such a vast scene, it is not possible to depict every detail, so there are suggestions for the right proportions of component parts: "In painting a landscape, make the mountain ten feet high, the tree one foot, the house one-tenth of a foot and the human figure the size of a pea." Then there are conventions which show the oriental attitude toward perspective (*q.v.*). "A mountain at a distance shows no ledge-marks; water at a distance, no waves; a man at a distance, no eyes. Not that these things are absent, but they appear as if they were absent." In executing a painting, the idea of perspective is indicated by three successive planes, one above the other, nearest objects being represented in the lowest plane. The general tones of ink or colour also indicate variations in distance—dark tones for the foreground, light for the far distance and medium tones for the intermediate spaces. The effect, therefore, is not linear but aerial perspective. Instructions in landscape painting deal, not with methods whereby to copy real scenery, but with suggestions how to compose such a picture. As the oriental conception of a landscape is "mountains accompanied by water," the artist who attempts such a theme cannot escape from introducing water in some phase, be it a river, a lake or a waterfall. He selects interesting parts from several scenes for his landscape, and then groups them to form complete unity, thereby creating an entirely new world. However, there should always be a clear distinction between the principal and the subordinate parts. Essays on the subject of landscape speak further of the general characteristics to be associated with scenery in the different seasons: "Mountains in spring should appear as if smiling; in summer as if freshly bathed; in autumn, bedecked; in winter, as if sleeping."

In the Far East, trees, plants, fruits, animals, insects and even fish are often included in the category of "Flower-and-Bird" paintings. The mode to follow in treating these motives is, first, to observe the innocence or the elegance of the flowers, or the instincts of the birds and animals, and then to paint the character or spirit of the subjects. Attempts have been made to establish rules governing the order for making the component parts. Both in China and Japan there are guide-books for painting orchids, chrysanthemums, plum blossoms and bamboos which, because of their virtuous characteristics, are together called the Four Sages. Rules explain the general arrangement of compositions, in particular showing the relation between the *principal* (or guest) and the *subordinate* (or host). The former is the chief portion of the design and the latter its adjunct. Broadly speaking, by *principal* is meant that portion of the design which occupies the centre of attraction, larger in size and more abundant in details. The *subordinate*, which is small in proportion, supports the *principal* by maintaining proper balance in a composition. Balance, in this case, does not denote a symmetrical arrangement of parts, but agreeable spacing in relation to the shape of the paper or silk on which the painting is done. There are also instructions which prescribe the order of brush-strokes to be followed when developing the theme. In painting a picture of bamboo, for example, the main stalk is drawn first in light ink, from the bottom upward, in a few sections which are graduated in length, the lowest being the shortest. The next step is to make the joints with darker ink. Then follow strokes for the branches, in light ink, each drawn by starting from one of the joints. The leaves are painted next, and the artist must bear in mind that each one grows from a branch; they are executed in a variety of ink-tones, due attention being paid to differences in distance, those nearer being drawn in dark ink. Among painters there are those who would define various arrangements or combinations of leaves by their resemblance to Chinese ideographs, a fact which proves the fastidious manner in which some rules have been formulated. In the main, it is important that a painter of bamboo or of other plants should always remember the natural order of growth, from the root gradually heavenward, and that he should follow in painting the same orderly process. Furthermore, the artist must strive to convey the characteristics of his subjects—the stern quality of the ever-bending but never-yielding bamboo, the courage of the plum which blossoms in winter, the purity of the orchid which unfolds its beauty in solitude and the nobility of the chrysanthemum which possesses the mind of a hermit. Likewise in painting birds, animals, etc., the artist must try to understand their special attributes—the beak and claws of an eagle, the plumage of a peacock, the horns of a deer, etc.; and he must emphasize their significance almost to the point of exaggeration.

Portrait and figure-painting have never attained, in China and Japan, a height corresponding to landscape or flower-and-bird subjects. Painting a figure merely for the sake of showing physical beauty, or a portrait from a model, has not been customary. On the other hand, portraying ideal or imaginary likenesses of historical or legendary persons has been common, which explains the existence of treatises on figure-painting. The latter, however, refer to types of features and facial expressions: an emperor should always look dignified; a general, brave; a recluse, noble; a lady, refined; a farmer, rustic; etc. In addition to this generalization, the essays discuss appropriate accessories to be included in these pictures—palaces, chairs, mountain-scenery, ponds, farms, etc. They also give scales of proportion for a figure: the height of a body in standing pose should be seven times the size of the head; the body when seated should be three times the size of the head; the size of the head itself should be twice the open palm of the subject's hand, etc. Further, the discussion covers varieties of brush-strokes to be used in depicting the draperies of figures, mention of which has already been made. Of course stress is laid upon the importance of revealing the soul of the subjects, but there is no reference to anatomical correctness. The absence of modelling in portraits, as in all subjects, is one of the peculiarities of oriental paintings. The contours of the face, the features and the muscles are indicated by lines. This linear treatment in two dimensions, though it fails to suggest a sense of relief, nevertheless produces a state of animation. In a composition, a figure or a tree often lacks indication of the ground on which it stands; the reason being that the artist, as well as the beholder, prefers that such an obvious element be disregarded entirely. A "filled-up picture" is wearisome, while an empty space allows the beholder's imagination to roam about. When asked what part of a painting is most difficult of execution, a Japanese painter replied: "The space which is to be left unpainted."

Far Eastern paintings are executed in ink and water-colours, usually on either paper or silk that has been sized with a thin solution of a mixture of transparent glue and alum. On the receptive surface of either paper or silk, the work of the artist is executed by one of three methods: (1) by painting immediately without any preliminary sketch; (2) by indicating in charcoal a skeleton of the design; or (3) by preparing a careful outline drawing of the design on a sheet of paper and tracing it upon the surface proper.

Copying and Tradition.—In the art of the Far East certain pictorial subjects frequently recur, each bearing a well-appointed title, usually somewhat fanciful and often poetic. Moreover, their treatment is similar, if not identical. The reason is not far to seek, for the artists of the Orient come of races which not only view the old with reverence, but always revert to the past for inspiration. It has been remarked that a pupil's training consists in copying and recopying his master's works and that there are model-books which show the proper methods of painting various subjects. So much stress upon tradition, at once a safeguard against radicalism and an obstacle to free development, naturally gave birth to pronounced school mannerisms and to restrictions which extend even to choice of subject and result in inevitable repetition. It may be added that artists of the East often select themes which cannot be studied from nature or observed at first hand; consequently, dependence upon old pictures for general guidance is necessary. It is probable, however, that the special reference in the "Six Canons" to copying old masters was not intended to mean mere copying; rather it should be interpreted as emphasizing the importance of preserving that part of tradition which ever lives as an eternal principle and of transmitting it to the next generation. A work of art may betray its maker's individuality, and however hard he may try, he cannot free himself from the influence of the past; so that orientals praise, rather than condemn, one who turns to classic pieces as models. A Chinese in the 4th century pointed out that the art of painting may be developed from copying old masters. There are four recognized methods of copying (1) tracing; (2) reproduction which consists in faithfully copying the original without resorting to the process of tracing; (3) interpretation, being a near copy of the design and characteristics of the original but embodying much of the copyist's personality; (4) reduction, which is usually sketchy in nature. The third method must have been the type of copying recommended by the formulator of the canons. Thereby the copyist preserves what is good of the past and develops it to meet his ideals as well as the conditions of his time. The art of the Far East has been evolving in this manner from the time of its inception.

BIBLIOGRAPHY.—William Anderson, *The Pictorial Arts of Japan* (Boston, 1886); Laurence Binyon, *Painting in the Far East*, 3rd edition (1923); *The Flight of the Dragon* (1911); Henry P. Bowie, *On the Laws of Japanese Painting* (San Francisco, 1911); Ernest Fenollosa, *Epochs of Chinese and Japanese Art*, 2nd edition (New York, 1913); John C. Ferguson, *Chinese Painting* (Chicago, 1927); Okakura-Kakuzo, *The Book of Tea* (New York, 1906); *The Ideals of the East with Special Reference to the Art of Japan* (1903); Raphael Petrucci, *Encyclopedie de la Peinture Chinoise* (Paris, 1918); *La Philosophie de la Nature dans l'Art d'Extrême Orient* (Paris, 1911); *Chinese Painters* (translation) (New York, 1920); Sei-ichi Taki, *Three Essays on Oriental Painting* (London, 1910). (K. T.)

LANDSCAPE PAINTING. Far East.—Early in the 16th century commerce and the consequent exchange of thought developed between Europe and Asia. We can guess that the artists of Europe, China and Japan studied the prints of the age and in some degree appreciated the subtleties of each other's art. French art took from the Japanese only what it liked—a delight in lovely contrast of movement.

Until her ports were forced open, Japanese art had been feudal, but with this event the popular and vulgar school of painting arose. It produced Japan's greatest landscape artist, Hokiisai, who did the 100 views of Fujiyama and other sets of masterpieces in landscape drawing. Hiroshige is the second famous and very fine painter of Japanese landscapes. Some of his work has been compared to Claude's because his colour print landscapes give a revelation of light in a masterly intellectual statement in line drawing. (D. Ga.)

WATER-COLOUR PAINTING. Japanese Art.—From the 6th century the development of painting may be shown as follows: (1) middle of 6th to middle of 9th century: naturalization of Chinese and Chino-Buddhist Art; (2) middle of 9th to middle of 15th century: establishment of great native schools under Kose no Kanaoka and descendants—pure Chinese school falling into neglect; (3) 15th to latter part of 17th century: revival of Chinese style; (4) latter part of 17th to latter part of 18th century: popular school; (5) 18th to 19th century: introduction of European influence—naturalistic school—acme and decline of popular school; (6) 1875 to present: a period of transition.

Painting began in the 5th century, brought by Nawrin from China. By the middle of the 6th century a real art of painting, of which Buddhism was the main theme, had begun. The art was thereafter carried out under Korean and Chinese immigrants. Toward the end of the 9th century, two exotic styles of painting flourished, and on these a native style had been founded which featured landscape of a romantic kind, animal life, trees, flowers

JAPANESE PAINTING AND PRINTS

PLATE I

BY COURTESY OF (1) THE MUSEUM OF FINE ARTS, BOSTON, (2) THE METROPOLITAN MUSEUM OF ART, NEW YORK

KORIN AND KOYETSU SCREENS

Korin and Koyetsu were two of the most famous painters of Japan and the two screens shown herewith represent their styles. The top screen, with its almost incandescent coloration of the jagged rocks around which raging waves lash, shows the strength and verve of Korin's art; while the lower screen, in its grasp of the colour and mood of autumn, gives an idea of Koyetsu's understanding of nature. Another piece by Korin is shown in "Screens," Plate II

JAPANESE PAINTING AND PRINTS

PLATE II

BY COURTESY OF THE TRUSTEES OF THE BRITISH MUSEUM

PORTRAIT OF YORITOMO

Copy of a portrait of Yoritomo, the first shōgun (commander-in-chief) of Japan
(1192–98), attributed to Takanobu, 12th century, Kamakura period

and designs representing legends of olden times. The exotic Buddhist style brought a change. Of Indian origin or influence, it was brilliant and decorative, with a lavish use of gold, and confined to representations of sacred personages and sacred places. The principal painters of this period, extending into the succeeding centuries, were of the Kose, Takuma and Kasuga lines, descending from Kanaoka, Takuma Tameuji, and Fujiwara respectively. Last and greatest was Meicho, or Chō Densu, who died in the year 1427.

The beginning of the 11th century shows adaptations of Chinese canons to motives selected from poetry, court life, and legends of Old Japan. This art was characterized by a lightly touched outline and tinted with flat and bright body-colour. Verdigris-green dominated the schemes. Important names are Fujiwara no Motomitsu (11th century), Nobuzane and Tsunetaka (13th century), Mitsunobu (15th and 16th centuries), Sishu (1421–1509), Shūbun and Kano Masanobu (1424–1520), Mitsushige and Mitsuōki (17th century).

A popular period began with the establishment of a school of art by Hishigawa Moronobu (1646–1713). He created a progressive and trustworthy life about him, expanding his followers' artistic natures. After this came a development of realistic art, which compares in time with the European style. This manner has its importance in the great harm it did to Japanese art. It attempted to reproduce nature and all forms exactly, combining European chiaroscuro and linear perspective with the Japanese style. Glass, tapestry and furniture suffered as well as pictures. Except for the existence of water-colour painting, the loss would have been still greater. (See JAPANESE ART; JAPANESE PAINTING AND PRINTS; JAPANESE SCULPTURE.) (G. P. E.)

JAPANESE PAINTING AND PRINTS.

Although Japanese painting originated in China, it is a mistake to suppose that in art the Japanese have been merely imitative. It was inevitable that the great empire of the continent, with its ancient civilization, should be to Japan even more than Italy and Greece have been to Western Europe. But in their art there is always a difference; and in certain schools and periods the Japanese genius has triumphantly asserted its special gifts and qualities.

General Characteristics.—Japanese painting ignores the cast shadows of nature. It attempts no sculptural effects. It insists very little on the relief of objects portrayed, and prefers the suggestion of modelling to its actual representation. It employs an empirical system of perspective. It does not aim at the complete representation of a scene, but, selecting the significant elements, uses blank space as a factor in the design. Though the Japanese artists study nature with ardent attention, their aim is to train the memory so that when what they wish to paint is completely visualized they shall be able to record the mental image with the utmost vividness and truth. They concentrate on life, movement, character, but always with an eye to decorative effect. Their technique follows that of the Chinese. The medium is Chinese ink, a substance yielding tones that range from deepest lustrous black to silvery grey and water-colours, to which rice-paste or diluted fish-glue is sometimes added according to the pigment used. Paintings are either in ink alone, or light-coloured or full-coloured. The material is silk or absorbent paper. Anything like the elaborate confection of a European oil-painting is therefore unknown. The expressive strokes of the brush are valued as a direct communication of personality, like the handwriting which, also employing the brush, not a pen, is an invaluable training for the painter.

Fresco-painting was practised in early times, but never to the same extent as in China. Pictures are usually in the form of *kakemono*, hanging-paintings, or *makimono*, horizontal-scrolls, which are sometimes of immense length. But some of the finest Japanese paintings are in the form of screens, usually six-fold; these, if in colours, are generally on a gold or silver ground. There are also paintings on sliding-panels, and framed pictures. The *kakemono*, mounted on fine brocade, are kept rolled up, and when shown, are hung in a sort of alcove called the *tokonoma*, reserved for this purpose.

The motives of Japanese painting are often similar to those of Chinese art; but except in periods when Chinese influence was paramount, the life of action becomes a far more prominent and fruitful theme. The Japanese, being essentially martial, while the Chinese are pacific, found congenial matter in the painting of heroic episodes of the civil wars which raged so long in mediaeval times. Where the Chinese tradition was followed, the Japanese painters tended to use a smaller scale. The national instinct for

AN ACTOR PRINT BY KUNISADA, DATING FROM THE MIDDLE OF THE NINETEENTH CENTURY

neatness, for fastidious and cleanly order, is reflected in their art. The high spirit that goes with a martial temper, and a frank gaiety, are also distinctive qualities that find expression in art. Perhaps the chief bane of Japanese painters has been an extreme dexterity, tending to sacrifice inner significance to clever manipulation of the brush. Nevertheless it must be emphasized that the Japanese have for centuries shown an instinctive taste that amounts to genius; and perhaps in no country has fine taste been so widely diffused. The colour-prints of the 18th century were produced by men of the artisan class solely for a public of the same class. Despised by connoisseurs in their own country because of this association, they were appreciated as miracles of refinement and exquisite design by Europeans familiar with the art of the whole world. China has nothing comparable to show of the kind. Nor, so far as we know, have the Chinese ever produced anything like the superb array of screen-paintings by great masters which are among the greatest glories of Japanese painting. If in general Japanese art is less profound than Chinese art, yet among the early religious paintings are some sublime masterpieces. In the portrayal of swift and vehement action Japanese draughtsmen of mediaeval times are unsurpassed. In the art of the later periods there is a world of humorous vivacity and observation. Japanese painting represents a continuous tradition of 1200 years, perpetually renewing itself and alive to-day. But the fact that nearly all its great masterpieces have remained in Japan has prevented the real range of its achievement from being appreciated by the world at large.

History: Early Buddhist Art.—In the 6th century A.D. Buddhism, in its triumphal progress from India, overflowed, by way of Korea, into Japan. Such rudimentary efforts at mural painting as had existed before hardly need a mention; the real tradition of Japanese painting starts from the introduction of Buddhism. Of its earliest phase the one existing relic is the so-called Tamamushi Shrine, a portable wooden shrine painted with Buddhist figures and legendary scenes in an oil medium and in Chinese Buddhist style. The earliest independent painting is somewhat later in date. It is a portrait of the Crown Prince Shōtoku with his two sons. Shōtoku was a great and enlightened prince, who as regent under the empress Suiko (reigned 593–628) was the chief influence in the propagation of Buddhism and in the fostering of the arts. In this painting, now thought to have been made after Shōtoku's death, and in the few other works surviving from the 7th and early 8th century, such as the "Beauties under the Trees," a screen-painting, and the exquisite "Kichijōten" in Yakushiji temple, the style of the earlier T'ang period in China is very closely followed. The same full and rounded type of face, the same fashions in coiffure and dress, the same suavity of demeanour, are found in some fragments of Chinese secular painting discovered by Sir Aurel Stein at Turfan (Turkistan) in a tomb of the early 8th century. The grandest works of this time, however, are the frescoes in the Hōryūji temple at Nara: they are no doubt closely modelled on T'ang wall-paintings. Tradition ascribes both these and the portrait of Shōtoku to Korean artists. In 756 the consort of the Emperor Shōmu dedicated the belongings of her dead husband to Buddha. These have been preserved to this day in the Shōsōin at Nara, and bring vividly before us the outward signs of the Chinese civilization of the period, as reflected in the Japanese court. To what extent these objects of noble design and exquisite workmanship were Japanese productions, it is difficult to say. But it is certain that the Japanese adopted the arts and graces, the costume and ceremony, the literary and aesthetic pastimes, of Chinese life in no spirit of barbarian mimicry, but with a responsive appreciation. Fine taste and a sensitive docility are qualities in which the Japanese have been surpassed by no other race.

In 794 the capital was moved from Nara to Kyōto, then called Heian; and from this date to 1100 extends the Heian period, the later part of it being often called the Fujiwara period from the ascendancy of the great clan of Fujiwara. We now begin to find recorded the names of individual artists. Among these is the priest and saint, Kōbō, who visited China in 804–806; a few pictures by him still survive, which show that he could compete with Chinese masters on equal terms. The greatest name of the 9th century is that of Kanaoka, who painted secular scenes, animals, birds and flowers, as well as Buddhist subjects. Tradition places him among the greatest of Japanese painters, but no work of his brush now remains. Some splendid pictures have borne his name for centuries, but are now judged to be of considerably later date. We may presume, however, that with Kanaoka Japanese art began to assume a character of its own. From the end of the 9th century to the 14th intercourse with China was almost suspended; and, shut up within herself, Japan sought to assimilate all the marvellous inheritance she had received from the continent, and at the same time to develop her art according to her own genius. Kanaoka founded the Kose School, Kose being his family name. Other schools which arose were the Takuma and the Kasuga schools, and later the Tosa School, all of them belonging to the Yamato or national tradition. The pictures that have survived of this early period are all of Buddhist inspiration; and though we know from records that the artists by no means confined themselves to religious themes, probably their grandest work was in the Buddhist style. Eshin Sōzu (d. 1017) ranks as the greatest of the religious painters of Japan. He is especially associated with beatific visions of Amida Buddha—rising in glory behind the mountains, or descending to welcome the blessed soul to Paradise—though some of the works attributed to him by tradition have been taken from him by modern criticism. During the Fujiwara period the painting of screens, panels and fans was fashionable; even more popular, towards the end of it, were the picture-rolls, often illustrating diaries or stories and combined with manuscript.

The Yamato or National Style.—A definitely Japanese style had now been created. Nothing that we know of in Chinese art prepares us for the amazing rolls of Toba Sōjō (1053–1140). The priest Kakuyu, who became an archbishop, is known in art by this ecclesiastical title. He painted a grand Death of Buddha, but is best known for the witty and animated drawings in which he satirized personages of the day, including the clergy, under the guise of frogs, monkeys, etc. Whether in drawing animals or human figures, his brush tingles with life. Nothing could stale the freshness of these masterly sketches.

The art of caricature is known in Japan after him as Toba-ye; but later artists, while imitating him in a fondness for animal travesties, exaggerate his methods to satiety. Nevertheless, this strain of buoyant fun, which is found thus early, is a notable characteristic of Japanese art. Contrasted with Toba Sōjō is Takayoshi, whose work reflects the life of the Court at the close of the Fujiwara days, its refined voluptuousness, its exquisite leisure, its devoted cult of beauty. It was Takayoshi who made the first illustrations to the Genji Monogatari, the marvellous novel written by the Lady Murasaki at the beginning of the 11th century. Here we find at its most splendid and original the fully-formed style of the Tosa school in which the Yamato tradition was to persist so vigorously. All that is truly Japanese, and least Chinese,

"THE STORY OF KASANE," AN ACTOR PRINT BY TOYOKUNI'S EMINENT PUPIL, KUNIYOSHI

in later painting derives from elements here established. It is an art of frank and audacious convention, quite unlike any other art in the world. The conception of life as a continual ceremony is reflected in the formality of the design, in which the play of curving forms against straight line and angle is enriched by the contrast of low-toned but glowing colour. It is an art of interiors chiefly; the profuse beauties of nature are symbolized by tree or flower detached in delicate isolation. There is no hint of Chinese impressionism; cloud and mist intervene in the design as solid bands of gold. About the middle of the 12th century the long

JAPANESE PAINTING AND PRINTS

PLATE III

BY COURTESY OF THE TRUSTEES OF THE BRITISH MUSEUM

18TH CENTURY JAPANESE PRINTS

1. The broken shoe-string, by Suzuki Harunobu (1718–70), the first painter to employ full colours in wood block printing
2. Two youths and a girl playing a flute, by Torii Kiyonaga (1752–1815)
3. Beauty in the mirror, by Kitagawa Utamaro (1753–1806) one of Japan's greatest masters of figure design
4. Theatre manager reading an announcement, by Toshiusai Sharaku

rivalry of the great clans of Taira and Minamoto came to a head, and Japan was given up to civil war.

Kamakura Period.—In the end the Minamoto triumphed, and Yoritomo took to himself the title of Shōgun. He established his capital at Kamakura, after which the ensuing period is named. The portrait of Yoritomo here reproduced (Plate II.) is an ancient copy of a picture preserved at Kyōto and ascribed to a contemporary painter, Takanobu. We observe the emphatic angles and straight lines on which the design is built; a certain squareness, contrasting with the grandly flowing curves of Chinese painting. Kamakura painting is indeed the most truly national phase of Japanese art, the art of a martial and heroic people. The swift and summary power of stroke, the animated intensity of delineation, which Toba Sōjō had shown so signally, were now applied to scenes of action and war. Mitsunaga, Nobuzane and Keion are the supreme masters of a vigorous school. "Keion," now thought to be a legendary name, is the traditional author of three picture-rolls of scenes from the civil war, one of which is in the Boston museum. For dramatic design, energy of movement, vehemence of action, the draughtsmanship here shown is not surpassed in the world's art. A detail from the Boston Roll is reproduced (Plate IV., fig. 1).

Mitsunaga is no less a master of expressive gesture and nervous line. Nobuzane is famed for a series of portraits of poets, but his masterpiece is the incomparable portrait of Kōbō Daishi as a child kneeling upon the lotus, an exquisite work. Takakane, Yoshimitsu, and Korehisa in the 14th century rival the preceding masters in splendour of colour and energy of line. This was a truly national school, and it is unfortunate that its masterpieces are so little known, and that the glories of this school can only be fully appreciated in Japan itself. (Many scenes from these rolls have been reproduced in colour in *The Kokka* magazine.) Besides the interiors with their scenes of court life and amorous intrigue, in which no one rivalled Takayoshi, and the battle-scenes, a favourite theme was the life of this or that saint; and here we find episodes and incidents taken from the ordinary life of the people, depicted with an intimacy of truth, a humour and pathos, which are emphasized by the contrast of the formal conventions of the background. Paintings of horse-taming and of demons on a journey are also famous. The school, usually styled the Tosa school, began to show signs of enfeeblement in time; and though Mitsunobu and Yukihide did admirable work in the 15th century, a strong reaction from China was already inaugurating a new era in art.

Ashikaga Period. The Chinese Renaissance.—During the 15th century a complete change was to come over the spirit of Japanese painting. During the civil wars of the Kamakura epoch the doctrines of the Zen sect of Buddhism had taken a deep hold of the samurai, or lesser nobility, as well as of the monks. Zen despised ceremony, the worship of images, dogmas; it relied on wordless communication, on contemplation of the absolute in oneself. Zen had been the dominant inspiration of the art of the latter part of the Sung period in China; and it was to the painting of Southern Sung that the Japanese now turned, and took for the supreme exemplars of this new movement or revival the great landscape masters Hsia Kuei and Ma Yüan and a master of the ink-sketch, Mu Ch'i. The Ashikaga line of Shōguns established their power in 1335 and were to remain in power till 1573. They removed from Kamakura, and Kyōto once again became the capital. During the early part of the period there was renewed intercourse with China; yet the contemporary art of the Ming period had little or no influence at this time in Japan. On the other hand, the ink-paintings inspired by Zen doctrine during the Sung era were eagerly collected. Zen had no longer any power or following in China; it was therefore Japan's opportunity, and in this phase of Chinese painting Japanese collections are particularly rich.

This revival had already a few precursors in the 14th century, notably Chō Densu, known also as Minchō (1351–1427), famous as a painter of Arhats or Buddhist Apostles and one of the greatest religious painters of Japan. And before the 15th century was over the talent of the rising generation was drawn more and more to the Chinese style. From the long rolls depicting in rich colour heroic stories, or ceremonious scenes of court life, or saintly legends, men turned to the swift ink-sketch, charged with concentrated energy—a spray of blossom, a bird poised on a reed, a glimpse of mountains among the mists, a sage absorbed in thought; the theme, whatever it was, being not so much the thing represented as what it evoked in the spectator's mind: fact transmuted to symbol and idea. To find the spiritual reality in oneself was

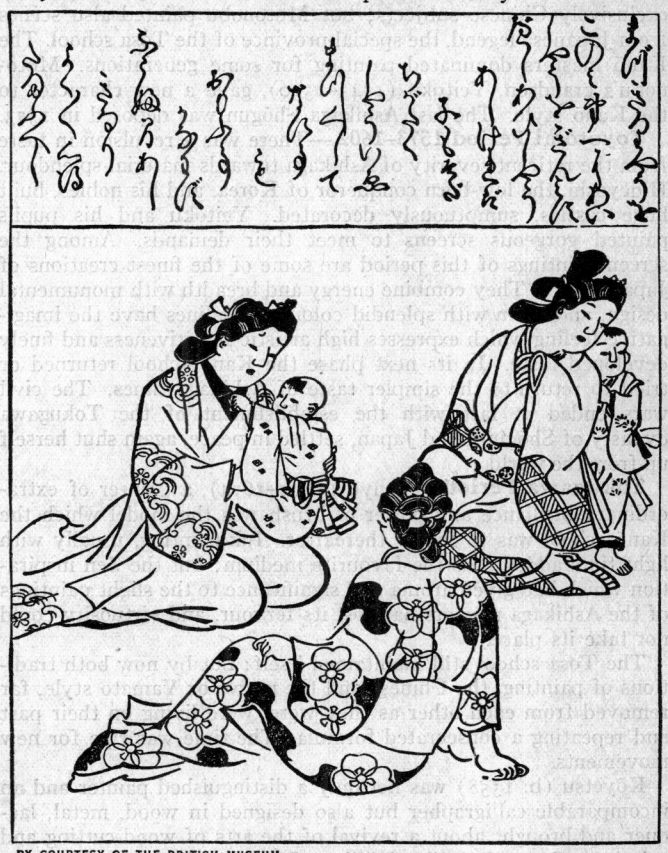

BY COURTESY OF THE BRITISH MUSEUM
"WOMEN AND CHILDREN," A 17TH CENTURY WOODCUT BY MORONOBU
A translation of the script is: "In choosing a wife (or husband), first, she must be beautiful; then love, and then sympathy comes. And finally there must be conjugal affinity (determined by the signs of the zodiac at birth); if not, the children will be frail, and suffering from poverty will come. Everything will be unsuccessful, causing continual quarrels between husband and wife. Remember these words well."

the Zen aim; and "an impulse from a vernal wood" embodied by the painter's brush in a hinted scene, could be of more potency than all the teaching of the sages. Soga Shūbun, a Chinese artist who settled in Japan, was a pioneer of the revival; he founded a line of painters, among whom his son Soga Jasoku is the most famous. Other pioneers were Josetsu; Bunsei, an artist till recently confused with Josetsu; and Shūbun the Priest (to be distinguished from Soga Shūbun). These were followed by Oguri Sōtan; Nōami and his son and grandson, Gei-ami and Sōami; Keishoki, and other masters. All of these belong to what became known as the Chinese School.

A yet greater artist, Sesshū (1420–1506), formed a more personal style and founded the school known by his name. He visited China, but found no peer among the Chinese. The force and intensity of his conceptions are matched by the vehemence of his brush strokes. In Japanese esteem Sesshū probably ranks as the greatest painter of Japan. His follower Sesson at times rose almost to Sesshū's height. A third school was originated by Kanō Masanobu, the first of the long line of Kanō artists, which has lasted into our own day. Though the art of this whole movement can never mean so much to Western minds as it means to Japanese, because of its subjective character, and though its achievements cannot be regarded as equalling those of the Chinese masters it adored, still the revival was of inestimable value to an art which was becoming impoverished through isolation, by re-uniting it to the main stream of Asiatic culture. It is permeated by ideas, and its art breathes a lofty atmosphere. The Kanō tradition would not have become so powerful had it not been for the genius of Motonobu, son of Masanobu, who is one of the greatest masters of Japanese painting (1476–1559). In his work the Kanō manner assumes the well-marked character which it was to preserve so long. The painters of the Ashikaga revival painted almost exclusively Chinese subjects; but Motonobu painted also scenes from Japanese legend, the special province of the Tosa school. The Kanō masters dominated painting for some generations. Motonobu's grandson, Yeitoku (1543–1590), gave a new character to the Kanō style. The last Ashikaga Shōgun was deposed in 1573.

Toyotomi Period 1573–1602.—There was a revulsion in taste from the reticent severity of Ashikaga towards material splendour. Hideyoshi, the low-born conqueror of Korea, and his nobles, built huge castles, sumptuously decorated. Yeitoku and his pupils painted gorgeous screens to meet their demands. Among the screen-paintings of this period are some of the finest creations of Japanese art. They combine energy and breadth with monumental design, and often with splendid colour. The lines have the imaginative feeling which expresses high artistic sensitiveness and finely developed taste. In its next phase the Kanō school returned or tried to return to the simpler taste of Ashikaga times. The civil wars ended at last with the establishment of the Tokugawa dynasty of Shōguns, and Japan, settled in peace, again shut herself up from the world.

Tokugawa Period.—Tanyū (1602–1674), a painter of extraordinary brilliance and power of brush, was the model which the Kanō school was to follow thereafter. Ink-painting, usually with light tints added, was the favourite medium; but the Zen inspiration which had given aroma and significance to the slight paintings of the Ashikaga masters had lost its fervour, and virtuosity could not take its place.

The Tosa school still maintained itself; but by now both traditions of painting, the Chinese and the native or Yamato style, far removed from each other as they were, were living on their past and repeating a consecrated formula. The time was ripe for new movements.

Kōyetsu (b. 1558) was not only a distinguished painter and an incomparable calligrapher but also designed in wood, metal, lacquer and brought about a revival of the arts of wood-cutting and printing. Somewhat like William Morris, he presided over a village in which his craftsmen pursued their various crafts under his direction. The screen in the Metropolitan Museum, New York, reproduced (Plate I.), used to be considered the work of Kōyetsu; but, as is often the case with screen-paintings, the actual authorship is problematic. Kōyetsu sometimes collaborated with his friend and follower Sōtatsu, the one supplying the calligraphy, the other the painting. They formed a style which is the most intimately Japanese of all the schools. Yeitoku had already created in his screen-painting a style of 'mural' art which, while taking over some of the Tosa conventions and its traditions of colour, drew from Chinese example a synthetic power, an emotional concentration, and a massive grandeur such as none of the old Tosa artists either aimed at or achieved. Kōyetsu and Sōtatsu, who founded their art on Tosa principles, completed this fusion of styles and refined on it with the sensitive delicacy of Japanese genius. Starting from an abstract design consisting of related or opposed forms, masses, tones, they fit or melt into the design whatever they choose of natural form and colour. Kōrin (1661–1716) carried the style to yet further audacities. He uses a freedom and extravagance which in Europe only caricaturists have ventured on to express a superbly decorative idea. The Wave Screen at Boston (Plate I.) is even more an imaginative conception than a glorious decoration. Kōrin's masterpieces were in lacquer as well as painting. His brother Kenzan was a fine painter, but even more distinguished as a potter. The style was to be revived later by the exquisite but rather cold Hōitsu (1761–1828).

Ukiyo-ye.—Another school which arose in the early 17th century was Ukiyo-ye, the painting of the transient world of daily life. The old Tosa rolls had often portrayed the doings of ordinary folk, but only as accessories to an episode in saintly or heroic lives. Certain Kanō painters, chiefly Sanraku, ventured at times on the kind of subject which we call *genre*, though without avowing their authorship of such pictures. Iwasa Matabei (1578–1650) was the first to make this kind of picture his main concern and to take pride in it. His authentic works, one of which is reproduced (Plate VI., fig. 1), are extremely rare; but paintings by his followers are numerous. Although the Chinese in far-off T'ang times had made masterpieces in this kind, especially of the occupations of women, this was a genuinely Japanese movement and fertile in results. Later in the century Moronobu, an admirable painter, exploited the woodcut as an inexpensive means for mirroring the contemporary life of the people; and the woodcut, first hand-coloured then colour-printed, became the medium of a truly popular art which yet was of singular refinement. It is by the colour-prints that Ukiyo-ye, and indeed Japanese pictorial art as a whole, is best known in the West (they are separately treated below). But all the masters of the colour-print were also painters, and a few of the best Ukiyo-ye painters, like Chōshun, designed no prints. The chief masters of this school, Okumura Masanobu, Harunobu, Kiyonaga, Utamaro and others in the 18th century, Hokusai and Hiroshige in the 19th, are notable artists who have received fuller appreciation in the West than in their own country, where they have not the prestige of the classic schools. Ukiyo-ye was almost exclusively the art of the populace of Yedo. Meanwhile in Kyōto, during the 18th century, other movements were stirring.

In 1731 a Chinese painter Shên Nan-pin came to Nagasaki and stayed two years. He was greatly admired and imitated. A school often known as the Neo-Chinese school, since it was different in its aims and inspiration from the Chinese revival of the 15th century, took for models the decorative, coloured style of later Ming or the light, freely-handled landscapes in ink of the Bun-jin-gwa or Literary Man's Painting. Bunchō, Riurikiō, Taigadō, Buson, Kwazan and others worked with distinction in these Chinese styles. A pupil of Buson's, Goshun, broke away to some extent from this school, craving for a stronger element of the naturalism which was in the atmosphere of the time. Of this naturalism Okyo (1733–95) was the protagonist. Gifted with extraordinary preciseness of vision and wielder of an unerring brush, Okyo studied more directly from nature than any Japanese before him, though he never deserted the main conventions of his country's art. His conceptions are sometimes grandiose but never impassioned. His impeccable, fastidious art is rather cold. Ganku (1745–1834), who is sometimes reckoned as the founder of a separate school, expresses a more impulsive temperament. He is famous for his tigers.

The naturalistic movement which Okyo did most to influence is embodied in the Kyōto painters known as the Shijō school, with whose style that of the followers of Bunchō and the neo-Chinese movement tended, during the 19th century, to coalesce. Mori Sosen (1747–1821), an exquisite painter of monkeys, deer and other animals, which he studied in their native forests, is the most eminent of these masters of a graceful naturalism. Contemporary with Okyo, Soga Shōhaku harked back to the great times of Ashikaga, and tried in his ink-pictures of Chinese sages to recover, with some measure of success, the fire and inspiration of the 15th century. Jakuchū was another contemporary artist who pursued an independent line; he recalls the rich colouring of Ming pictures in his gorgeous paintings of cocks and hens and fishes. The Kanō school still produced its academic repetitions of old themes; but its best pupils tended to break away, like the brilliant Itchō (1652–1725) who painted Ukiyo-ye subjects. In the early 19th century there was a revival of the Tosa style by two gifted painters, Totsugen and Tameyasu. Formed in the Kanō school, Yōsai (1787–1878) made a style of his own; he is famous for his pictures of heroic subjects. Contemporary with him were Zeshin, the distinguished lacquer-designer and painter, and Kyōsai, a various and vigorous master.

Meiji Period.—From the 17th century onwards European influence begins intermittently to be felt. Yamada Emosaku in that century learned oil-painting from the Dutch. In the 18th century Shiba Kōkan painted in European style; and European perspective is attempted in many Ukiyo-ye prints. During the first

JAPANESE PAINTING AND PRINTS   PLATE IV

BY COURTESY OF (1) THE MUSEUM OF FINE ARTS, BOSTON, (2, 3) THE FREER GALLERY OF ART

JAPANESE PICTURE ROLLS AND SCREENS

1. "Flight of the Court," detail from the "Burning of the Sanjo Palace," a horizontal picture roll or makemono representing the civil war, by "Keion," perhaps a legendary name, Kamakura period. 13th cent.
2. "Two Geese Flying over a Beach," ink-picture on four-fold screen. Kyōto school, 18th century, formerly attributed to Ōkyō
3. "Cryptomerias and Cedars on a Snowy Hillside," by Yeitoku or of his time (1543–90), ink-picture on a six-fold screen, with a lavish use of gold. Kanō school, Ashikaga period and Toyotomi period

PLATE V JAPANESE PAINTING AND PRINTS

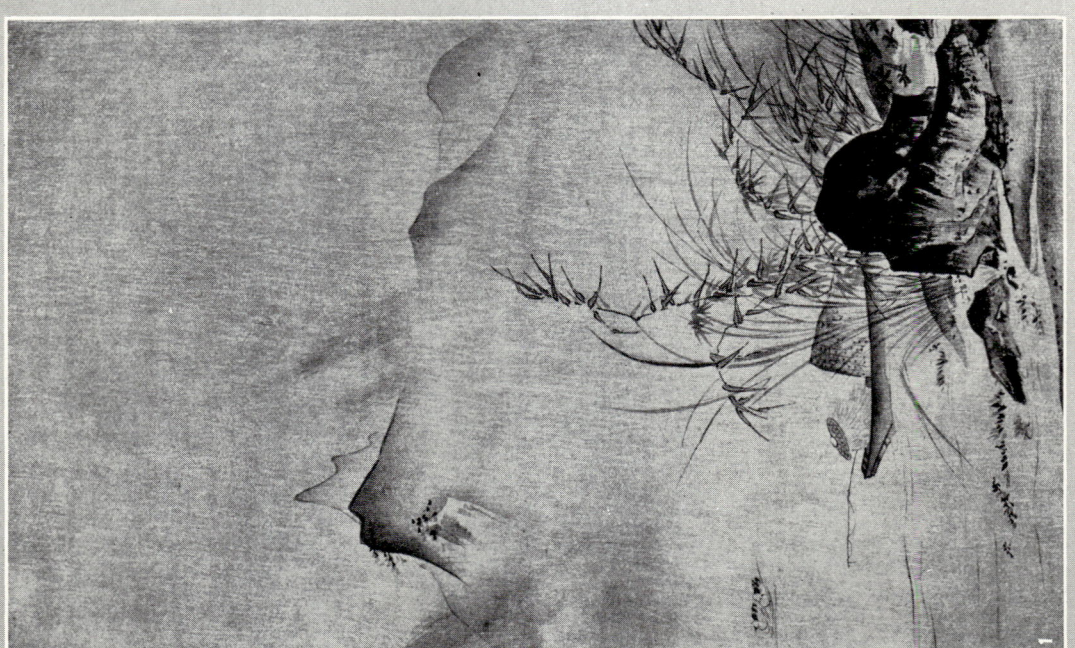

BY COURTESY OF THE KOKKWA MAGAZINE, TOKYO

JAPANESE PAINTERS OF THE ASHIKAGA PERIOD—THE CHINESE RENAISSANCE

1. Landscape, by Sōga Jasoku, 15th century, Ashikaga period. Sōga Jasoku was the son of a Chinese artist who settled in Japan
2. Winter scene, by Motonobu (1476–1559), Kanō school, Ashikaga period. Motonobu who followed the Chinese tradition and chose many Chinese subjects, also painted scenes from Japanese legend
3. Jurōjin, by Sesshū (1420–1506), Sesshū school, Ashikaga period. Jurōjin, symbolising in this painting the genius of immortal old age, is represented as a venerable figure, looking out from blossoming spring trees

JAPANESE PAINTING AND PRINTS

PLATE VI

BY COURTESY OF (1) THE KOKKWA MAGAZINE, TOKYO, (2) THE MUSEUM OF FINE ARTS, BOSTON

PAINTINGS OF THE KANŌ SCHOOL

1. "Men of Leisure," by Iwasa Matabei (1578–1650), Kanō school, founder of Ukiyo-ye school of *genre* painting. Matabei, a Samurai, was the first to make "the painting of the Transient World of daily life" his chief concern and to lead a genuinely Japanese movement in this field. The faces of the women in this painting illustrate the typical feminine face of Matabei, with short nose, long, full cheeks, and round chin

2. "Mist Rising," by Shokei (1628–1717), signed "Hokkyo Shokei, aged 86"; Kanō school. Landscape in ink on paper, size 290 mm. x 530 mm. Bigelow Collection, Museum of Fine Arts, Boston

JAPANESE PAINTING AND PRINTS

years of the Meiji period (1868–1911) when Western ideas were being eagerly adopted, the European or Dutch style of painting was more cultivated than any other. An English artist, Charles Wirgman, who came to Japan in 1857, had a number of pupils, of whom the best was Takahashi Yuichi. In 1876 the Government invited an Italian artist, A. Fontanesi, to teach painting; he was very successful for a short time. In 1878 E. F. Fenollosa, an

BY COURTESY OF THE BRITISH MUSEUM, FROM THE SHIMBI SHOIN REPRODUCTION
SELECTION FROM TOBA SOJO ("SATIRICAL DRAWINGS OF ANIMALS")
The scripts are identical, standing for "Kozanji" or "Takayama Tera," in English, "High Mountain Monastery," and indicate where the drawings were made

American critic, became professor of philosophy in Tokyo. He was the first to open the eyes of the West to the beauty and importance of the older art of Japan and China; but he also had great influence in Japan. He persuaded the Government to forbid the temples to sell works of art, and to schedule as national treasures all the most precious objects. His enthusiasm for the old traditions reacted on Japanese artists. The School of Fine Art set up with Italian professors had been a failure. A new school was established in 1887, and among the teachers were Kawabata Gyokushō, Hashimoto Gahō and Kanō Hōgai, all eminent painters in traditional styles, though not quite unaffected by Europe. In 1898 a secession from this school, under Okakura Kakuzō, founded the Nihon Bijutsu-in for the teaching of national styles of painting. To this movement belong Yokoyama Taikwan and Shimomura Kwanzan, distinguished living artists. Takeuchi Seiho and Kawai Gyokudō are among the most eminent artists of to-day who maintain the Asiatic traditions of art. Many gifted painters practise oil-painting and follow Western methods; but though the adoption of so much of Western civilization must inevitably modify the mental outlook, it does not seem likely that Japan's ancient inheritance in art will ever be wholly superseded. (A full account of contemporary painting is given in Elisséev's *Peinture Contemporaine au Japon*.)

ENGRAVING

Copper-engraving and etching, learned from the Dutch, were practised by some Japanese in the 18th and 19th centuries, but the medium did not prove congenial. The woodcut is the national mode of engraving and has been carried to a pitch of marvellous perfection. The art of the woodcut was introduced into Japan from China in the wake of Buddhism. It was used for the printing both of texts and pictures. Actually the earliest surviving specimens of printed texts in the world are Japanese, and are in the form of Buddhist charms enclosed in miniature wood pagodas distributed among the temples in the 8th century A.D. For a long period the woodcut was confined to the reproduction of popular images of piety, similar to the Chinese prints discovered at Tunhuang by Sir Aurel Stein. Some remarkable woodcuts were made in 1414 to illustrate a block-printed history of the Yūdzū Nembutsu but there was no real development of the art till the 17th century. In 1608 an illustrated edition of the Ise Monogatari appeared with woodcuts attributed by some critics to Kōyetsu.

Other illustrated editions of classic stories followed. But it was Hishikawa Moronobu (1618–1694) who transformed the art and made possible all the brilliant work of the Ukiyo-ye designers of the 18th century. A desire for the pleasures of art had sprung up among the lower classes, now that they at last enjoyed the peace of a settled Government. Paintings were too expensive. Moronobu saw the enormous possibilities of the woodcut, and adapting his style to the limitations and possibilities of the medium, devoted himself to supplying the need of the people. He designed chiefly for books, with or without text. A comparison of his early work (c. 1660) with his later books shows the immense stride forward that the engravers made under the stimulus of Moronobu's genius. There was soon a demand for colour. Moronobu and his pupils produced broad-sheets as well as books, and these were often coloured by hand, *tan* or red-lead being the dominant colour; hence the name *tan-ye* for these prints.

The theatre was a passion of the Yedo populace; and an actor Torii Kiyomoto, who designed posters for the Osaka theatre, came to Yedo in 1687 and, though his own work has not survived, he founded a famous dynasty of artists. His son Kiyonobu was the first to design portraits of actors, which were to remain one of the staple themes of the print-designers. Kiyonobu's son, Kiyomasu, rivalled his father. Competing in popularity with the portraits of actors were the portraits of fashionable beauties, especially courtesans. The Kwaigetsudō group of artists during the early years of the 18th century produced some stately prints of women. But in this field Okumura Masanobu was much more inventive and fertile; he designed idyllic groups and enlarged the whole range of the woodcut, while the Torii masters kept almost entirely to the stage. Kiyonobu died in 1729, but prints signed with his name continued to be published till the mid-century. This second Kiyonobu has not yet been identified with certainty.

In 1740 or 1741 was published the first two-colour print. The colours chosen were *beni* or rose-red, and green. Colour-printing had been practised for at least a century before this in China; but the Yedo printers seem to have learned the art afresh. (In a work called Jinkō-ki, 1627, one of the woodcuts is printed in colours. "Block-Printing and Book Illustration in Japan," by L. Norton Brown, p. 29.) The cherry-wood used was cut on the plank with a knife, as in Europe till the days of Bewick. A separate block was cut for each colour; so for a two-colour print there would be three printings. An accurate register was secured by the simple means of a guide-mark in the form of a right-angle at the lower right corner of the key-block and a straight line parallel to the lower edge at the left corner. There was no press. Colour-printing soon ousted the hand-coloured print in popularity, though the latter was still practised for some years. The two-colour or *beni* print continued till 1764, and a marvellous range of colour-design was accomplished within this narrow compass. In 1764 the first polychrome prints were made by Harunobu, who till his death in 1770 was to reign undisputed over Ukiyo-ye. Everyone imitated his style. He created the fashion for a smaller sheet, with smaller figures of exquisite grace. He was an enchanting colourist. His chosen subjects were youthful idylls, and he avoided the stage. Harunobu's closest follower was Koryūsai who after his death developed a more personal style, specially excelling in the *Hashira-ye* or pillar-print. Shunshō revived the prestige of the theatrical print, neglected by Harunobu, and produced a long series of extremely fine designs before his death in 1792. But from about 1780 to 1790 Ukiyo-ye was again dominated by a single master, Kiyonaga (1752–1815) in whose designs the almost infantine grace of Harunobu's types was supplanted by tall and stately figures, and his interiors were exchanged for out-door scenes. Kiyonaga designed some masterpieces, especially in the form of diptychs and triptychs, and was closely imitated by a whole generation; there is an unrivalled poise and dignity in his groups, and his drawing is masterly; but he had little invention in figure-composition and is apt to be monotonous. Utamaro (1754–1806) is the greatest master of figure-design in the whole school. Among his earlier works are picture-books of insects and shells, exquisite in quality; but his absorbing theme is woman. In the last few years of his life there is a falling-off, but a was a time of rapid decline in the general taste. In the discovery of beautiful relations between figures, and in a sort of intensity of design, Utamaro is incomparable.

During the 1790's Yeishi and Toyokuni competed with Utamaro for popular favour. Sharaku published in 1794–95 a series of actor-prints surpassing in power all his predecessors in this line, and now immensely sought after. Artists admired them, but the public disliked their pungency. After Utamaro's death in 1806, the decline became a downfall. The school was regenerated by Hokusai (1760–1849), who found a new inspiration in landscape. His Thirty-Six Views of Fuji and other sets (c. 1820–1830) contain some of the finest landscape designs ever made. A little later Hiroshige (1797–1858) in countless sets of prints depicted every aspect of his own country in every weather, with extraordinary intimacy and freshness. Meanwhile Kuniyoshi and Kunisada were the outstanding masters of figure-design. After Hiroshige's death aniline dyes were introduced. The school which had mirrored the popular life of Yedo for two centuries now virtually came to an end. During Meiji period (1868–1911) there was a revival, but the art had lost its character. From the days of Moronobu the artists had designed for the woodcut; now, the woodcut was merely the reproduction of a painting. The use of cheap pigments sadly affected the quality of these clever prints. Yoshitoshi, Toshikata and Gekko were perhaps the best of the designers in this period.

All the artists of the colour-print designed illustrations for books, the number of which is almost incredible. Many, however, of the book-illustrations were the work of artists who designed neither single-sheets nor colour-prints, and some of these artists did not belong to the Ukiyo-ye school at all. O-oka Shunboku (1688–1768) was an Osaka artist, who published a number of picture-books; one of these, a copy of a Chinese work of 1702, was printed in colours in 1746. An older contemporary of his, Tachibana Morikuni, was a notable book-illustrator, also at Osaka. Sukenobu was extremely popular as a designer of picture-books of women and children, and strongly influenced some of the earlier Ukiyo-ye artists. Tsukioka Tange made drawings for many of the *meisho* or guide-books. Some of these artists devoted much of their work to reproducing classic pictures or furnishing decorative designs for artisans. The first colour-printed book was produced at Osaka by Sukenobu in 1745. In Yedo, Harunobu produced some beautiful picture-books. Among others too numerous to mention, Shunshō and Shigemasa's *Beauties of the Green Houses* ranks as one of the finest colour-printed books, with Utamaro's *Insect Book* in quite a different style. Hokusai's *Hundred Views of Fuji* and *Mangwa* are famous books in black and white or with a faint tint only. Among more modern works Yōsai's *Zenken Kojitsu* and Bairei's books of birds deserve mention.

A new style of colour-printing began in 1889 when the *Kokka* began to reproduce old paintings. For the woodcuts printed in this magazine and in the sumptuous publications of the Shimbi Shoin body-colours are used, and sometimes as many as 100 blocks. Not as faithful as photographic reproductions, these prints have an extraordinary beauty of texture and in their way are unrivalled. See ART: *Far Eastern Methods*; SCREEN.

BIBLIOGRAPHY.—Seigai Omura, *History of Japanese Pictorial Art* (1909); Arthur Morrison, *The Painters of Japan* (1911); E. F. Fenollosa, *Epochs of Chinese and Japanese Art* (1912); L. Binyon, *Painting in the Far East* (1908); S. Elisséev, *La Peinture Contemporaine au Japon* (1923); E. F. Strange, *Japanese Illustration* (1904); S. Tajima, *Masterpieces selected from the Ukiyoyé School* (1906–09); W. von Seidlitz, *History of Japanese Colour-prints* (1910); Vignier and Inada, *Estampes Japonaises* (1910–14); Binyon and Sexton, *Japanese Colour Prints* (1923); F. Rumpf, *Meister des Japanischen Holzschnittes* (1924). (L. Bi.)

IRON IN ART. Iron began to take its place in the brilliant bronze age culture of China about 500 B.C. By the end of the 2nd century of the present era bronze weapons had been almost completely supplanted, while iron had been generally substituted for bronze in common use in utensils and vessels of various kinds, tools, chariot-fittings and even small pieces of sculpture. These were commonly cast in sand-moulds, were patterned after bronze prototypes and were typical in style and decoration of the Han period.

The Iron age in Japan is supposed to have begun in the 2nd century B.C., though the chief early remains are weapons from the dolmens of the 2nd to the 8th centuries A.D. The Japanese iron founder attained a considerable skill at an early date and acquired a social position which was never attained by the bronze caster, or by the iron workers in China where the bronze age tradition was much stronger.

From the 9th century iron increasingly took the place of bronze in China as a material for sculpture, especially in the north and under the Sung dynasty....

Several iron pagodas, ranging in size from miniature models to towers 30 or more metres in height, and dating from the 10th to the 14th century, give further evidence of the dexterity of the Chinese iron caster. These imitate in detail both the structural and decorative effects of the more common tile-roofed brick pagodas. Iron for temple furniture has long been in use, and a large number of the braziers, censers, caldrons and bells found to-day in the temples are of iron.

In China in the 17th century the iron picture was developed, the craftsmen seeking to reproduce in permanent form through the medium of wrought iron the effects of the popular ink-sketches of the master painters. When completed, these pictorial compositions were mounted in windows, in lanterns or in frames as pictures. When in the latter form a paper or silk background often bore the signature and seal of the maker, heightening the resemblance to a painting. The craft flourished in Anwhei province and is still practised, though with less patience and fineness.

Embellishment of Armour.—It is apparent that iron has been used in China chiefly as a substitute or imitative medium, worked often with great skill but with little artistic invention. In Japan, however, the iron worker developed a distinctive and original means of expression and high artistic attainment in furniture for the sword. With the rise of feudalism and the establishment of the samurai class after the wars of the 12th century, the equipment of the warriors became an object for the efforts of the artist. At first these efforts were devoted to the embellishment of defensive armour, but from the 15th century the sword became the centre of attention. The blade is not properly part of our subject, but in the mountings, especially the guards (*tsuba*), we find exquisite artistry expressed chiefly in iron. A remarkably soft and pure variety of the metal especially free from sulphur was employed. It was worked by casting, hammering and chiselling; and innumerable surface effects were obtained by tooling, inlaying, incrustation, combination with other metals and patination by various, usually secret, processes. Simple conventional patterns, crests and pictorial designs were the bases for the decoration. As these were often furnished by painters or designers the criterion of connoisseurship in Japan is the unsurpassed technical quality of the handling of the iron itself. With the promulgation of the edict of 1876, prohibiting the wearing of swords, this art came to an end, but the skill of the Japanese iron worker may still be noted in numerous small decorative objects.

BIBLIOGRAPHY.—B. Laufer, *Chinese Clay Figures, Part 1, Prolegomena on the History of Defensive Armor* (Chicago, 1914); H. C. Gunsaulus, *Japanese Sword-mounts in the Collection of the Field Museum* (Chicago, 1923); E. Boerschman, "Eisen-und Bronzepagoden in China," *Jahrbuch der Asiatischen Kunst*, pp. 223–235 (1924); B. March, "Iron Pictures: A Chinese Craft," *Chinese Economic Monthly*, vol. iii., pp. 312–313; O. Sirén, *Chinese Sculpture* (1925); G. Soulié de Morant, *Histoire de L'Art Chinois* (1928). (B. Mar.)

> PUBLISHERS' NOTE—Following the Britannica custom, we have retained at the end of signed articles the initials and not the full name of the author. The reader, however, can always identify the author by referring to the Table of Contents where the full names of the authors are given together with their initials.

FLOWER PAINTING. The close observation and contemplation of nature by the artists of the East have produced in their work a rare character and charm. Their flower paintings vibrate with life and force; they are beautifully rhythmic. Their lilies nod and sway on delicate stems; lotus flowers vigorously grow from earth and water into light and sunshine. Their vines hang and sway in the breeze, their peonies unfold, their plum blossoms

IRON IN ART

PLATE V

CHINESE CAST IRON WORK

BY COURTESY OF (1) WARREN E. COX. (2) THE MUSEUM OF FINE ARTS, BOSTON, (3, 4, 6) THE FIELD MUSEUM OF NATURAL HISTORY, CHICAGO, (5) THE METROPOLITAN MUSEUM OF ART, NEW YORK

1. Cast iron vessel of the Han dynasty (206 B.C.–A.D. 220)
2. Cast iron head of a Bodhisattva, Sung dynasty (960–1280)
3. Cast iron figure, Ming dynasty (1368–1644); dated, equivalent to A.D. 1618
4. Cast iron bell, Sung dynasty (960–1280)
5. Cast iron statuette, Ming dynasty (1368–1644)
6. Cast iron vase, Han dynasty (206 B.C.–A.D. 220)

PLATE VI   IRON IN ART

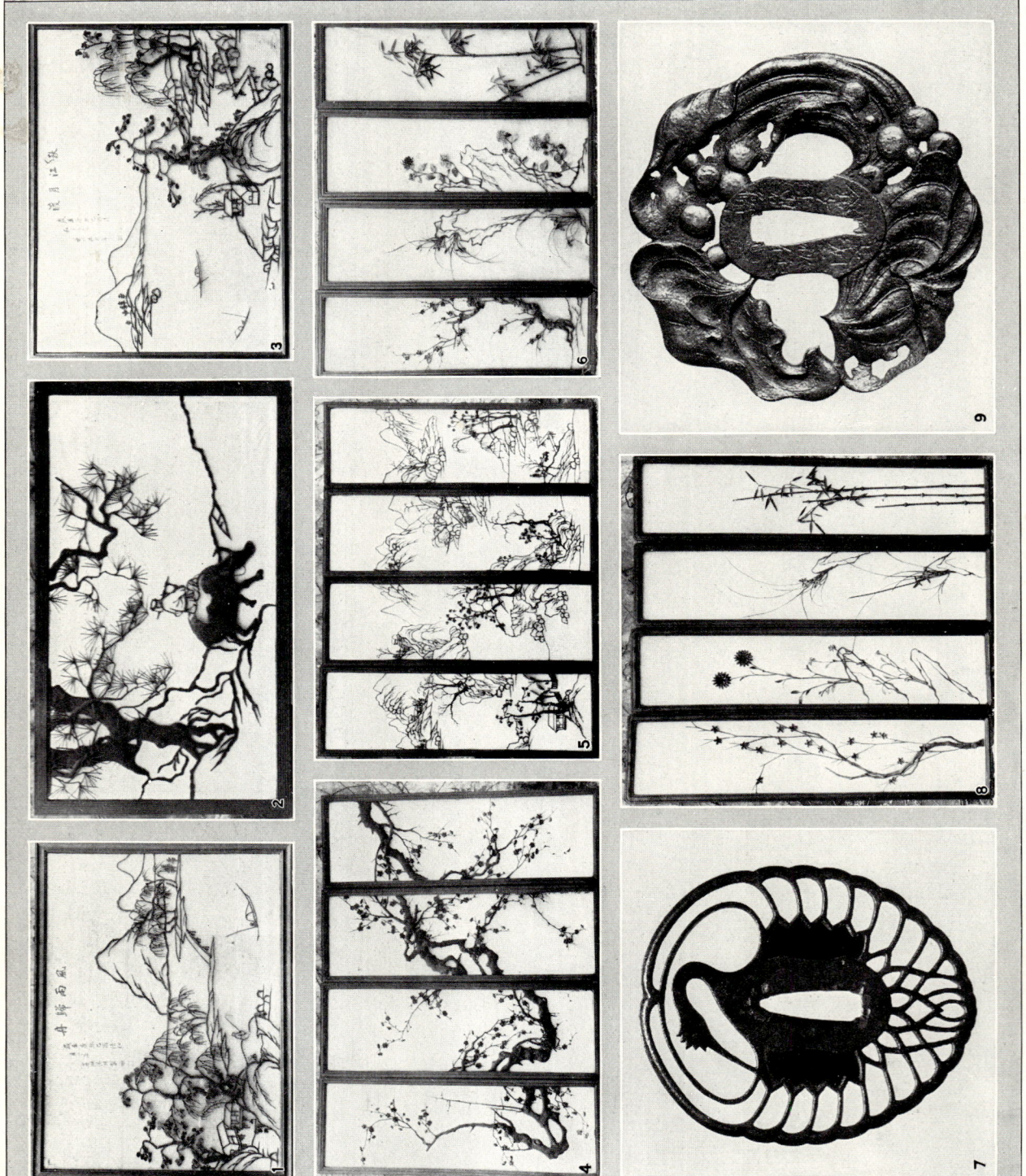

GROUP OF CHINESE IRON PICTURES WITH PAPER OR SILK BACKGROUNDS AND JAPANESE SWORD GUARDS

BY COURTESY OF (1-6, 8) JOHN REILLY, JR., (7, 9) THE MUSEUM OF FINE ARTS, BOSTON

1 and 3. Chinese wrought iron landscapes signed by T'ang P'eng (dated equivalent to A.D. 1705)
2. Wrought iron landscapes, with figures, 18th century
4. Set of panels of the Prunus wrought in iron
5. Iron landscape panels
6. and 8. Two groups of four iron panels each, depicting the four seasons
7. Japanese iron sword guard, 17th–18th century
9. Japanese iron sword guard by Yukinaka (11.?), 18th century

PLATE II — FLOWER PAINTING

BY COURTESY OF THE TRUSTEES OF THE BRITISH MUSEUM

JAPANESE AND CHINESE FLOWER PAINTING

1. "Lotus, White Heron and Kingfishers" by an unknown Chinese painter of the Sung dynasty (960–1268), an example of the work of the period when flower painting advanced to a great art in China
2. "Chrysanthemums" by Tawarayo Sotatsu, an outstanding figure of the Tokugawa period in Japanese art. He worked between 1624–1643 and was the first to use gold as a pigment, mixing it with ink and colours

spread their petals and gently float away in the breeze almost as they open. Flowers in their paintings are associated with the passing of the seasons and the moods of nature. Generally they are painted with the birds of the seasons naturally associated with them at the time of flowering, in their natural habitat, and always with a great understanding of their life and growth. The Chinese artists ever communed with nature. It is said of Chao Ch'ang, of the early 11th century, that "every morning he would walk round the gardens and examine some flower carefully, turning it over and over in his hand. Then he would paint." Of I Yüan-chi, it is said that "he laid out a garden, planted it with bamboos and rushes, and kept there a variety of water fowl, so as to be able to watch them in movement and repose." Kuo Hsi writes about this same time: "Those who study flower painting take a single stalk and put it into a deep hole and then examine it from above, thus seeing it from all points of view. Those who study bamboo painting take a stalk of bamboo, and on a moonlight night project its shadow on to a piece of white silk on a wall."

Of the early Chinese flower paintings few remain to the present day, but of those known, the earliest are of the T'ang dynasty (A.D. 600–900) and show an art that must have been highly developed through many earlier centuries. Pien Luan, of the late 8th century, was noted for his paintings of birds and flowers. Hsiao Yüeh of the same century painted the bamboo exclusively. Hsü Hsi, of the early 10th century, was famous for his painting of flowers. "Peonies in the Wind" and "Ducks in a Lotus Pond" are typical titles. In his time he was considered an artist of the front rank, and has been called "the father of bird and flower painting." He was famous for his paintings of the lotus flowers which were the inspiration for many painters in later times both in China and Japan. Huang Ch'uan and his son Huang Chü-ts'ai were noted painters of flowers of this same century. Two pictures, "Fowls" and "Peonies," in the British Museum are attributed to the father, while there is record of a large number of paintings of birds and flowers by the son.

The three centuries of the Sung dynasty (960–1260) saw flower painting advanced to a great art. It was a period of intense nature study, a period where a passion for flowers was common, a period when flowers were associated with nature and with every mood of nature. Many flower painters flourished, and their paintings are filled with an elusive poetic quality, combined with accurate form and rhythmic beauty of growth. In this phase of Chinese art, the Sung artists are pre-eminent. Hsü Ch'ung-ssŭ was a painter of flowers and insects, and is accredited with being the first to paint directly without first sketching the subject. Chao Ch'ang, who followed something of his methods, attained great fame. It is said of him that he "not only produces an accurate resemblance, but hands over to you the very soul of the flower" also. Ch'êng T'ang was famous for his paintings of bamboo, as was Chou Shun. Li-Ti excelled as a flower painter, Chao-Mêng-Chien delighted in painting the plum and narcissus, while Cheng Ssŭ-hisao devoted himself to the painting of orchids.

In the Yüan period, 1260–1368, there are few outstanding flower painters. Ch'ien Hsüan, born in the earlier dynasty, was noted, and Li K'an achieved great fame as a painter of the bamboo. In the Ming dynasty, 1368–1644, though a decline had set in, much of the tradition of the golden age of the Sung period was carried on, and a number of flower painters are found. Mr. Fenollosa claims for Lin Liang first place of all Ming artists. Lü Chi painted his flowers and birds with a landscape background. Sun K'an specialized in the painting of the chrysanthemum. Other flower painters of this time were Ch'ên Shun, Kao Ku, Sun K'o-hung, whose paintings were noted for beauty of movement in flowers, and Chou Chih-mien, also noted for the rhythm and spirit he attained. In the Ch'ing or Manchu dynasty, 17th to the 20th century, though no new vigour has been added, and marked signs of decadence are seen, many of the traditions in flower painting of the earlier Sung and Ming periods were maintained with vitality, at least to the beginning of the 18th century.

In Japan, flower painting, inspired greatly by the Chinese masters of the T'ang, Sung and Ming periods, possess many of their characteristics, grafted often on to the traditions of their own Japanese native schools of painting.

The most impressive periods were the Ashikaga period (1335–1573) and the Tokugawa, from about 1600 into the 19th century. The first strongly upheld traditions of the Sung painters. The native Japanese tradition slumbered, and a sort of Chinese renaissance in Japan took place. The gorgeous coloured scrolls, which had been typical, were replaced by bold simple ink paintings of birds and flowers and landscape. It was the philosophic, contemplative art of earlier Chinese painters. So far as flower painting was concerned, it was the interpretation of the life and growth of the flowers and their association with nature. Sesshiu and Kano Masanobu, the first of the great Kano school, both of whom had great influence and many followers, painted flowers in the classic Chinese style. Utanosuke, son of Kano Masanobu, achieved a great reputation for his distinguished painting of flowers and birds. He died in 1575. About 1600 began the Tokugawa period of Japanese art. Chinese ideals were developed along with the Japanese tradition for rich colour and sumptuous decorative effects. Artists with great skill and understanding vied with each other in producing a phase of flower painting, combining all the beauty of the growing flower with superb design and gorgeous colour, that remains unique in the entire field of painting. The three outstanding masters of flower painting of this period are Koyetsu (1557–1637), the leader in this movement, Sotatsu, considered by Japanese critics as the greatest of flower painters after Utanosuke, and Korin (1661–1716) who "is perhaps the most Japanese of all the artists of Japan." Their influence carried forward to recent times, but there are few, if any artists since who have inherited their skill or genius. . . . (G.W.D.)

JAPANESE SCULPTURE. It is surprising that so many pieces of sculpture should still be preserved in Japan when we know that they have been housed in wooden buildings which have been reduced to ashes again and again by recurrent conflagrations. Such preservation has been mainly due to the important part sculpture has always played in religion, and in later times to the reverent attitude towards those works of art tolerated by the "tea men" when the *cha-no-yu* (commonly known as the tea ceremonies) came into the life of the people in the 15th century. A commission was created in 1897 for the systematic preservation and care of works of art, and up to the beginning of 1928 no fewer than 1,800 pieces of sculpture, together with about an equal number of objects of aesthetic and historical value, have been scheduled as "national treasures" in addition to the 1,100 old buildings which likewise have been placed under "special State protection."

Few examples in stone remain of the sculpture of the pre-Buddhist period. The stone warriors discovered in the province of Higo date from the second decade of the 6th century A.D. and are rude in workmanship. There survive, however, from this early period a large number of *haniwa,* or baked clay figures of men, women, animals and birds, which decorated the burial mounds of illustrious personages. The expression of peace and amiability on the faces of all these human figures is noteworthy.

Historic Period.—The real history of Japanese sculpture may be said to date from the official introduction of Buddhism from Korea in A.D. 552. Fortunately, there are preserved to this day a comparatively large number of Buddhist images of that time. Most of them are of impassive character, reminiscent of the North Wei dynasty, and showing in bronze and wood the technique of stone. Naturally, there are some that are of Korean type, as Japanese of Korean descent were among the noted sculptors of that time. Among the relics of this period mention may be made of many bronze figures in the Imperial Household collection, including a Kwannon (Avalôkitêsvara) bearing the date 591, and the famous group of 48 figures. Among others, there is a gilded bronze Sakyamuni, dated 623, with two attendants, in the Kondō of Hōryuji, where the group was originally placed by the sculptor Tori, who modelled them. A standing image of Kwannon, of a Korean type, also belongs to the Hōryuji monastery, and in the Dream hall there is another wooden image of Kwannon attributed to Shōtoku Taishi; there is also in the nunnery of Chūguji, close by, a seated image of Nyo-i-rin Kwannon, and a similar figure is in the temple of Kōryuji at Uzumasa. The peculiarly Japanese grace softening the stiff uncouth style of the last two pieces is remarkable.

A noticeable development occurred in the sculpture of the Hakuhō period (645–707), when magnificent figures in bronze were cast, as may be seen from the Yakushi (Bhâishajyaguru) trinity in Yakushiji of Yamato, all measuring about 10 ft. in height, and with Aryan rather than Chinese features. A masterful achievement in refined workmanship may be seen in the bronze Amitâbha trinity, which belonged to Tachibana Fujin.

Tempyo (708–781) was a great period of sculpture when thousands of Buddhistic images were created in clay, wood, dry lacquer and bronze. The gigantic seated Buddha of Tōdaiji, measuring some 53 ft. in height, was cast at that time, though the head had to be recast twice after being destroyed by fire. The four Deva-kings in the Kaidan-in of the Tōdaiji monastery and the Twelve Generals in Shinyakushiji are excellent examples of the period in clay. Miroku Bosatsu (Mâitrêya) of Hōryuji, and the Eight Genii and the Ten Great Disciples of Buddha in Kofukuji, are among the works in dry lacquer, a technique peculiar to this and the next period. Power and strength may be said to characterize the sculpture of this age, with a tendency to combine realistic with idealistic elements.

The new sects of esoteric Buddhism, Tendai and Shingon, infused a new life into sculpture in the early Heian period (782–888), many learned priests and talented sculptors devoting themselves to the production of deities in wood so faithful to the originals in the *sutras* that they long served as models for forms. Many of the masterpieces of this period are preserved in the temple of Tōji and Jingoji in Kyoto, as well as in Muroo-dera in Yamato. The best of them are executed in bold and deep-cut lines and are characterized by great dignity. The exquisite statue of the 11-faced Kwannon in the Hokkeji nunnery, commonly attributed to the Tempyo, may also be included among the works of this period.

The Fujiwara Periods (889–1183).—At the beginning of the early Fujiwara period (889–1068) sculptors simply followed in the footsteps of their predecessors, until the appearance of the great master, Jōchō. With the assistance of his pupils, Jōchō completed a wooden image of Dainichi (Mahavâirôcana) 32 ft. high for Hōshōji, and hundreds of smaller statues. As in architecture, the nationalist spirit was at work in sculpture, modifying the original type of Buddha. The face became fuller, with narrow benevolent eyes, the lines of the robes took an eloquent flow, the whole figure was realistically represented in beautiful proportions, and the colouring was in accordance with a refined taste, all tending to nobility and dignity. Among the best examples of works of the period now remaining are: the Amitâbha of Hōkaiji in Yamashiro, the 9 statues of Amitâbha of Joruriji and the Amitâbha trinity of Sarzen-in both in Kyoto and the Amitâbha in Hōwōdō at Uji.

In the later Fujiwara period (1069–1183) a tendency became apparent in the direction of excessive detail, elegance and overemphasis, and by the end of the Fujiwara period the work had become weak and effeminate. In the products of masters only were vigour and life maintained. The use of cut-gold for decoration (leaf-gold cut into strips and applied to form patterns, etc.) which began to be an important factor in early Fujiwara, became profuse towards the close of late Fujiwara.

From Kamakura to Momoyama (1186–1602).—The over-refinement and effeminate delicacy of feeling developed by the end of the preceding era was succeeded in the Kamakura period (1186–1335) by something bold and strong, the romantic giving place to the dramatic. Naturalistic representations were introduced, such as the insertion of rock crystals for the eyes and the use of strong colours and cut-gold for the decoration of robes, etc. There were two elements to be noted: a new school with Sung elements, and the tenacious Fujiwara school of Kyoto which was not eclipsed till the period that came after Kamakura. There was a style in which the figures were of short stature and impressive force, and another in which they were represented in long, flowing robes that partly overhung the pedestal; both these styles reveal the influence of Sung and Yuan. Though wood was the most common material, the masters worked in bronze as well. A great masterpiece is the big bronze Buddha at Kamakura, seated in perfect serenity, with eyes whose gaze penetrates into the very soul of each worshipper standing before him. Two master sculptors, Kaikei and Unkei, made themselves famous, not only during this period, but throughout the history of Japanese sculpture. Their joint work may be seen in two Deva-kings guarding the great south gateway of Tōdaiji.

In the Nambokuchō (1336–93) and Ashikaga (1394–1573) periods the art of sculpture stagnated, though some dignified portraits in wood were produced. Representation reached the extreme of elaboration, and the statues of deities became more human in character. The Kwannon in the Tokyo Imperial Household museum, minutely decorated all over with coloured lacquer and cut-gold, with rock crystals inlaid for the eyes and lips, may be considered one of the best examples of the period. It is to be noted that many sculptors of the time turned their attention to carving masks used in the *Nō* drama, which flourished among the feudal lords.

The aversion from monks shown by Oda Nobunaga and Toyotomi Hideyoshi resulted in the destruction of many temples, and in the Momoyama period (1574–1602) circumstances were not at all conducive to the development of Buddhistic sculpture. The great castles and palaces, however, were profusely decorated externally and internally.

Modern and Recent Sculpture.—During the peaceful Tokugawa régime (1603–1867) the talent of sculptors was mainly turned to the production of articles of luxury for the people. *Nō* masks required a high degree of skill, and a great demand was created for smaller carvings in wood and ivory, such as *netsuke*, or the ornamental piece fastened to the end of the cord attached to the tobacco pouch or the *inro* (small medicine cases hung from the sash). With the restoration of the temples, many images were carved, but these were merely reproductions of the old works of art. Work characteristic of the period is to be found, however, in the carvings adorning temple buildings and shrines. Some localities, such as Kyoto and Nara, produced peculiarly characteristic wooden dolls.

With the restoration of power to the imperial throne in 1868, which was followed by the abolition of the feudal system, a change came over Japanese sculpture. The introduction into Japan of Western clay-modelling, first taught at the Tokyo School of Arts, gave a great impetus to the development of sculpture in Japan. Not only has the new technique found a large number of followers, but the traditional wood-carving has received a great stimulus which has led to improvement. The traditional school, however, still continues to work mainly in wood, while the exponents of foreign ideals choose bronze, marble and clay, as well as wood. In spite of the aggression of the younger school, the older school courageously struggles to hold its own and to preserve that which is characteristically Japanese. (*See* CHINESE SCULPTURE; IVORY CARVING, JAPANESE; WOOD CARVING, FAR EASTERN; MASKS; JAPANESE ARCHITECTURE.)   (J. HAR.)

LACQUER or **LACKER,** a general term for coloured and frequently opaque varnishes applied to certain metallic objects and to wood. The term is derived from the resin lac, which substance is the basis of lacquers properly so-called. Technically, among Western nations, lacquering is restricted to the coating of polished metals or metallic surfaces, such as brass, pewter and tin, with prepared varnishes which will give them a golden, bronze-like or other lustre as desired. Throughout the East Indies lacquering of wooden surfaces is practised, articles of household furniture, as well as boxes, trays and toys, being decorated with bright-coloured lacquer. This process of applying the lacquer to decorative articles of wood is also known as *Japanning*.   (X.)

CHINESE AND JAPANESE

The lacquer of the Far East, China, Japan and Korea must not be confused with other substances to which the term is generally applied; for instance, the lac of Burma, which is the gummy de-

JAPANESE SCULPTURE

PLATE I

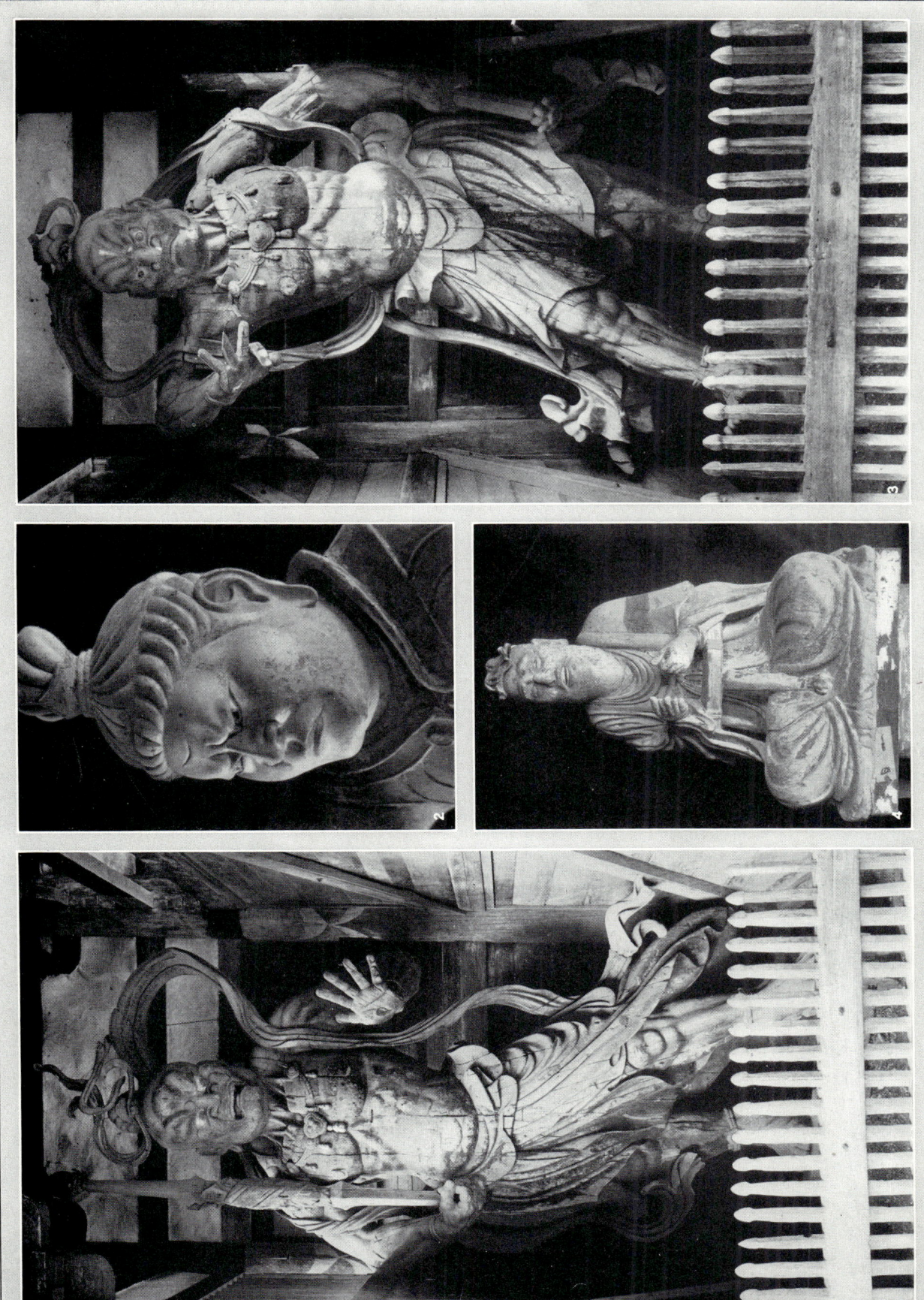

BY COURTESY OF JIRO HARADA

JAPANESE SCULPTURE OF THE TEMPYO AND KAMAKURA PERIODS

1 and 3. Pair of Deva Kings guarding the Great South Gateway of the Todaiji Monastery, Nara. Wood sculpture, joint work of Unkei and Kaikei. Kamakura period (1186–1335)   2. Head of one of the Four Maharajas of Heaven, in Kaidan-in, Todaiji, Nara. Tempyo period (708–781)   4. Yuima-koji, clay figure; Tempyo period. Kept in the five-storeyed pagoda of the Horyuji

PLATE II — JAPANESE SCULPTURE

BY COURTESY OF JIRO HARADA

BUDDHISTIC IMAGES IN CLAY, WOOD AND DRY-LACQUER

1. A Bodhisattva, clay figure; Tempyo period (708–781). Kept in the five-storied pagoda of the Horyuji
2. Kwannon (Avalokitesvara) wood sculpture; Asuka period (552–644); belonging to the Horyuji
3. Amitabha, wood sculpture, gilded; 11th century, in the Howodo, Uji
4. One of the Ten Great Disciples of Buddha, dry-lacquer; Tempyo period; belonging to the Kofukuji, Nara
5. A Bodhisattva, wood sculpture; Asuka period; belonging to the Horinji

posit of an insect, *Coccus Lacca*, and the various solutions of gums or resin in turpentine of which European imitations of Eastern lacquer have been and are concocted.

TECHNIQUE

Lacquer, properly so-called and as used in China and Japan, is a natural product, the sap of a tree, *Rhus Vernicifera;* subject to the removal of impurities and excess water, it can be used in its natural state, though it was frequently adulterated. The tree, which is indigenous to China, and has certainly been cultivated in Japan at least since the 6th century A.D., is tapped at about the age of ten years, lateral incisions being made in the bark and the running sap collected during the months of June to September. Branches of a diameter of one inch or more are also tapped, the bark having first been removed. Smaller branches are cut off, soaked in water for ten days, and the sap collected, producing a lacquer (*seshime*) of particular quality, used for special purposes. These processes kill the tree, but the wood, when of sufficient size, is of some use for carpentry. From the roots five or six shoots spring up, which become available for the production of lacquer after about six years, and the operation can be thus continued for a considerable length of time before the growth is exhausted. The Chinese and Japanese methods are practically identical in this respect, but the cultivation of the tree does not seem to have been so systematic in China as in Japan. The sap, when extracted, is white or greyish in colour and about the consistency of treacle. On exposure to the air it turns yellow-brown and then black. It is strained through hempen cloth to remove physical impurities, after being pounded and stirred in shallow wooden tubs, to give it uniform liquidity. It is then slightly heated over a slow fire or in hot sunshine and stirred again to evaporate excess moisture, and stored in air-tight vessels. The characteristic constituent of lacquer is termed by chemists *urushiol* (from the Japanese name of lacquer, *urushi*), and its formula has been stated as $C_{14}H_{18}O_2$. Japanese lacquer is said by Prof. K. Mijama to contain from 64.00 to 77.6% of *urushiol* as compared with an average of 55.84 for Chinese; the difference being due, probably, to inferior methods of cultivation and extraction, and perhaps in some cases to climatic differences. Lacquer is a slightly irritant poison, but workers in the industry soon become inoculated. A series of implements used in the preparation of lacquer with an illustration of the system employed in the actual gathering of the sap is exhibited in Museum No. 1 of the Royal Botanic gardens, Kew, England.

Lacquer-ware.—The basis of lacquer-ware, both in Japan and in China, is almost always wood, although it was also occasionally applied to porcelain and brass and white metal alloys. In some instances, objects were carved out of solid lacquer. The wood used, generally a sort of pine having a soft and even grain, was worked to an astonishing thinness. The processes that follow are the result of extraordinary qualities of lacquer itself, which, on exposure to air, takes on an extreme but not brittle hardness, and is capable of receiving a brilliant polish of such a nature as to rival even the surface of highly glazed porcelain. Moreover, it has the peculiar characteristic of attaining its maximum hardness in the presence of moisture. The Japanese, therefore, place the object, to secure this result, in a damp box or chamber after each application of lacquer to the basic material (wood, etc.). The Chinese are said (in an account of the industry dating from A.D. 1621–28) to use a "cave" in the ground for this purpose, and to place the objects therein at night in order to take advantage of the cool night air. It may, indeed, be said that lacquer dries in a moist atmosphere. The joiner's work having been completed, and all knots or projections having been most carefully smoothed away, cracks and joints are luted with a mixture of rice paste and *seshime* lacquer, till an absolutely even surface is obtained. It is then given a thin coat of *seshime* lacquer to fill up the pores of the wood and to provide a basis for succeeding operations: in the case of fine lacquer, possibly as many as 20 or 30 or even more; of each of which the following may be taken as typical. On the basis, as above described, is laid a coat of lacquer composition, allowed to harden, and ground smooth with whetstone. Next comes a further coat of finer composition, in which is mixed some burnt clay, which is again ground, and laid aside to harden for at least 12 hours. On this is fixed a coat of hempen cloth (or rarely in Japan, but more often in China, paper) by means of an adhesive paste of wheat or rice flour and lacquer, which needs 24 hours at least to dry. The cloth is smoothed with a knife, and then receives several successive coats of lacquer composition, each demanding the delay necessary for hardening. On this is laid very hard lacquer, requiring a much longer drying interval, afterwards being ground to a fine surface. Succeeding coats of lacquer of varying quality are now laid on, dried and polished; and this *preliminary* work, occupying in the case of artistic lacquer-work at least 18 days, produces the surface on which the artist in lacquer *begins* his task of decoration. A large number of processes were at his command, especially in Japan, but the design was first generally made on paper with their lacquer and transferred to the object while still wet, or drawn on it direct with a thin paste of white lead or colour. In carrying it out he made use of gold or silver dust applied through a quill or bamboo tube, or through a sieve to secure equal distribution. Larger fragments of the precious metals (*hiraine* or *kirikane*) were applied separately by hand, with the aid of a small, pointed tool. In one typical instance the writer has counted approximately 500 squares of thin gold foil thus inserted, within one square inch. These decorative processes each entailed prolonged hardening periods and meticulous polishing. Relief was obtained by modelling with a putty consisting of a mixture of lacquer with fine charcoal, white lead, lamp-black, etc., camphor being added to make it work easily. Lacquer was sometimes engraved, both in China and Japan.

The carved lacquer of China (*tias ch'i*) which, although imitated in Japan was never equalled in that country (as the Chinese have never reached the perfection of the Japanese gold lacquerware), needs particular notice. In this, the lacquer was built up in the method above described, but to a considerable thickness; and, when several colours were used, in successive layers of each colour, arranged in the order in which they were to predominate and of uniform thickness. When the whole mass was complete and homogeneous, it was cut back from the surface, so as to expose each colour as required by the design. The carving was done with a V-shaped tool kept very sharp, and when the lacquer was cold and hard. The cutting was done with amazing precision—no correction of faults was possible, for each layer had to be exactly and accurately reached, and the final result precisely foreseen and allowed for from the beginning of the work. The red lacquer (*tan sha*), so well known and justly appreciated, was coloured with cinnabar (red sulphuret of mercury). Other colours which are employed include a deep and a lighter olive-green, buff, brown, black and aubergine.

In Japanese lacquer, the following are the chief processes used:—*Nashiji* (pear-skin), small flakes of gold or silver sunk to various depths in the lacquer. *Fundame;* fine gold or silver powder worked to a flat, dull surface. *Hirame,* small, irregularly shaped pieces of sheet gold or silver placed on the surface. *Togidashi,* the design built up to the surface in gold, silver and colours with many coats of lacquer and then polished down to show them. *Takamakiye,* decoration in bold relief. *Hiramakiye,* decoration in low relief. *Rōiro,* polished black. *Chinkinbori,* engraved lacquer. *Kirikane,* square dice of sheet gold or silver, inserted separately on the surface. *Raden,* inlaid shell and metal. From the earliest times of which we have record, shell was used in the adornment of lacquer in China as well as in Japan, being inlaid on the surface in patterns, as well as in small squares like *kirikane* and dust. For this purpose various shells were used, mother-of-pearl for larger work and that of nautilus, pear-shell, sea-ear (*Haliotis,* Jap. *Awabi*) and *Turbo Cornutus* (Jap. *Sazaye*). For a very charming form, called by the French *Lac Burgantée,* the shell of the sea-ear, of iridescent blue and green, was employed in combination with gold and silver and delicately engraved, as early as the Ming period (A.D. 1368–1644) and also in Japan. Chinese lacquer was also inlaid with hard stones such as jade, aralachite, etc., as well as coral, soapstone, ivory, porcelain and other decorative substances.

HISTORY OF LACQUER IN JAPAN

The earliest definite record of the existence of a lacquer industry in Japan consists in an allusion in the *Nichonge* (Chronicles of Japan) to a high court official who was probably in control of it in the year A.D. 587. This implies some development already achieved; and during the following two or three centuries it is certain that the cultivation of the lacquer tree and the use of the material were fostered and controlled by a Government department. Lacquer, for instance, was accepted in some districts in payment of taxes. But the history of the art, so far as concerns definite evidence still extant, begins with the 8th century, and the specimens to which reference may be made are those still preserved at Nara and in the Hōryuji temple referred to above. Although a number of these are of Chinese origin, the collections certainly include treasures that must be given an authentic Japanese origin. Among those may be mentioned the sword scabbard of the emperor Shomu (A.D. 724–749) himself, in gold on black lacquer and others decorated with leaves of gold and silver inlaid in lacquer. The emperor Kwamma (A.D. 781–806) removed the capital from Nara to a new city, Heiankyō—the modern Kyōto; and an increased luxury in the style of living brought about further developments in the art, especially in the use of gold lacquer, due largely to the spread of Buddhistic influence. This period, however, saw the beginnings of a Japanese national style as distinct from the Chinese methods and manner, imported by Buddhist missionaries. Lacquer was used at this time in the decoration of important buildings; and inlay of shell also became popular. The organization of the industry was extended, and as early as A.D. 905 sumptuary edicts began to be issued regulating the dimensions of and quantities of material to be used in the domestic utensils—chiefly of black or red polished lacquer—which now began to come into general use. From this time, it is no exaggeration to say that, to a considerable extent, lacquer filled the place occupied in China by ceramic wares. A remarkable development of this period which must not be overlooked was the production of statuary of considerable merit, made with lacquer composition (*kanshitsu*), a process derived from China, but carried to a high standard in Japan for a brief period, till it was superseded by wood sculpture. Some few authentic examples remain of the fine lacquer of the Heian period, notably the Case for Buddhist Scriptures in the Ninnaji temple at Kyōto, made by order of the emperor Uda at the beginning of the 10th century. This is in black lacquer, sprinkled with gold dust and with a pattern of flowers, clouds, birds and Buddhist angels. Several other historic pieces were exhibited, either in original or very accurate reproduction in the Japan-British exhibition of 1910. During the Kamakura period (A.D. 1192–1333), in spite of the disturbance caused by the famous struggle between the Minanioto and Taira clans, and the establishment of the feudal shogunate at Kamakura, which gives its name to the period, the art of making fine lacquer continued to progress, under the patronage of the Fujiwara family, who maintained the imperial court at Kyōto with ever-increasing luxury. Marked features of this time are improved methods of inlay of precious metals and shell, and especially an attractive form of design in which beautifully written poems are interwoven with the pattern (*ashide-ye*). The process called *Kamakura-bori*, carved wood thickly lacquered with red or black, also dates from this period and continued to flourish for another two centuries or so. Modern imitations of this work have to be reckoned with by the collector. During this epoch, we see the beginnings of the characteristic Japanese treatment of landscape and flower subjects in design, generally in flat gold lacquer, with nastiji and pewter inlay. The Ashikaga period (A.D. 1336–1573) saw a further technical and artistic development, largely under the patronage of the Shōgun Yoshimasa; who, after holding office for two years only, retired in 1451 and devoted himself to a life of luxury. He gave great impetus to the Tea and Incense ceremonies, to the latter of which was especially due a whole series of new applications of the art, in respect of the exquisitely wrought small utensils required by that ritual. The ostentatious simplicity of the Zen sect of Buddhists was displayed in the use of black lacquer of the first quality with little or no ornament. Excellent work in shell inlay was also a characteristic of the time. The gold lacquer of the Ashikaga craftsmen gained so great a reputation in China that artisans from that country came to Japan to learn the methods by which it was produced, though they seem to have had little success in introducing it into their own country. Among the leading Japanese craftsmen of the period may be mentioned Kōami Dōchō, Taiami, Seiami, and Igarashi Shinsai, but attribution of specific works to them is largely a matter of conjecture. The civil wars which continuously infested Japan during the later middle ages checked the growth of the industry for a while; but the short Momoyama period (A.D. 1574–1603) which followed saw at least the work of one of the greatest of Japanese artists in lacquer, Honami Kōyetsu (A.D. 1557–1637). He was the founder of a striking and original style of ornament, essentially national in character. His designs were bold and simple in detail, generally executed in high relief with masses of shell or metal inlay. The great Shōgun, Toyotimi Hideyoshi (d. 1598) who secured the peace of the country with a strong hand, was an enthusiastic patron of the arts; and under his patronage a real revival took place. At his death, his widow erected the Kōdaiji temple at Kyōto, in which a new method of lacquer decoration was used (*Kodaiji-makiye*). It still contains examples of this ware presented by her. In 1603 began the rule of the Tokugawa Shōgunate, which continued without a break until the restoration of the imperial family to actual power in 1868. The first of the line, Iyeyasu, established at Yedo (the modern Tōkyō) the great school of lacquer artists which is responsible for almost the whole of the artistic ware known outside Japan. Technical processes were still further developed with additions such as the engraved lacquer (*chinkinbore*) derived from China, carved red and black lacquer from the same source, and the so-called *Somada* ware of shell inlay on black, but different in character from the Chinese *lac burgantée* already mentioned above. This period also saw the introduction of a class of work made by workmen, as a rule, specially devoted to it, namely the now well-known *inro* or portable medicine-cases, worn on the girdle and an indispensable addition to the national costume so long as the latter was uncontaminated by Western influence. These were small in size, generally oval or cylindrical in section and from $2\frac{1}{2}$ to 4 in. in length. They consist, as a rule, of from two to five compartments, beautifully fitted into each other and held together by silken cords running along each side, secured by a bead or toggle (*ojime*) and kept from slipping through the sash by a *netsuké*, sometimes of lacquer, but more often of cunningly carved wood, ivory bone, or other material. On this class of work was lavished some of the finest artistry of the Japanese craftsmen, and the convenient size and intrinsic charm of these dainty utensils (originally, perhaps, made for seals) has caused them to be much favoured by collectors. The earlier years of the Tokugawa period saw a considerable Chinese influence in the design of lacquer, especially in *inrō*; but the work of the greatest of Japanese lacquer artists, Ōgata Kōrin (A.D. 1661–1716), followed and extended the style originated by his master, Kōyetsu. Ritsuō (1663–1747) and Hanzan (18th century) maintained this tradition and a considerable revival of the style took place in the early years of the 19th century, when Hoitsu published his memorial volumes of the designs of the great master. To the latter period belong not a few objects which have been accepted as the original work of Kōrin himself. The more formal school of lacquerers included Kōami Choan and Koma Kitō-ye, who was appointed court lacquer artist to the Shōgun Igemitsu in 1636 and died in 1674. His successors held this post for 11 generations. A set of three stands made by Kōami Nagashige in 1637 as a wedding present from Iyemitsu to his daughter on her marriage with the Daimyō of Owari is considered by Japanese experts to be the finest extant piece of Japanese lacquer. It is now in the collection of the Marquis Tokugawa. Lacquer artists followed the practice of other craftsmen in Japan, in transmitting their names to sons or selected pupils. Thus, there were ten generations of the family of Yamamoto Shunshō, who died in 1682, aged 63. The Kajikawa family continued the tradition of its founder well into the 19th century, and the same must be said of Shiomi Masanari (Kyōto, *c.* 1716–36) whose work was notable

LACQUER

CHINESE LACQUER WORK OF THE 16TH, 17TH AND 18TH CENTURIES

1. Formal-garden seat of carved lacquered wood, Khang H'si period (1622–1723). 2. Screen of black lacquered coromandel wood with designs incised and painted in gold and colours. 18th century. 3. Vase of cinnabar lacquer, coloured by the brilliant red mercury or cinnabar ore or oxide, carved. Attributed to reign of Ch'ien Lung (1736–1795). 4. Ewer with panel decorations inlaid with shell, coloured ivory and carved red lacquer, 16th century. 5. Throne, in flat lacquer of various colours on black. Early 17th century

IVORY CARVING

PLATE VII

BY COURTESY OF JIRO HARADA, AND THE IMPERIAL HOUSEHOLD MUSEUM OF JAPAN

IVORY CARVINGS OF JAPAN

1 and 2. Ivory foot-rules, stained pink, carved and coloured, dating from 8th century A.D. In the Imperial Treasure-house, Shosoin, at Nara

3. Ivory plectrum, stained pink, carved and coloured. The plectrum is used for the playing of the *Samisen* and other plucked string instruments. It dates from the 8th century A.D. In the Imperial Treasure-house, Shosoin, at Nara

4. Reverse of fig. 3

5. Ivory *netsuke* helmet, by Shinshisai

6. Paulownia box, inlaid with ivory and shells, by Asahi Gyokuzan (1842–c. 1900)

PLATE VIII IVORY CARVING

BY COURTESY OF (1, 3, 8, 9) JIRO HARADA, (2, 4, 5, 6, 7, 10, 11, 12) JIRO HARADA, AND THE IMPERIAL HOUSEHOLD MUSEUM, TOKYO, JAPAN

JAPANESE IVORY ORNAMENTS AND WORKS OF ART

1 and 3. Carved ivory tusk, by Nomura Tomekichi. 2a. Ivory *netsuke* (ornamental piece fastened by cords to purse or *inro*), masks by Mitsushige (18th–19th c.). 2b. Ivory *netsuke*, kirin, unsigned. 4a and b. Ivory *netsuke*, by Yoshinaga (19th c.). 5a. Ivory *inro* (medicine case), inlaid with mother-of-pearl and coral, with *netsuke* similarly inlaid, by Shibayama (18th–19th c.). 5b. Ivory *inro*, carved with peony and butterfly; ivory *netsuke*, with the signs of the zodiac, by Dōshōsai (19th c.). 6a. Ivory *netsuke*, by Rantei (18th c.). 6b. Ivory *netsuke*, by Yoshimasa (17th c.). 7. Ivory carving, by Soma Senrei, modern. 8. Fishermen with net, by Ikeda Shoten. 9. Falconer, by Ishikawa Mitsuaki, modern. 10. Skull, by Asahi Gyokuzan, (1842–c. 1900). 11. "Watching fireworks," by Ōno Hōfū, modern. 12. Boy with a fowl, by Asahi Meido, modern

for the quality of the rubbed-down gold and colour lacquer called *togidashi*. The *Genroku* epoch (1684-1704) saw, perhaps, the ultimate perfection of style and technique; but the work of the later 18th and, to some extent, of the early 19th centuries has many exquisite qualities. The later periods were characterized by more elaborate detail; but adulteration of the gold with bronze and other metallic powders was too often prevalent. A fiery brown tint of the *nashiji* is a certain mark of quite late date. Nevertheless, there is plenty of good work of the early 19th century, and to this period belongs the last of the great artists of the industry, Shibata Zeshin, who was born in 1807, was a pupil of Koina Kwansei and died in 1891. His work will bear comparison even with some of the greatest of his predecessors, both in technique and in design. There may still be a few men capable of producing artistic lacquer on the old lines; but modern industrial conditions have practically killed this ancient and beautiful art. It would not have survived so long had not the country been closed to alien influences for two and a half centuries. The applications of lacquer to various purposes were much more extended in Japan than in China. In addition to the medicine cases already described, and the use of lacquer for all sorts of domestic utensils (it is capable of resisting great heat and is impervious to acids) and for furniture such as sets of shelves, cabinets, screens, etc., the greatest skill of the craftsmen was applied, for instance, to sets of writing materials including the writing-box with its inkstone, water-pot and rack for brushes, a document box, and a low table or stand. Boxes of every kind, saké cups, trays and sword-scabbards were made of lacquer of the best quality and decorated by the leading artists of the industry, while, on a large scale, lacquer was extensively employed in the decoration of temples and other architectural works. Many cabinets imported into Western countries from the 17th century onwards and often attributed to China, were products of Japan exported through the British, and after the closure of the country, the Dutch and Chinese settlements at Nagasaki, but the first organized display of Japanese lacquer in Europe was at the Paris Exhibition of 1867.

BIBLIOGRAPHY.—Chinese Lacquer: P. le Bonnani, *Traité de la composition des Vernis* (1723, reprinted 1780); P. d'Incarville, "Mémoire sur le Vernis de Chine" in the *Mémoires* of the Académie Royale des Sciences (Paris, 1760); S. W. Bushell, *Chinese Art*, vol. i. (1904-06; new ed., 1921); O. Muensterberg, *Chinesische Kunstgeschichte*, 2 vol. (Esslingen a. N., 1910-12); W. P. Yetts, *Symbolism in Chinese Art*, publ. by the China Soc. (1912); A. A. Breuer, "Chinese Inlaid Lacquer" and "Chinese Incised Lacquer" in the *Burlington Magazine*, vol. xxv. (1914); E. F. Strange, *Catalogue of Chinese Lacquer in the Victoria and Albert Museum* (1925), and *Chinese Lacquer* (1926).

Japanese Lacquer: *Report by Her Majesty's Acting Consul at Hakodate on the Lacquer Industry of Japan* in *Accounts and Papers*, vol. lxxii. (1882); O. Korschelt and H. Yoshida, "The Chemistry of Lacquer" in Asiatic Society of Japan, *Transactions*, vol. xi. pt. 2 (1883); E. Hart, *Lectures on Japanese Art Work*, publ. by the Society of Arts (1886); and "Notes on the History of Lacquer," Japan Soc. *Transactions*, vol iii. (1893-95); J. J. Rein, *The Industries of Japan*, vol. ii. (1889); M. Tomkinson, "Inro," Japan Soc. *Transactions*, vol. iii. (1893-95) and *A Japanese Collection*, 2 vol. (1898); *Catalogue of Specimens of Japanese Lacquer and Metal-work*, Burlington Fine Arts Club (1894); *L'Histoire de l'art du Japan*, Paris Exhibition (1900); W. H. Smith, "A Description and History of Lacquer down to the end of the Genroku period, 1681-1708," Japan Soc. *Transactions*, vol. vii. (1905-07); F. Brinkley, *Japanese Temples and their Treasures* (1910); *Official Catalogue of the Japan-British Exhibition* (1910); E. F. Strange, "The Incense Ceremony and its Utensils," Japan Soc. *Transactions*, vol. xxi (1923-24) and *Catalogue of Japanese Lacquer and Inrō in the Victoria and Albert Museum* (1924).

Chinese and Japanese lacquer: F. Brinkley, *Japan and China*, 12 vol. (1901-02; 2nd ed., 1903-04); Toyei Shuko, *Illustrated Catalogue of the Ancient Imperial Treasury, called Shōsoin* (1909); Omura Seigai, *Record of the Imperial Treasury, Shōsoin* (1910); A. A. Breuer, "Influence of China on Lacquer in Japan," Japan Soc. *Transactions*, vol. xii. (1913-14). See also *Kokka*, a monthly journal on Fine Arts, Archaeology, etc. (Tokyo, 1890, etc.). (E. F. S.)

IVORY CARVING

History.—In the Shōsōin (imperial treasure-house at Nara) collection, which consists mainly, if not entirely, of objects dating from the 8th century A.D., still housed in the original wooden structure, there are a number of ivories carved in the style known as *bachiru*. The name implies the method of decorating an ivory object in which an article with a finished surface is generally dyed or stained, and then designs are carved on it, the unstained parts, wherever the carving is deep, being either left plain or treated with other colours, producing a very beautiful and decorative effect. In some articles the carving is done on unstained ivory and colours are applied to the designs carved. In that unique collection there are several ivory foot-measures in blue and bright red, an ivory plectrum of bright red colour for the *biwa* (a stringed musical instrument) a large number of bright red and blue ivory *go* (a game resembling chess) pieces, a few ivory knife-hilts and several ivory scabbards, etc., which are all decorated in the *bachiru* style with minute carvings of birds, animals, flowers, etc., the colours still retaining their original freshness. Not only those so decorated, but a number of plain ivory pieces of sceptres, combs, flutes and foot-measures, are also found in that collection. Though ivory must have been imported into Japan, it was used extensively with horn, bone and wood in minute inlaid works, such as decorated *go* boards, arm rests, musical instruments, and various small boxes preserved in that treasure-house belonging to the imperial household of Japan.

For nearly ten centuries after the Tempyo period (708-781), to which most of the articles mentioned above belong, nothing is known about ivory carving in Japan, there being left practically no examples worthy of note from an artistic standpoint. It was Yoshimura Shuzan of Osaka who first began in the Kyoho era (1716-36) carving ivory *netsuke* (ornamental pieces fastened to the cords attached to a tobacco pouch, purse or *inro; i.e.*, medicine case) which became very popular among the people. Of course, the wooden *netsuke* was already known to have been used with a bunch of keys in the Ashikaga period (1394-1573) and with *inro*, when they came to be a great fashion in the Tensho era (1573-92). However, Shuzan seems to have popularized them in ivory, and he was followed by many artists who carved mostly *netsuke* and rarely *okimono*, or ornaments for the alcove, in ivory as well as in wood. Among the ivory carvers who worked under the Tokugawa régime, which came to an end in 1867 after continuing for about two and a half centuries, are Shibayama Senzo, who is known to have devised a method of inlay in the An-ei era (1772-81), using corals, ivory, horns, etc.; Garan of Osaka, who was fond of carving birds, animals and insects for *netsuke* at about the same time; Izumiya Tomotada of Kyoto, who is known to have excelled in the Temmei era (1781-89) in *netsuke* of cows and oxen in realistic carving; Tametada of Owari, an expert relief carver; Tomotane of Kyoto, whose favourite subjects for *netsuke* were warriors, angels, insects and animals; Hōshin of Kyoto, skilled in carving palaces and landscapes in half-opened shells and miniature figures in buildings; Masanao of Kyoto, who generally drew his subjects from hermits, animals, birds and insects, especially frogs in the act of jumping; Masatoshi, also of the Temmei era, who was an expert *netsuke* carver, being fond of figures, demons and masks for his subjects; Nakayama Yamatome of Yedo, skilled in minute carving, such as 53 stages of the Tokaido road, or portraits of 36 famous poets, on a single small piece; Noriaki, who was well-known in the Kwansei era (1789-1801) for figures and animal subjects; Miyasaka Hakuryu of Kyoto, who excelled in carving tigers, monkeys and dragons; Genryosai Minkoku, whose favourite subjects were grotesque hermits, animals and fishes; Ranko of Izumo, who left good works in a variety of subjects, such as figures, animals, birds, flowers and attempted landscapes on *netsuke;* and such others as Masaharu, Rantei, Yoshimasa, Yoshinaga, Shokyusai, Mitsushige, Tadachika, Ikkosai Tōun, Rakuwosai, Masakazu, Shinshisai, Tomochika, Gyokuyosai, and his pupil Ozaki Kokusai, some of whom have left masterpieces in ivory *netsuke* and other carvings.

Scope.—Immediately after the Restoration of 1868, ivory objects found their way abroad, having attracted the attention of foreign collectors. So great was the foreign demand for the ivory carvings that they became quite an item in the Japanese export for some time. It was a great encouragement to the carvers, as their native patrons were becoming scarce, and the call for *netsuke* in Japan came to an end when the cigarette drove away tobacco pouches. However, the demand was for a greater and cheaper production, rather than for a high quality of work, and the standard of the craft deteriorated in consequence. Nevertheless, there were a number of masters who did produce works of high merit. Among them Asahi Gyokuzan and Ishikawa Mitsuaki stand pre-eminent. The former made his reputation in wonderfully minute and realistic carving of skulls in ivory and in intricate and beautiful inlaid works, while the latter produced excellent figure ornaments as well as exquisite low relief in ivory. Among other well-known ivory carvers of more recent times mention may be made of Shimamura Toshiáki, Asahi Meidō, Sōma Senrei, Kaneda Kenjiro, Nishino Kōgyoku, Otani Mitsutoshi and Ōno Hōfū, whose works have been much admired.

Designs in ivory *netsuke* are manifold, embracing almost every imaginary subject. However, the striking feature was the rounded corners, avoiding sharp edges, so as not to scratch the *inro*, which is generally in lacquer of costly decoration. Influences of contemporary artists like Hokusai and of such comic styles of painting as Otsu-ye are shown in the choice and treatment of the subject. Taoists and, later, *genre* figures commonly supplied the motives, and various animals, especially those in the 12 signs of the zodiac, were treated in all moods and attitudes.

Uses.—Apart from the *netsuke* and ornaments for the alcove, ivory has been used extensively as an ornamental piece for the *kakemono*, the mounted hanging paintings that can be rolled up when not in use. For plectra for *shamisen* (popular three-stringed musical instruments) ivory has been invaluable. Moreover it has long occupied a dignified position as an important accessory to the *cha-no-yu* (ceremonial tea) utensils. The lid of the tea caddy (*cha-ire*) is almost exclusively made of ivory, the bottom being lined with gold foil. It is generally in a simple but graceful form, having a knob in the centre with concentric circular lines or relief as ornaments. However, the portion of the tusk with black stains or flaws is often chosen for making a lid, care being taken to let such a flaw appear as an ornament or "scenery," as it is called, which often constitutes a striking feature in the ware. Tea scoops also are sometimes made of ivory, though most commonly they are made of bamboo by bending the flattened end of it to scoop out pulverized tea leaves from the caddy in preparing the tea.

It is for *kakemono*, *shamisen* plectra, tea caddy lids and tea scoops, though these are not of very great artistic value, that ivory is chiefly used in Japan at the present time, since *netsuke* are almost entirely out of fashion. One still sees in shop windows ivory carvings of wide variety, and there are some skilled carvers in ivory producing works of unquestionable merit, but it cannot be denied that most of them cater for the taste of Europeans and Americans, and that the true refined taste of the Japanese rarely admits an ivory carving to the *tokonoma*.

See A. Brockhaus, *Netsuke-Versuch einer Geschichte der Japanischen Schnitzkunst* (Leipzig, 1905). (J. HAR.)

BON-KEI ("tray-landscape"), generally acknowledged to be an evolution of *hako-niwa* (q.v.), is a popular branch of the Japanese art of making miniature landscapes with earth or its substitutes, representing trees, grass, houses, figures, etc., on bronze, concrete or porcelain trays and used as decorations for windows or rooms. The art is occasionally called *bon-tei* (tray-garden), and the name *bon-kei* is then given to another branch popularly known as *bon-seki* (q.v.), but this is not generally accepted. *Bon-kei*, in its present phase, has not been in existence very long, having taken a new life at the dawn of the 20th century, when *keto-tsuchi*, a sort of peat, was introduced by Idzumi Chisen as a substitute for earth for modelling not only hills, but rocks and stones also. Nowadays actual stones are hardly ever used. As the art gained popularity, all sorts of devices were tried, including old newspapers soaked in water, as substitutes for the earth. Usually, on a round, oval or rectangular tray of from 1 to 3ft. in extreme dimension, hills, rocks and ground are modelled with *keto-tsuchi*, newspaper preparation, or earth by means of a spatula, and then are painted to give an appearance of snow, a water-fall or distant scenery, the nearer parts being covered with fine moss and planted with vegetation of appropriate size and form. Different coloured earth is strewn to indicate a path, and sand is used to represent water. The views may be embellished with miniature houses, towers, bridges, figures, birds, etc., of baked clay. *Bon-kei* very strongly resembles *hako-niwa*, though the latter is meant to be kept for years, while the former is primarily to meet a temporary need (though with care it may be preserved for months in its original freshness and proportion), and is very quickly made; it is entirely different from *bon-seki*, in which neither earth nor vegetation is used.

BON-SAI (potted dwarf tree). Strictly speaking, the name applies only to dwarf trees planted in shallow vessels, those in deeper pots being called *hachi-uye* (pot-planted). But both are known as *bon-sai*, irrespective of the vessels they grow in. The growth of the plants is controlled by pruning, fertilization, etc., so that the trees are trained into the stately shapes of ancient big trees, the vacant space in the pot suggesting plains or distant mountains. The trunk of the tree, the spread of the roots, the distribution of branches, all of which may be used to give an aged appearance to the tree, are especially important. Without showing any trace of artificiality, each tree should develop its own characteristics. The deciduous should have the dignity of age either with or without the leaves, as in nature, though in some the leaves, while in others the flowers or fruits, may constitute the main attraction, according to the season. The *bon-sai* may consist (1) of a single tree (*ippon-dachi*) either in an upright or leaning attitude; (2) of two trunks (*ai-oi*) growing out of a single stump, or planted closely together to appear as such; (3) of groups (*yose-uye*) of similar or different kinds of trees to suggest a forest or wooded mountain side; it may also have (4) high exposed roots (*ne-agari*); (5) trees or vines drooping down (*ken-gai*) as if overhanging from a cliff; or (6) roots growing out of and embracing a rock (*ishi-zuki*). The pot in which the trees are planted plays an important part in the scheme, shapes and sizes being determined by the kinds of plants contained. The pots are generally plain, but some have considerable decoration in relief or in painting. They are of earthenware, with a hole in the bottom for drainage lest the roots rot, in shape round, oval, rectangular, octagonal or lobed, etc., of varying depths, and chosen to be in harmony with and in right proportion to the tree. For centuries the Japanese have cultivated the art of dwarfing trees, using them as ornaments for rooms, and *bon-sai* still remains a hobby among the aristocrats as well as among the working people of Japan.

BON-SEKI (tray-stone) is the Japanese art of creating a landscape on a tray with stone and sand. Its origin in Japan is traced to the reign of the empress Suiko (593–628) when stones of rare shapes were presented to the court from China. Placed on a board or tray, the stone was admired on account of its beautiful lines or shape that might, perhaps, suggest a stately mountain or a tremendous precipice. Furthermore, the people appreciated it for its own qualities—its solid reality, its unchanging and lasting virtues which they believed to have a power of "softening the hardened hearts of men." Later, sand was used in conjunction with the stones to suggest mountains and water, and the art of arranging them came to be known by the name *bon-zan* (tray-mountain). A further development led to its use to represent sentiments of poems or to reproduce famous scenes in all their complicated phases, showing distant ranges of mountains as well as nearer hills, with villages, temples and pagodas overlooking a shimmering lake or sea, with sailing boats and flying geese, etc., all portrayed by means of stones, pebbles and sand. When the art attained this stage of development it was for a time called *bon-kei* (q.v.) by some. That name was soon dropped, however, for the original name *bon-seki*, *bon-kei* being given to another branch of the art, a development of *hako-niwa* (q.v.), in which earth, or its substitutes, and living vegetation were used to make a landscape on a tray.

In *bon-seki*, it is needless to say, the selection of the stone is of greatest importance. One that resembles a mountain or a range of mountains, an island or a chain of isles, is highly valued. However well shaped it may be, if it has been chiselled to get the desired form it is despised as a "dead stone"; it must be natural, and those found in mountain streams are considered to be the best. Greenish stones are used for a spring landscape to suggest a fresh verdure; black ones for summer, indicative of dark shad-

BON-KEI

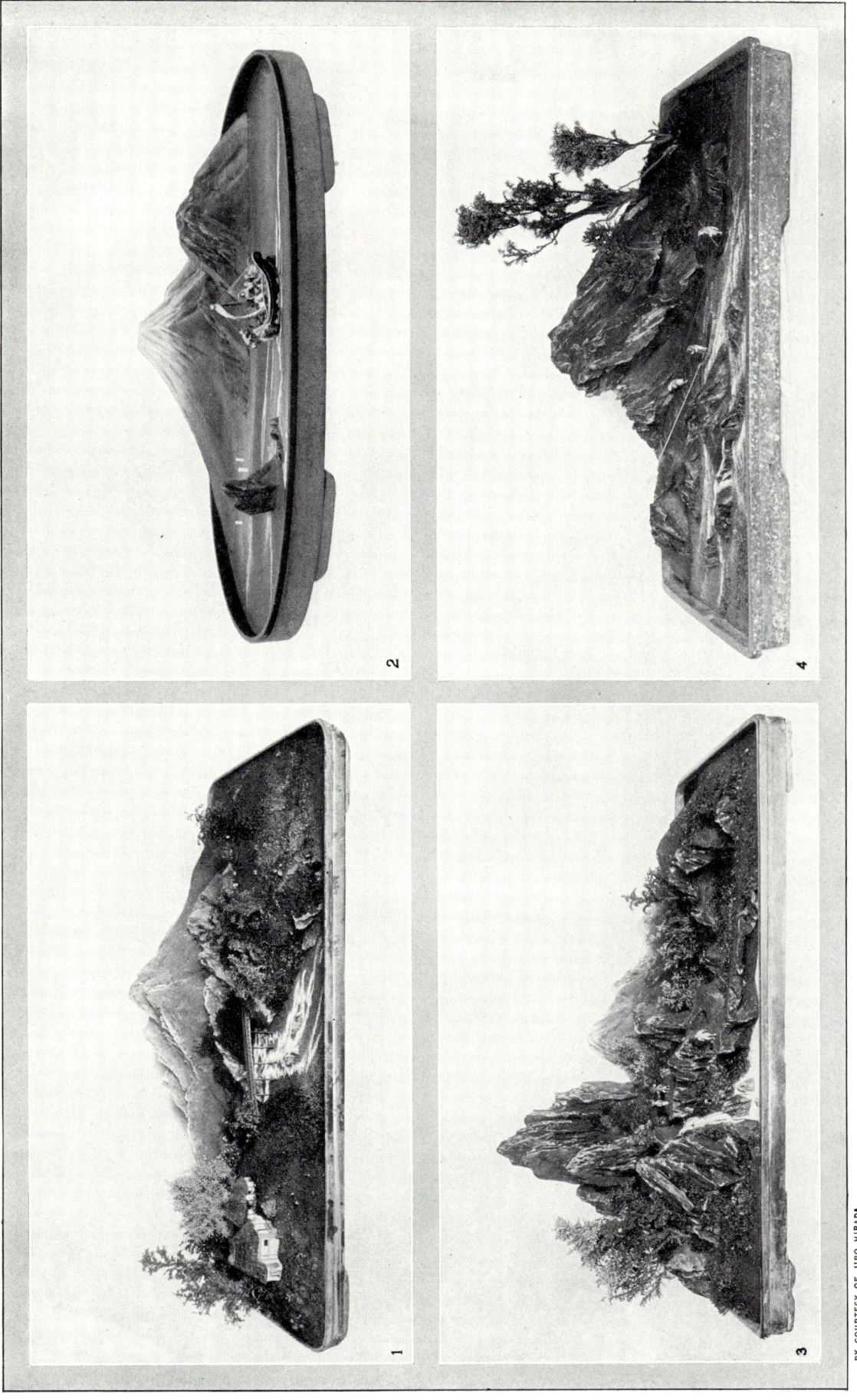

BY COURTESY OF JIRO HIRADA

MINIATURE LANDSCAPES MODELLED ON TRAYS OF BRONZE, CONCRETE OR PORCELAIN

1. A rolling landscape modelled from earth or a substitute for earth. Sand is used for the water and the scene is embellished with tiny plants representing trees, and with miniature houses and a bridge
2. A seascape, the mountains are modelled with a spatula and sand is used for the sea
3. A rocky landscape, with a waterfall; tiny figures are climbing the steep cliff
4. A landscape on the edge of the sea; little figures can be seen in the boats

BY COURTESY OF JIRO HARADA

THE JAPANESE ART OF DWARFING TREES FOR ORNAMENTATION

1. A potted dwarf tree which has developed the characteristics of an ancient tree with great gnarled trunk and wide-spreading branches
2. A single tree (*ippon-dachi*) growing in an upright attitude, planted in an oblong flat pot meant to suggest a plain
3. A withered and deformed tree drooping down (*kengai*) as though overhanging a cliff
4. A deciduous tree, the earth receding from its roots, its few remaining branches and leaves discoloured and brittle

PLATE II
BON SAI

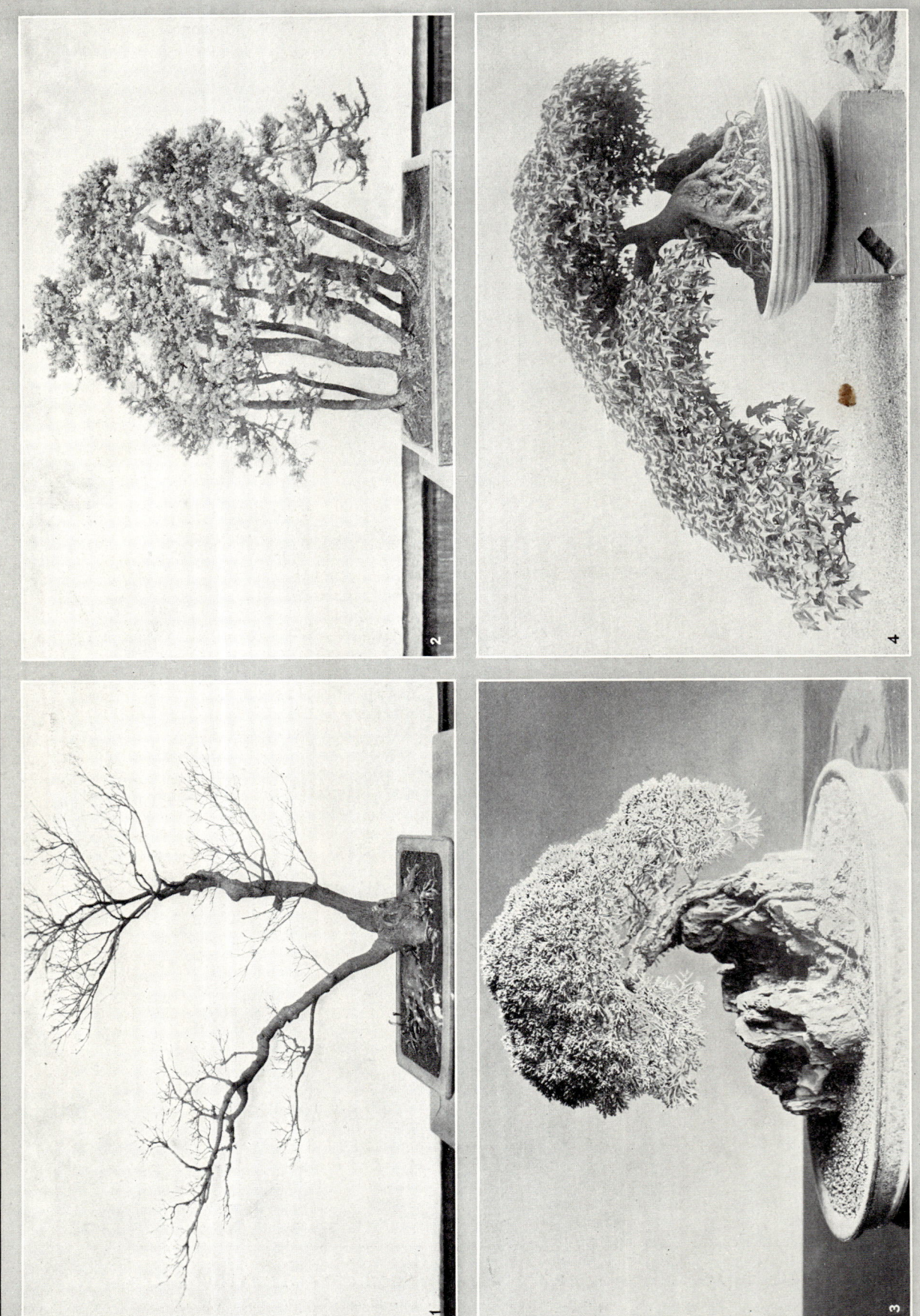

BY COURTESY OF JIRO HARADA

DWARF TREES TRAINED INTO VARIOUS SHAPES BY PRUNING AND FERTILIZATION

1. A tree with two trunks (*ai-oi*) growing out of a single stump, trained to give an appearance of age by the gnarled trunks, the spread of the roots and the distribution of the bare branches
2. A group (*yose-uye*) of similar trees planted close together in a shallow vessel, the whole intended to suggest a forest
3. A tree with its roots growing out of and embracing a rock (*ishi-zuki*) which seems to surmount a precipice over the sea
4. A tree with high exposed roots (*ne-agari*) and overhanging branches suggesting by its droop its place on a cliff-side

BON SEKI

PLATE I

BY COURTESY OF JIRO HARADA

JAPANESE TRAY LANDSCAPES AND THE PARAPHERNALIA FOR MAKING THEM

1 and 2. Examples of Bon Kei. Earth or a substitute is used for modelling these miniature landscapes, which are then embellished with moss and small plants to represent grass and trees, and with miniature houses, towers, bridges, figures, etc., of baked clay. Bon Kei is different from Bon Seki, examples of which are shown below, in that the former is fashioned from perishable materials and the latter is fashioned from imperishable ones

3. Bon Seki, entirely made of stones and pebbles used in conjunction with sand, in this case to represent the river Fuji, in Japan. Stones are used for the landscape, and sand for the water and the beach

4. Bon Seki, called Moonlight on the Sea. Black stones, indicative of dark shadows, are used for the summer landscape. The markings on the sea, made with a heron's plume, are meant to suggest calm, rippling summer waters

5. The flight of geese at Kobado, the land- and sea-scapes are of stone and sand, the geese are portrayed with pebbles

6. Stones with sand between them, the whole designed to represent a waterfall. Black stones are used here, and in fact are most commonly used, because they look well with the white sand

7. Stones of shapes that suggest mountains are used here together with sand flowing through them to represent the river Isuzu, in Japan

8. The brushes that sweep the sand together, the plumes that do the modelling and marking of the sand, and all the other paraphernalia that go to make up the equipment of an artist in Bon Seki

BON SEKI

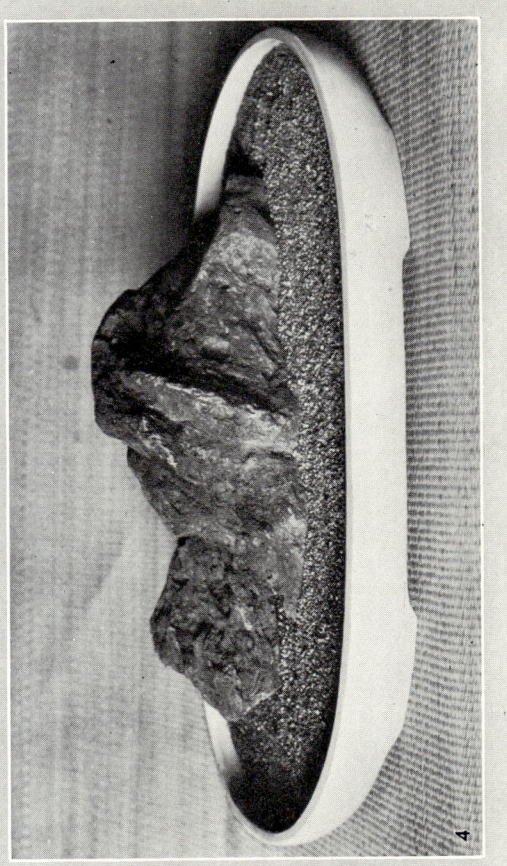
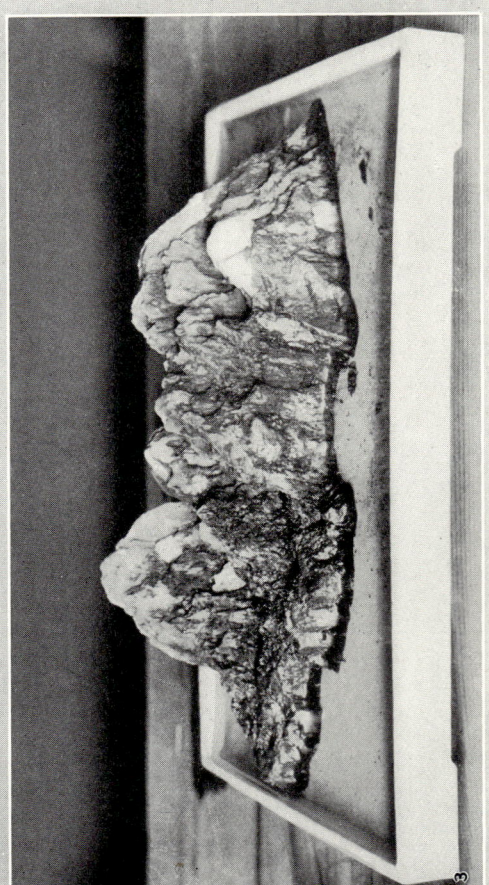

AN ARTIST IN BON SEKI AND SOME ARRANGEMENTS OF STONES AND SAND ON TRAYS (KI SEKI)

BY COURTESY OF JIRO HARADA

1. A Japanese artist with his materials about him for the making of bon seki; combinations of stones of beautiful outline and colour with sand on trays to make house ornaments

2. A stone placed on a tray with low growing grass, the latter intended to emphasize the immensity of nature as suggested by the stone

3 and 4. Stones of desirable shapes in trays with sand. Natural stones are greatly valued by the Japanese, who have an old custom still prevailing of enjoying stones in themselves, for their form and colour and for their unchanging virtues. These stones are called ki seki

WOOD CARVING

ows; reddish ones for autumn, suggestive of tinted hill-sides; whitish ones for winter, to denote snow. Black stones, however, from the provinces of Kii, Satsuma and Echigo are most commonly used for all scenes, irrespective of seasons, as they go well with the white sand. The desirable size of the principal stone is considered to be about 7 or 8in. long, and 4 or 5in. high, though a considerable latitude is allowed in practice. Stones of smaller sizes are also necessary to get variation and perspective. The bottom of the stone is usually sawn flat for stability and is covered with silk so that it may not scratch the surface of the lacquered tray. Besides the principal stones there are *soye-ishi* (auxiliary stones), *sute-ishi* (thrown-away stones), sacrificed to emphasize the more important ones, and *ashirai* (small stones for creating details of the scene). Agate, ruby, serpentine and rock crystals of various shades are also used, though very rarely, for forming islands or as *ashirai*.

Sand is indispensable to *bon-seki*. White sand from the provinces of Bizen and Bingo has been popular, but now-a-days crushed calcareous spar is most generally used. It is generally prepared in ten different grades. Grades from 1 to 5 are used to add details to the scenery, the 6th, 7th and 8th grades for making promontories and seashore, the 9th for streams and waves, and the 10th, the finest, for mists, snow or clouds. Not only calcareous spar, but also agate and corals are granulated and used as sand, though rarely, except the red coral for the rising sun to distinguish it from the moon.

Black lacquered trays are generally preferred, either oval (with extreme length and width of about 16 and 10in. respectively) or fan-shaped in a smaller size, with low borders, or rectangular, without any border.

Brushes are used very effectively by some masters of this art, but plumes are indispensable. Feathers of hawks, cranes, swans and herons are employed for various purposes. One kind is used to sweep the sand together or remove unnecessary sand from the tray, another, with the aid of a small ruler, to make mists. Still another is required to mark streams and waves of different varieties, for each season has its characteristic waves; for spring they are peacefully long and continuous near the beach and higher off the shore; for summer, ripples cover the calm sea; for autumn, they are rough, intermingled with more peaceful ones; for winter waves, the feather is brushed roughly to right and left, making a choppy sea with roaring surges. The directions of wind peculiar to each season must not be overlooked; the front of the principal stone is always considered as facing south. Other paraphernalia required in *bon-seki* include sieves to sift different grades of sand, a metal spoon and a tube for the sand, a pair of chop-sticks to manage small pebbles, forms for making crescent or full moon, and miniature models in silver or bronze bridges, temples, pagodas, etc.

Bon-seki has had a long history, for it was already in vogue at the time of Ashikaga Yoshimasa (1436–90) and the period that followed, when *cha-no-yu*, commonly known as ceremonial tea, being "a cult founded upon the adoration of the beautiful amidst sordid facts of everyday life," flourished. As in other branches of Japanese art, there arose different styles or "schools," some of the more prominent being Takeya-ryu, Kiyohara-ryu, Tōzan-ryu, Hōshō-ryu, Ikuta-ryu, Uda-ryu, Sekishyu-Tōyama-ryu, Kōno-ryu and Hosokawa-ryu. The last-mentioned school is most active at present, having for its chief master Katsuno Hakuyen, of Nagoya, who revived the school with his rare talent, and established branches all over Japan and her colonies.

There is a special kind of *bon-seki* called *kake-gaku* (hanging picture) or *tome-ye* (fastened painting). The sand is mixed with powdered paste and the completed picture steamed, so that it sticks to the tray. Usually a fine grade of sand is used for this purpose, though recently some masters have contrived to stick even stones by means of gum arabic. There is a similar art known as *bon-ga* (tray-pictures), an evolution of *suna-ye* (sand-painting), which men on the street were accustomed to practise at various times in Japanese history, record showing that the custom existed in the era of An-ei (1772–81). Sands, not only of natural colours, but artificially dyed, are used in depicting almost any subject: trees and houses, flowers and birds, natural scenes and historical events—a pictorial art in sand. *Bon-ga* is distinct from *bon-seki*, though the latter sometimes appropriates for itself what is practised in the former, and the former does not enjoy either the artistic prestige or the popularity of the latter. Still another branch of art in which sand is used is *suijo-sunaye* (sand-pictures-on-water) or *sui-ga* (water-picture) for short. Using wax-coated sand of different colours, the artist draws pictures on the water contained in a tray. In order to prevent the rippling of the water, which would prevent the sand from floating, pulverized white cowpeas and alum are previously stirred in. This art was in vogue in the era of Bunkwa (1804–18), but is now seldom practised.

Apart from *bon-seki*, there still prevails among the Japanese their ancient custom of enjoying rare stones by themselves. While some of them are too large, others may be used in *bon-seki* as well. They call these stones *ki-seki* (rare or strange stones), or merely *ishi* (stone), and some are among heirlooms of ancient families. Provided with individual wooden stands, they are placed on one's writing desk or in *tokonoma* (alcoves in the guest room), that the gazer may be led into reveries by the fancies their shapes suggest, such as mountains, immense cliffs or some natural phenomena. A stone with a white streak or vein may suggest a waterfall, the sound of which may be heard, or rather felt, in the momentary solitude of one's room, for "heard melodies are sweet, but those unheard are sweeter."

Some stones are placed on a tray with low-growing grass or bamboo in order to emphasize the immensity of nature suggested by the stone. Another way of enjoying them, which has been for centuries and still is popular among the Japanese, is known as *sui-seki* (water-stone). A natural stone of desirable shape is placed in a porcelain or bronze tray or dish with sand and water. Months and years of patient watering and care may, according to the kind of stone used, bring forth a thin coating of moss, enlivening the stone with a verdure like a mountain or an island with forest and meadows. (J. HAR.)

WOOD CARVING. Splendid examples of Japanese 8th century wood-carving may be found in the phoenix and musical angels adorning the canopy hung in the Kondō of Hōryuji and in the *gigaku* masks carved in paulownia wood and preserved in the Imperial treasure-house Shōsōin, the Hōryuji monastery and other ancient temples in Japan. The *gigaku* masks in the Shōsōin, numbering 164, the majority of which are in wood, the most of which are in paulownia, if not all, the rest being in dry-lacquer, are believed to have been used in connection with religious services observed at Tōdaiji, especially at the inauguration ceremony of the Great Buddha which took place on April 9, 752. The belief is substantiated by the carvers' signatures and dates written on the inside of the masks, and also on the original bags which contained them. Inscriptions on some of the masks indicate the number of days spent in carving the mask, some being 5 and 7 and others 9 days. The wooden masks used in *bugaku*, the music of which is still preserved and occasionally performed in the Palace, are smaller and less grotesque in appearance, as may be seen from the old masks scheduled as "national treasures" and preserved in some temples. The *no* masks, all carved in wood, which came into existence in the 16th century, taxed the resources of the talented carvers, and a large number of masterpieces are now in possession of the head families of the different schools of *no* drama.

Up to the 15th century, the work of the wood-carver was confined to the embellishment of the temples: carvings on the pedestals, nimbus, and baldachins of Buddhist figures, and some slight ornamentations on the building itself, such as the carving of the beam-ends into animal heads and the use of the *kaeru-mata*, a simple decoration between the beams. But in the second half of the 16th century, the decorative wood-carving came to assume an importance in palatial mansions of the shōguns and in shrines where wood carvings were inserted into the *kaeru-mata* between the beams, attached under the rafters, used as the panels of the gate, etc., a large number of which may still be seen at Kitano Jinsha and Nishi Hongwanji of Kyoto, Chikubushima Jinsha in Lake Biwa, etc. The predominance of wood-carving as an architectural decoration in the 17th century may be seen at the mausoleums of the Tokugawa shōguns at Shiba, Tokyo, and at Nikko, where both the interior and exterior of the buildings are profusely covered with wood-carvings ranging over a wide variety of subjects faithfully executed and realistically coloured.

The taste for simplicity has not tolerated wood-carving in the architecture of dwelling houses. The only place the carver could display his art was in *ramma*, the ventilating panel in the narrow partition wall over the sliding screens that separate one room from another. The *ramma* carving has made a special development of its own, all sorts of subjects being treated: flowers and birds, animals and insects, figures in history and romance, landscapes and mists, clouds and waves, etc., carved on board to give, together with the decoration on the sliding screens, a character to the room.

Some fine carving in wood, the temple decoration in miniature scale, may be seen in the family shrine (*butsu-dan*) where the ancestral tablets are kept, generally fitted into a recess in the room. In their profuse and minute decoration some of the portable shrines (*mikoshi*), used in the procession at the festival, are also beautiful examples of the art of wood-carving. So also are the small ornaments for cabinet decoration or for the *tokonoma*, the recess in the guest room for objects of art. Some wonderful workmanship in wood has been produced by the *netsuke* (ornamental button for suspending a pouch or medicine case) carvers when many of the talented sculptors in wood turned their attention from carving Buddhist figures to the production of smaller objects in greater demand.

The Chinese have utilized the wood-carving more lavishly than the Japanese in their home architecture. They have carved their heavy beams on the ceiling and the massive pillars as well with delicate tracery. The simplest of their chairs and tables are invariably carved in the "key"-pattern, some simpler than others, and the doors are in delicate trelliswork design or ornamented with carvings in low relief. Lanterns with diapers or some other interesting designs in pierced work are held by brackets or arms carved in forms of dragon heads. Although rich in variety, the designs used in the wood-carving, show a fondness for geometric patterns that is distinctly Chinese. The following are some of the other motives resorted to by the wood-carvers: emblems of richness and happiness, clouds and thunder patterns, the curious mask of a creature "TaoTieh," "The Eight Trigrams" or "Pa Kwa," "The Four Quadrants," "The Five Elements," etc. Sacred scenes and figures incised in floral scrolls, intermingled with series of conventional emblems of one religion or another form subjects for woodcarvers in decorating the Buddhist, Taoist and Confucian temples. Sacred to Buddhism are the eight symbols, the chief among which is the lotus, an emblem of purity, chosen because the lotus lifts out of the mud its rosy or white blossoms unsullied, forming a fitting resting place for the Buddha. Taoists have their symbols of eight immortals and derive many floral emblems of longevity from sacred plants, the most prominent among which is the peach, the tree of life of their paradise, bearing fruits ripening but once in 3,000 years which confer immortality to those who partake of it. While Confucianism has no distinct emblem of its own, the symbol of culture and examples of filial piety, such as the well known 24 examples of filial piety, are sometimes attributed to it.

Artistic vitality characterizes even the highly conventionalized designs of the Japanese wood-carvers, but the bulk of the Chinese work reveals a sense of laborious and mechanical execution. On the whole, the Chinese wood-carvings are more effective as a design and ornament compared with the Japanese work, which while the thing carved on is well decorated, carry a far less decorative value. The former aims more for the effect, while the latter pays much greater attention to the mode of execution and technical skill. The former covers the carving with paint or lacquer, while the latter delights in appreciating, whenever possible, the clear cut chisel marks in natural wood. Even the decorative panels in the temples and shrines which are coloured, show traces of the Japanese wood-carver's pleasure and satisfaction derived from the clear cuts of his chisel. There is a tendency in both for an effort to surmount formidable difficulties in design and execution, defying time and labour, with little regard for the artistic merit in the result achieved. (See INDIAN ART AND SINHALESE, INDONESIAN and FURTHER INDIAN ART AND ARCHAEOLOGY.)

BIBLIOGRAPHY.—*Temples and their Treasures*, Dept. of Interior, Japan; F. T. Piggott, *The Decorative Art of Japan* (1910); S. W. Bushell, *Chinese Art* (1904–1909). (J. HAR.)

PUBLISHERS' NOTE

Since the publication of the New 14th Edition of the Encyclopædia Britannica, we have received thousands of requests to publish in separate form the articles in certain fields of knowledge so that these articles may be the more available for continuous reading, for students' use, etc. Accordingly we have prepared booklets containing all the Britannica articles on Painting; Mammals and Birds; Chinese Art; Botany: Plants and Gardening; the Earth, the Seas and the Heavens; Japanese Art; Fishes, Reptiles and Insects; The Theatre and Motion Pictures; Graphic Arts; and expect to follow these with many others. We trust they will prove useful, not only in themselves but also as evidence of the wide scope and the fullness of information in the Britannica itself.

The articles in this booklet are all taken *verbatim* from the New 14th Edition of the Encyclopædia Britannica except that material not essential to the subject has been omitted and in a few unimportant instances certain material has been condensed for mechanical reasons. The plates, too, are reproduced unchanged but the numbering is not always consecutive because the original numbering has been retained in order to agree with the text. A number of cross references to articles not in this booklet have also been retained for the benefit of those who possess the Britannica.

Following the Britannica custom, we have retained at the end of signed articles, the initials and not the full name of the author. The reader, however, can always identify the author by referring to the Table of Contents where the full names of the authors are given together with their initials.

POTTERY AND PORCELAIN. Japan, like every other country, has its primitive pottery, a rough hand-made material sometimes mat-marked like the primitive Chinese. A more advanced type is found in the dolmen burials which date from the 3rd century B.C. to the 7th A.D. The dolmen-builders were invaders from the mainland, doubtless from Korea, and the dolmen pottery closely resembles the Korean wares of the Silla period. The development of the potter's art in Japan was slow—perhaps it was retarded by the preference for other materials, such as lacquer, for the articles of every day use—and it seems at first only to have moved forward under the stimulus of foreign influences. The first foreign influence was Korean. The next was Chinese, and this must have been felt as early as the 8th century, for the treasure of the Emperor Shomu, preserved at Nara, includes a few specimens of motley glazed pottery of T'ang type. In the 13th century Kato Shirazaemon is said to have gone to China to study the work of the Sung potters, and to have set up kilns in Seto on his return. Reputed specimens of his work are tea jars and tea bowls with thick treacly glazes of black, amber brown, chocolate and yellowish grey colour. This type of pottery took a firm hold in Japan and variations of the Seto glazes were subsequently made in many factories throughout the country. A second and more potent wave of Korean influence flooded Japan after Hideyoshi's campaigns in the 16th century,

PLATE IV

WOOD-CARVING

BY COURTESY OF (1, 2, 3, 5, 6) THE DIRECTOR OF THE VICTORIA AND ALBERT MUSEUM

EXAMPLES OF FAR EASTERN WOOD-CARVING

1, 2, 3. Chinese shop front
4. Carved ramma in the crane room of the Nishi Hongwanji, Kyoto
5, 6. Carved beam from a Chinese house
7. Wood-carving under the eave of Kitano Jinsha, Kyoto
8. Chinese screen with carving
9. A Chinese temple
10. Wood-carving on the famous gateway (Yōmeimon) of the Nikko Shrine, Japan
11. Wood-carving on the wall of the Nikko Shrine
12. Sleeping cat at the Nikko Shrine carved by the left-handed Jingoro
13. Carved ramma in the wave room of the Nishi Hongwanji, Kyoto

POTTERY AND PORCELAIN

PLATE XLII

BY COURTESY OF (1, 3) THE FREER GALLERY OF ART, (4, 5, 6, 11) THE MUSEUM OF FINE ARTS, BOSTON, (2, 7, 8, 9, 10) THE TRUSTEES OF THE BRITISH MUSEUM

JAPANESE POTTERY

1. Jar, Hagi, Nagato province, 18th century
2. Jar, Kutani, Kaga province, 17th century
3. Jar, Karatsu, Hizen province
4. Tea bowl, by Goroshichi, Hizen province, c. 1530
5. Wine bottle for offerings, Imbe, Bizen province, c. 1780
6. Bowl, by Ninsei, Yamashiro province, c. 1650
7. Teajar, Seto, Owari province
8. Incense box, Raku
9. Bottle, Karatsu, Hizen province, 17th century
10. Dish, Kakiemon, Hizen province, 18th century
11. Jar for cake, Tada, Suo province, c. 1770

from which he brought back a large number of Korean captives. It happened too that about the same time the famous aesthete Senno Rikiu organized the tea ceremony, which has played ever since an important part in Japanese social life. The masters of the tea ceremony decided that pottery was the most fitting material for the tea vessels; and the Japanese potters soon learnt from the Koreans how to meet the demand satisfactorily. Hence the numerous imitations of Korean Yi dynasty wares to which allusion was made in the last section. Indeed many of the best known Japanese potteries, such as those of Karatsu, Satsuma, Shigaraki, Takatori and Hagi, owe most of their importance, and also very often their origin, to Korean teachers. From the 16th century onward Japanese pottery developed rapidly and many new and original types were invented, of which the *raku* ware is one of the most important (Plate XLII., fig. 8).

Though the credit for the invention of *raku* ware is given to a Korean family settled in the Kioto district, the ware itself is essentially Japanese. It is a soft, hand-made earthenware, requiring only a slight firing, and covered with a peculiarly waxen, treacly and semi-opaque glaze of various colours of which the black and salmon are the earliest and the yellow, green, cream white and mixed colours later.

Another successful Japanese creation is the antithesis of the *raku* ware. It is a hard reddish brown stoneware unglazed as a rule, except for an accidental smear, and evidently well suited for figure modelling. Its habitat is the province of Bizen, where the industry can be traced back to the 14th century. A fine, hard, buff pottery with closely crackled cream glaze is another Japanese specialty. It is a development of the Korean *koma gai*, or white ware; and it reached its finest expression in Satsuma. Here and at numerous factories in Kyoto it was used as the vehicle for enamelled decoration.

The art of enamelling on porcelain was learnt from China, the story being that Sakaida Kakiemon, an Arita potter, was instructed in it by a Chinese ship's master about the middle of the 17th century. One of the most celebrated Japanese potters, whose art-name is Ninsei, adapted its use to the cream glazed pottery and developed a special style of enamelling in purely Japanese taste. Ogata Kenzan, another of the great Japanese ceramic artists, at the end of the 17th century found a way of using enamelled decoration on the soft *raku* glazes (Plate XXVII., fig. 1). From this time onwards Chinese influence was discounted in the pottery which displays much originality and a true national style.

Japanese Porcelain.—Meanwhile the manufacture of porcelain had started in Japan. Needless to say the technique was learnt from the Chinese, a potter named Gorodayu go Shonzui visiting Ching-tê Chên itself to study in the 15th century. Shonzui's difficulty on his return to Japan was to find suitable raw material and he was forced to work with imported Chinese clays. Not till the beginning of the 17th century did the discovery of the important deposits of porcelain stone on Izumi Yama, in the Arita district of Hizen, permit the establishment of the Japanese porcelain industry on a firm basis. The Arita district was the chief centre of the manufacture; and it was here, at the seaport Imari, that the Dutch traders obtained the "Old Imari" porcelain with which they flooded Europe. Here too Kakiemon practised his new-found art of enamelling, in a style which is for ever associated with his name. The Kakiemon enamels were soft orange red, grass green and lilac blue, supplemented by pale primrose yellow, turquoise green, gilding and occasionally by underglaze blue; and his decorations are slight and in the best Japanese taste. A few blossoms, a floral medallion, a flowering prunus tree, a banded hedge with birds, quails and millet, a tiger and bamboos (Plate XXVII., fig. 3) a dragon and sometimes children are motives of the nicely balanced Kakiemon designs which have been imitated wherever porcelain has been made (Plate XLII., fig. 2). The "Old Imari" of the Dutch importers included another highly specialized but less artistic kind of porcelain. It was painted with masses of heavy impure blue supplemented by red and gold and to a less extent by enamel colours. The designs are irregular and confused, asymmetrical panels enclosed by mixed brocade patterns. Over-loaded, but not without decorative value, they appealed strongly to the Dutch taste.

Many factories were started in the Arita district, those of the princely houses of Hirado and Nabeshima being the most noted; and the industry soon spread to other provinces. It was early established in the Kutani district of the province of Kaga and at a little later period at Seto in Owari, Mino, Kioto and many other places. The Kaga potteries in the 19th century popularized a special kind of decoration in red and gold; but on the whole Japanese painted porcelain follows closely on Chinese lines, and the highest ambition seems to have been to make wares which could be mistaken for Ming porcelain. The Koto factory on the shore of Lake Biwa was noted for its enamelled porcelain in the middle of the 19th century; and good imitations of Chinese celadon were made in the Arita district at an early date and at Sanda and Kioto since the end of the 18th century. In the early 19th century remarkably fine porcelain of "egg-shell" thinness was made at Mikawachi, in Seto, Shiba and Mino.

Since the reopening of Japan to the foreigner in 1868 vast quantities of pottery and porcelain have been made for the Western market. These wares, usually overloaded with ornament, do not represent true Japanese taste, which requires that a piece of pottery be made strictly to serve its useful purpose and decorated soberly in a style appropriate to its form and use.

It is not practicable within the compass of this article to describe the work of individual potters, and the mere mention of famous names, such as Banko, Hozan, Dohachi, Eisen, Rokubei and Zengoro Hozen, cannot serve any useful purpose. The potteries are very numerous, being for the most part small family concerns; and as each had its individual mark or seal and a proper pride in using it, the list of Japanese potter's marks is a formidable one, for which the reader must consult works cited below.

BIBLIOGRAPHY.—F. Brinkley, *Japan, Its History, Arts and Literature* (1904); A. W. Franks, *Japanese Pottery*, Victoria and Albert Museum Art Handbook (1906), *Catalogue of the Franks Collection of Oriental Pottery and Porcelain* (1879); E. S. Morse, *Catalogue of the Japanese Pottery in the Museum of Fine Arts* (Boston, 1901). (R. L. Ho.)

INTERIOR DECORATION. The refinement of simplicity, which finds its aesthetic ideal in the natural beauty of materials and is compatible with the austerity of architectural form, is a keynote of a Japanese house-interior.

The Walls.—Rooms of various sizes are made by the use of walls and *fusuma* (sliding partitions of wood covered with patterned or painted paper or silk), running in grooves, which usually measure some 6 ft. in height and 2¼ to 4½ ft. in width. *Shōji*, the equivalent of windows, consist of light lattice-work to which is pasted white translucent paper, and also slide in grooves. The grooves run between squared wooden posts, and allow the screens to pass one another, rendering hinged doors unnecessary, and permit of the screens being lifted out altogether, thus throwing a series of rooms into one great apartment. The "filling" (varying in height from 2 to 4½ ft.) between the beam over the screens and the ceiling, is generally, in good class houses, of latticed wood or bamboo or of pierced woodwork called *ramma*. The carving of the *ramma*, often elaborate in palaces and mansions, should be in harmony with the character of the room. Those in certain palaces and temples in Kyoto are exquisitely carved, some having intricate designs in pierced work carved from a single piece of wood.

The Floors.—The floor boards are completely overlaid by *tatami*, straw mats some 2 in. thick and measuring about 3 by 6 ft., each one covered by finely woven grass matting. The size of the room is computed in mats, according to whether it needs 4½, 6, 8, 10, 12 or 12½ mats to cover the floor. In ordinary dwelling houses a room is seldom larger than 15 mats. The spotless matting of closely-woven fresh reeds, bound on the long sides of each mat with a narrow strip of dark linen, with their pale green colour neutralized by light filtering through the paper screens, and their fresh fragrance, appeal strongly to the Japanese, and those who can afford it continue to preserve this freshness by reversing and changing the top matting from time to time.

The Ceiling.—The ceiling is equally simple. In an ordinary dwelling house it is about 9 ft. from the floor and formed of thin, slightly overlapping panels of unpainted wood about 12 to 18 in.

wide, whose monotony is broken by parallel strips some 18 in. apart running across the ceiling, and invisibly nailed from above. Since the grain of the wood forms part of the decorative scheme in the interior, the boards are cut from a single tree to insure uniformity. The panels, 6 ft. in length, must be so laid as to suggest continuity of the grain across the room, and must be carefully planed by the carpenter, for they are to be admired in their natural state and no flaw in human handicraft must be allowed to spoil their intrinsic beauty. All the woodwork of the interior must in the same way be left virgin, unspoiled by colour-stain or paint, with occasional exception of the narrow framework of the *fusuma*, and the *tokobuchi*—a piece of wood several inches in width and thickness running along in front of the *tokonoma* (see below) to its full extent—both of which may be lacquered in harmony with *tatami* borders or the *tokonoma* post. This is often made from a tree having some special tint or texture, or else made to conform to its natural curve of growth. A portion of its bark or the worm-eaten marks beneath it, or the stump of a branch or some other witness of nature, is preserved, thus focussing on the *tokonoma*—the most important feature of a Japanese interior—the significance of the design of the room.

The Tokonoma.—This slightly raised recess or alcove, usually built into the wall at right angles to the verandah, is commonly from 2 to 3 ft. deep and 4½, 6 or 9 ft. wide proportionately to the size of the room. In it are displayed the only independent decorations in the room. A painting or a set of two or three *kakemono* (hanging-paintings mounted on rollers) occupy the back wall of the alcove, and a vase holding the *ike-bana* or flower arrangement (*q.v.*), an incense burner or a wood-carving, or some other art object, is placed on its floor. They must each be in harmony with the season or with any special occasion which may befall, and are chosen with a view to give pleasure to an expected guest. There may be many *kakemono* put away, especially in old families, but only one is shown in the *tokonoma*, selected to do honour to the guest. If he is likely to enter other rooms having a *tokonoma*, a distinctive atmosphere must be created in each, while emphasizing some central harmonizing idea. The flower arrangement and other decorative art objects must be complementary to the painting. Thus a *kakemono* of the moon may be accompanied by a few sprays of autumn flowers, artistically arranged in a bamboo basket, and a small bronze censor in the shape of a cottage, thus suggesting a fishing hamlet on a tranquil evening of autumn. Or a painting of a waterfall may hang in the *tokonoma*, while on its floor is placed a rectangular bronze vessel well filled with water and with a few water-lilies appropriately arranged in it. In a small room the same atmosphere may be achieved by showing a narrow *kakemono* of a waterfall in a roughly-executed black monochromatic style and placing on the floor a single white blossom of *Hibiscus mutabilis*, half-concealed among its freshly moistened leaves, displayed in a slender bronze vase with very cold water so that the moisture collects outside and trails down over the beautiful patina, creating the suggestion of a miniature pool on the round flat lacquered board of liquid black upon which the vase stands.

Thus the guest is brought to feel the very spray from the waterfall, transforming the confined room into a fitting place in which to entertain visitors on the hottest of summer days. An alternative to the painting is a couple of lines of poetry on which the guest may meditate on his entrance into the room. His attention may next be led to a *bon-seki* (*q.v.*), a tiny landscape contrived with natural stones and sand, on a black lacquered tray at the foot of the *kakemono*. It may call to mind some familiar scene—a rocky promontory with an island near by, and beyond the moonlit sea the dim contours of undulating hills. The poem on the *kakemono* (for calligraphy is also treated as a pictorial art) thus quickens with new meaning for him and he can share the poet's inspiration.

Other Decorations.—In a companion recess adjoining the *tokonoma* are *chigai-dana*—shelves arranged stepwise—for additional art objects and there is usually a small cupboard with appropriately decorated sliding doors either above or below the shelves. There may also be a low writing-place built at the side from which the light comes, in front of the *tokonoma*, where lacquered boxes for paper and other writing paraphernalia can be placed, further decorating the room. What articles, and how and where they are to be arranged in these places to conform to the general scheme and to afford the maximum of decorative value and aesthetic pleasure, has been an aesthetic study for centuries. In the time of the Shōgun Yoshimasa (1444–73) a set of systematic rules of decoration had already been formulated, and is still followed by some of the "tea-men." There may also be placed by the low writing-table in the master's room, a portable lacquered set of shelves or a cabinet carrying a few objects of art for his delectation in moments of leisure.

Thus simplicity of display is fully compatible with wealth of possessions. The same object is rarely seen twice in a dozen visits. Hundreds of beautiful things may be stored in the treasure-house. Guided by his knowledge of the character and temperament of his guest, his recollection of the impression made by the things on view on former occasions, a Japanese host will select from his store, always aiming at giving pleasure and a delightful surprise to his guest.

Sometimes a skirting of strong white or grey paper about a foot high as a protection against the broom is seen on a Japanese wall, but it is never papered or covered up by paintings, although a *gaku*, consisting of a painting or a few written characters expressing or suggesting a poetical sentiment or a truth may be framed above the *fusuma*. Plastered earth and sand, variously coloured, and mixed with boiled *funori* (*Gliopeltis furcata*) to give solidity, is used for the interior surfaces of the lath and plaster walls, and the pounded shell of little fresh-water bivalves or iron filings is sometimes mixed with the sand for their decorative value. Plaster in tint of smoke, mist or cloud, often has a hard and resistant surface.

Furniture.—In the Japanese house the furniture is conspicuous by its absence. There is neither table nor chairs such as are used in China or in the West. Everybody removes his or her shoes, sandals or clogs upon entering the house, and even slippers or house sandals are left outside in the wooden corridor. People sit, or rather kneel and sit back on their heels, on the *tatami* on flat square cushions. Each person is provided with a *tabako-bon* (smoking set) in summer and a *hibachi* (charcoal brazier) in winter. In some houses to-day gas or electric stoves are fitted, but the brazier is the characteristic means of warming a Japanese interior. It may be of bronze, porcelain or wood decorated with lacquer, and is furnished with a pair of small tastefully designed and ornamented fire-irons like chopsticks. Braziers are usually small and portable.

Beds may be arranged on the floor in any room at night by piling up wadded quilts, which are folded and packed away in the closet, after airing in the sun, in the morning, leaving the room clear for other uses during the day. A *tansu*, a chest-of-drawers in plain paulownia wood, may betray the sleeping apartment, but this, too, is often packed in the closet, shut off by *fusuma*, so as not to be seen. A clothes-horse is as a rule also placed out of sight behind a screen. *Byobu*, ornamental folding screens of 2, 4 or 6 panels decorated with writing or painting, or carried out in plain gold, serve many a convenient purpose, warding off draughts or hiding an undesired view. A single-panelled screen called *tsuitate* is usually placed in the entrance-room, to allow of the front *shōji* being pushed open without exhibiting the interior of the house to a caller. Even the dining-room is without any sign of its use, a collapsible low table being brought in for family use at mealtime, or food being carried in and served to each individual on small low lacquer tables called *o-zen*, kept in the kitchen cupboard when not in use.

In the summer heat the ordinary *fusuma* and *shōji* are frequently removed and replaced by others specially made of rushes or split bamboo to permit the passage of any breath of wind that may happen to stray into the house. The floor, too, may be covered over with rattan matting, to impart coolness; and *misu* or blinds made of split bamboo or rushes, may be suspended from the eaves to give shade and privacy.

Simplicity the Keynote.—Japanese rooms are thus extremely

INTERIOR DECORATION PLATE XVI

BY COURTESY OF JIRO HARADA

JAPANESE HOUSE INTERIORS

1. The Prince's room in the shinden of the Ninnaji, near Kyoto
2. Suite of rooms in the shinden of the Ninnaji
3. A guest room in Mr. Tomita's home in Nagoya
4. A room in the home of Mr. Miyazaki, tea-master in Nagoya
5. A guest room in Mr. Hirai's home in Kyoto
6. A room in Mr. Ichida's home in Kyoto

PLATE XVII

INTERIOR DECORATION

BY COURTESY OF JIRO HARADA

JAPANESE INTERIORS AND FURNISHINGS

1. Interior of the Keiun-tei in the garden of Mr. Tomita at Nagoya
2. A room in the house of Mr. Nishimura, Kyoto, showing *tokonoma* (raised alcove) and adjoining recess with shelves
3. Shelves and cupboards in a room in the Katsura detached palace
4. Guest rooms in the Temple Hokyoji
5. Pierced screen of paulownia wood, carved by Kobayashi Jodei. In the Imperial Household Museum
6. Small bamboo cabinet of the 8th century. In the Imperial Household Museum
7. *Tokonoma* in the home of Mr. Hatton, Nagoya. The *kakemono* (scroll-painting) of Fujiyama is complemented by a few sprays of red-berried *nandin* in a bronze basin, and by *bon seki* (a miniature landscape made with stones and sand)

JAPANESE ARCHITECTURE

TEA PAVILION, A SHRINE AND OTHER JAPANESE BUILDINGS

1. Korin's *chaseki* (tea pavilion) in the garden of the Ninnaji, Kyoto   2. Shinto shrine   3. Nijo palace, Kyoto   4. Thatch-roofed cottages, Viscount Saga's villa at Atami

PLATE II — JAPANESE ARCHITECTURE

JAPANESE TEMPLES, AND OTHER BUILDINGS

1. Veranda of the Sanboin, Daigo, looking out on a 17th century garden
2. *Chaseki* (tea pavilion) in the garden of the Katsura palace
3. Veranda of the Chion-in temple, Kyoto
4. Hiunkaku, in Kongwanji, Kyoto; originally at Momoyama, 16th century

BY COURTESY OF JIRO HARADA

JAPANESE ARCHITECTURE

PLATE III

NIKKO SHRINE

Nikko shrine, showing Yomeimon, its principal gateway; built in the 17th century

BY COURTESY OF JIRO HARADA

PLATE IV JAPANESE ARCHITECTURE

BY COURTESY OF JIRO HARADA

VARIOUS FORMS OF JAPANESE ARCHITECTURE

1. Detail, five-storied pagoda of the Kofukuji, Nara. Kamakura period (1186–1335)
2. Pagoda of the Yakushiji; Tempyo period (708–781)
3. Castle at Hikone
4 and 5. Two views of the Kabukiza theatre in Tokyo; re-enforced concrete building; designed by Dr. Shin-ichiro Okada, executed by Obayashi-gumi
6. Shinto shrine at Nachi
7. Hōwōdō of Uji, built in the 11th century
8. Kondo of the Horyuji Monastery, built at the beginning of the 7th century; said to be the oldest wooden building in the world

simple, though neither barren nor cheerless, since every detail of form and colour is studied and harmoniously combined, even the joinery being so perfect that not a trace of a nail can be seen anywhere, with the result that, at least for beauty, the empty room is sufficient in itself. There is a sense of relief in this absence of furniture. These neat and airy rooms, so restful and so spacious, may be opened at will for their entire width onto a tiny landscape over which the eyes delight to wander. Or they may be closed up completely, leaving the occupant alone with an iron kettle (an object of art in itself) gently boiling on the charcoal fire, overlooked from no window, but companioned by the silhouettes of bamboo or pine branch in the garden forming countless attractive patterns on the creamy paper of the *shōji*. In such a room may be admired an ancient tree of stately form, growing in a pot placed in the *tokonoma*, and still retaining its dignity in its miniature form. Freed from the distraction of furniture, the men and women in the room recapture their dignity and significance. In the simple form in which the exigencies of construction determine the refined and reserved quality of the decoration, and the furnishings are reduced to the essentials, while the subtly blended colouring and the constant variety of the view on which it can be made to open build up a composition of delicate lines and graceful forms, the Japanese interior well fulfils its main and consciously recognized functions: it supplies an appropriate setting for clean and simple living. (*See* JAPANESE ARCHITECTURE; JAPANESE SCULPTURE; WOOD CARVING: *Far Eastern;* BON-SEKI; BON-SAI.)

BIBLIOGRAPHY.—E. S. Morse, *Japanese Homes and Their Surroundings;* R. A. Cram, *Impressions of Japanese Architecture and the Applied Arts.* (J. HAR.)

JAPANESE ARCHITECTURE. The physical features of the country and the national characteristics of cleanliness and simplicity have determined and guided the general trend of Japanese architecture; wood is the principal building material, for Japan is abundantly supplied with such splendid timber as *hinoki* (*Chamaecyparis obtusa*), which is still in excellent condition in buildings 12 or 13 centuries old. A commission was created in 1897 for the preservation and care of such buildings, as well as sculpture and other works of art, and up to the beginning of 1928 more than 1,100 buildings, in spite of the recurrent conflagrations, had been placed under "special State protection."

Pre-Buddhistic Period.—The primitive form of Japanese architecture is known as "primaeval palace construction." It consists in two posts set in the ground and supporting a ridge-pole, to each end of which are lashed slantwise two rafters reaching to the ground. To these rafters are tied horizontal beams to support a thatch which serves both as walls and roof; later a wooden floor was introduced, the whole structure raised, and the original shape of the roof retained while vertical walls were added. This simple form of architecture has been adhered to in some shrines sacred to Shintō. The oldest style is *Ō-yashiro*, the prototype of which is the shrine at Izumo; it developed into such forms as *Ō-tori* and *Sumiyoshi*, in none of which is there any evidence of the curves of a later date. These forms soon underwent slight variation, forming the style known as *Shinmei*, a perfect example of which is the Imperial Ise Shrine, which is rebuilt every 20 years, exactly the same to the minutest detail, with plain white wood and a thatch of chamaecyparis bark. It is recorded that the emperor Nintoku (A.D. 313–399) did away with palace decorations for the sake of economy, and "lofty architecture" is spoken of in connection with his reign as well as with those of two succeeding emperors, thus showing that the palaces at that time were no longer built in the simplest form. Their architectural development, however, was retarded, owing to the custom of changing the seat of the imperial court at the death of each emperor, and real growth, therefore, only came with the establishment of the court, first at Nara (708) and later at Kyoto, where it remained nearly 11 centuries before it was finally removed to Tokyo in 1868.

Early Chinese Influence.—The official introduction of Buddhism to Japan from Korea in A.D. 552 completely changed the architecture as well as other branches of Japanese art. Temples on a grand scale with elaborate detail were built. Some of the buildings of the Hōryuji monastery date from the beginning of the 7th century, and are considered to be the oldest wooden buildings in the world. With Buddhism, the influence of the six dynasties of China became evident, though those who built the Japanese temples were Koreans introduced at the same time. Soon afterwards, however, T'ang influence became irresistible, and monasteries assumed a still greater grandeur in scale, as may be seen from what remains of Tōdaiji at Nara (completed about 750), a representative work of the Tempyo period (708–781). The exterior of the temple was coated with red oxide of lead and the interior painted in vivid colours, especially in the shade known as *ungen;* the palace at that time was also probably gorgeous with red pillars and green tiles. With the rise of two powerful sects of esoteric Buddhism (Shingon and Tendai) in the early Heian period (782–888) temple architecture again underwent a change, as the tenets of those sects required the monasteries to be built on mountain tops; Shintō architecture changed also and a curve was given to gable and roof, such forms being evolved as *Kasuga, Nagare* and *Hiye.*

First Nationalist Movement.—In the second half of the 9th century intercourse between Japan and China was interrupted. Left alone, Japan enjoyed a period of self-realization which gave the native taste a chance to discriminate and reassert itself in architecture, as well as in other branches of art. Grace and finish were imparted to architectural detail without sacrificing the strength and harmony of the whole. To the roof was given a gentle sweep of exquisite grace; to the interior a richer, but more subdued tone. However, the later Fujiwara period (1069–1185) revealed signs of weakness and a tendency to over-refinement and delicacy, and a philosophical endeavour to amalgamate Shintoism and Buddhism resulted in the modification of Shintō architecture. Aristocrats began building their mansions much after the fashion of the imperial residences; a style of architecture—*Shindenzukuri*—consisting of a series of oblong houses systematically arranged and joined by corridors, with a garden laid out on the southern side in which was a big pond, became the fashion.

Second Chinese Influence.—Another great wave of Chinese influence began to be felt in the Kamakura period (1186–1335), when the Zen sect of Buddhists, which was destined to grip the mind of the people and to influence the art of the country fundamentally, was introduced from China. At the same time a peculiarity of the Sung dynasty under the name of "Tenjiku," or Indian, was introduced. Side by side with these imported styles the native architecture continued, and only later was influenced by the Zen principles; the "Tenjiku" style, apparently not congenial to native taste, was allowed to die out. In the Zen style the interiors were either plain, or coloured with utmost simplicity, a low relief generally constituting the only form of decoration. The period being strongly militaristic it was but natural that a style should arise, known as *Buke-zukuri*, for military aristocrats. It was a natural native growth, but its fuller development was seen in the Nanbokucho (1336–93) and the Ashikaga (1394–1573) periods. Generally speaking, the Ashikaga period emphasized detail, ignoring structural significance, and revealing weakness in place of refinement, though it produced some great works with far-reaching consequences.

Based upon the *Shinden* style of Fujiwara and the *Buke* style of Kamakura, already mentioned, and under the influence of Zen, there arose a form known as *Shoin-zukuri* (a study style) in connection with domestic and palace architecture. It admitted more light into the house and provided the room with *tokonoma* (a recess for paintings and flowers to serve as decoration) and shelves for ornaments, etc.—two characteristic and pleasing features in the Japanese house. However, a greater triumph of native architecture was the creation of the *Chaseki*, a place for *cha-no-yu*, commonly known as the tea ceremonies, which, with Zen at its foundation, has most vitally influenced all branches of Japanese art, especially painting, architecture and garden designing. In the *chaseki* variation was insisted on lest monotony should weary the mind, and harmony and balance lest freedom of soul should be disturbed. While *cha-no-yu* was in vogue—in the latter part of the Ashikaga period culminating in the Momoyama period (1574–1602)—there developed the art of building fortified castles, strong and massive, and resistant to earthquakes. In the Momoyama period, though the forms were too well established to suffer any material change, architecture sustained a great innovation. For the first time in its long history, there were built lay buildings which far surpassed the temples in splendour; among noteworthy examples now remaining may be mentioned the Hiunkaku and the Stork chamber, both in Nishi Hongwanji, Kyoto, but originally at Momoyama, and the sanctuary of Ninnaji at Omuro which was part of an imperial palace.

Second Japanese Nationalist Movement.—Another nationalist period began with the Tokugawa régime (1603–1867), a period of peace and wealth. Many new buildings were erected and ruined temples restored; but it was in the construction of mausoleums and great edifices built over the bones of Tokugawa Shoguns that the spirit of the age found its fullest expression. The best examples may be seen at Nikko. They are in a style known as *Gongen* or *Yatsumune*, suggesting a complicated system of roofs; the buildings were lacquered within and without, and profusely decorated with carvings. Many feudal lords of the period, following the example of the Shogun, erected such extravagant buildings that it became necessary to impose restrictions. The magnitude of the scale on which the Shogun kept his court may be conceived from the Nijō palace in Kyoto, still well preserved.

Dwelling-houses.—The evolution of the common dwelling-houses of to-day was completed in the Tokugawa period. It was based on the *Chaseki* and *Shoin* styles, where were adopted by the people in general, and it brought with it a great development in landscape gardens which became indispensable as an integral part of the dwelling. The ordinary dwelling-house is one or two storied, roofed either with grey tiles, or in the country, with thatch. The floor is covered with closely-fitted mats 2 inches thick, measuring 3 × 6 ft., the size of rooms being computed by the number of mats in them. The house is divided into rooms by sliding screens; light is admitted by a paper-covered lattice mounted as a sliding window, these screens are removable so as to throw the series of rooms into one. At night the house is closely shuttered by wooden panels running in grooves on the outside. It is now usual to have one reception room furnished in Western style. The kitchen, long neglected, has been much improved by the introduction of Western conveniences and labour-saving devices. The whole interior, however, remains essentially simple and refined.

Post-Restoration.—With the restoration of power to the imperial throne in 1868, which was followed by the suppression of the feudal system, an attempt was made "to abolish every institution in Japan which had no counterpart in the civilized west." Naturally, the Western style of architecture was welcomed with a zeal that led to the invitation of European and American architects to the country to demonstrate the art of building with bricks, stone, iron and concrete. Some attempts were made to harmonize the Western and native styles of architecture, but with little success. A certain reaction set in just before the great earthquake and fire of 1923 destroyed much of Tokyo and its vicinity, exposing the weaknesses of both styles. A tendency, however, is to be noted towards the adoption, on one hand, of Western architecture for public buildings, and on the other towards maintenance of the pure native style for private dwelling-houses, since the old customs are still kept up in private life and the taste for simplicity remains essentially unchanged. (*See* ARCHITECTURE; SCULPTURE; NŌ DRAMA; WOOD CARVING.) (J. HAR.)

FAN. In Japan also the use of the fan is very closely linked with the life and customs of the people. In Rhead's *History of the Fan* the author says that it is regarded as an emblem of life, widening and expanding as the sticks radiate from the rivet. It plays a part in almost every aspect of their existence: it is presented to the youth on the attainment of his majority; it is used by jugglers in feats of skill; the condemned man marches to the scaffold fan in hand. The earliest examples were made of palm leaves or feathers while the rigid screen fans were introduced from China in the 6th century A.D. Large screens were used for religious and civil ceremonial and as war standards. Most interesting of all the rigid fans is the Gumbai Uchiua, a type of battle fan of iron first known in the 11th century. It is, however, the folding fan, invented by the Japanese in the 7th century, that has played such an important role in their history and art. There are innumerable variations of its form each designed for a particular use and possessing individual characteristics. The Akomé Ogi is the earliest form of court fan having come into use in the 7th century; it is composed of 38 blades fastened with a rivet, formed of a bird or butterfly, and ornamented at the corners with artificial flowers and 12 long streamers of coloured silks; it was the type used by court ladies until 1868. The Gun Sen is the folding battle fan with sticks of wrought iron and the mount of thick paper painted with the sun, moon or star in red or gold on a black or coloured ground; its initial purpose in battle was as a signal. The Mai-Ogi or dancing fan dates from the 17th century; it has 10 sticks and a mount of thick paper usually decorated with a family crest. The Rikin-Ogi or tea fan, used in tea ceremonies celebrated in each province on the first day of every month, has only three sticks and the paper mount is simply decorated, the fan itself being used for handing around little cakes, fanning being prohibited during this dignified ceremony. Many early fans were designed with the infinite artistry of the great painters of Japan but these are rarely seen to-day. Those most often found in collections are the modern *brisé* of ivory or tortoise-shell decorated with lacquer and inlay and often made for exportation to Europe. (*See* DRESS: *Eastern.*) (E. B. SA.)

DOLLS. Dolls are among the first inventions of children, having been doubtless improvised in the earliest instances from natural objects such as sticks and stones. Aboriginal America and Japan are the chief sources of information.

In Japan a primitive type of child's doll consists of a shaved willow stick with shavings or strings for hair, and paper clothes, an obvious adaptation of the shaved willow sticks formerly set up on the banks of streams as scapegoats at the annual purification ceremony. An actual scapegoat doll, which was dressed and fed and generally treated as though alive, was given to mothers in old Japan to ward off evil from their children. Women desiring children presented dolls essentially emblems of maternity, at a certain shrine. Apart from these "magical" dolls, Japanese girl children have ordinary dolls as well as ceremonial dolls symbolizing the imperial court, which are not played with but exhibited formally at the girls' festival on May 5. Japanese boys have similar toy images of warriors, which are displayed at their festivals on the third of March.

In Korea little girls make their own dolls and cut a bamboo pipe stem about 5 in. long, in the top of which they put long grass, salted and made fine like hair. They never give these a face but sometimes paste a little white powder in its place. They dress the stick in clothes like those worn by women and sometimes put a pin, made by themselves, in the hair. The children's festival in Korea occurs on April 8, celebrated in Japan as the birthday of Buddha. On this occasion, the Koreans make an image of a woman of paper with a rounded base made of clay so that it stands erect. In Japan the corresponding toy is identified as the Buddhist *Daruma* and is purchased by boys at the festival of a certain temple. One which rises quickly to a vertical position is selected. The face is painted, but instead of eyes, two white paper discs are pasted. This doll is carried home, placed on the "god shelf" and a prayer is said. The god is promised eyes if he answers the prayer, and, this accomplished, black dots are made with ink on the vacant eye discs. In China this toy is made to represent an actor and described as a drunken man. . . .

BY COURTESY OF THE MUSEUM OF THE AMERICAN INDIAN

PRIMITIVE TYPES OF DOLLS OF THE CARAJA INDIANS, BRAZIL

FAN — PLATE IV

BY COURTESY OF THE IMPERIAL HOUSEHOLD MUSEUM OF TOKYO

JAPANESE FOLDING FANS

Top: Fan painted by Ogata Kenzan. Illustrating a type of folding fan widely used in Japan, having ten sticks and a decorated mount of thick paper

Bottom: Japanese folding fan, painted by Sakai Hoitsu. Fans are often regarded in Japan as an emblem of life, widening and expanding as the sticks radiate from the rivet

PLATE III · FAN

JAPANESE AND INDIAN FANS OF THE NINETEENTH CENTURY

1. Japanese fan with a paper mount, painted by Hokusai. The sticks and guards are of wood
2. Japanese brisé fan of ivory sticks decorated on both sides with lacquer
3. Indian brisé fan of lacquered ivory sticks

BY COURTESY OF (1) THE MUSEUM OF FINE ARTS, BOSTON, (2, 3) THE METROPOLITAN MUSEUM OF ART, NEW YORK

DOLLS

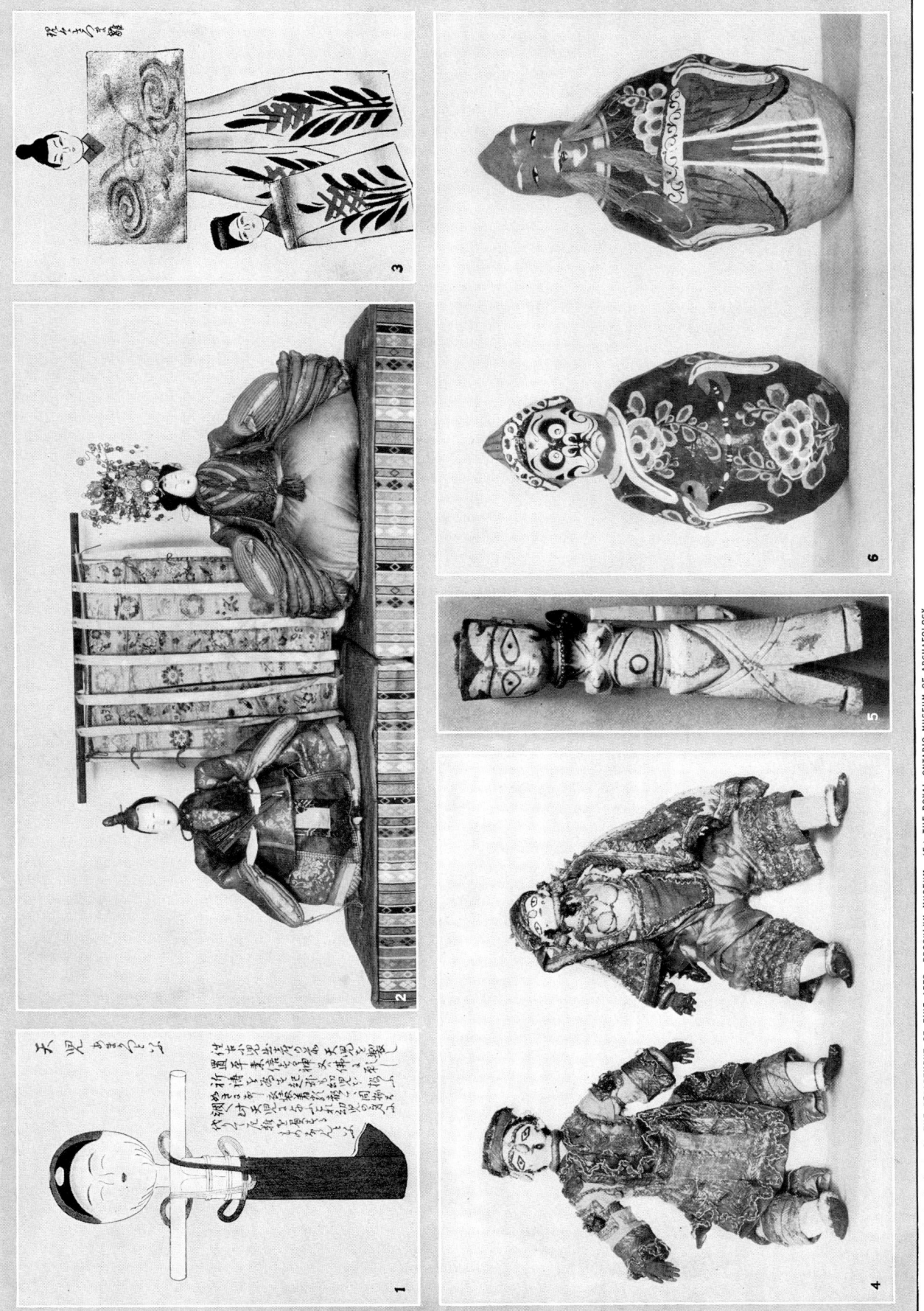

ASIATIC AND EGYPTIAN DOLLS

BY COURTESY OF (1, 2, 3, 4, 6) THE DEPARTMENT OF FINE ARTS, BROOKLYN MUSEUM, (5) THE ROYAL ONTARIO MUSEUM OF ARCHAEOLOGY

1. Wooden Japanese puppet doll mounted on a staff
2. Japanese court dolls
3. Satsuma standing dolls of Japan, made of paper
4. Indian dolls, sometimes used as wedding presents to child brides
5. Coptic doll of bone, seven and one half inches high
6. Chinese "tilting" dolls, made to represent actors

NŌ DRAMA

PLATE I

BY COURTESY OF JIRO HARADA

CHARACTERS IN THE NŌ DRAMA

1. Celestial being in dancing costume; in *Hagoromo*. Hōshō school
2. Hanako looking at her lover's keepsake; throwing the dress off one shoulder in this instance signifies insanity; in *Hanjo*. Hōshō
3. The ghost of a daughter of the well, dancing in the form of Narihira, her lover; in *Izutsu*. Hōshō
4. The ghost of Rokujo-no-Miyasudokoro, as conceived by Aoinouye; in *Aoinouye*. Hōshō
5. A god being pleased with the filial son of a wood chopper, who is rewarded by the Emperor; in *Yōrō*. Kita school
6. Geni of Atago Mountain and saintly priest of Sagano engaged in discourse; in *Kurumazō*. Hōshō
7. Mother praying for the spirit of her dead son, in *Sumita-gawa*. Kita school
8. Tomonori's ghost attacking his living enemy; in *Funabenkei*. Hōshō
9. Soga brothers about to set out to avenge their father; in *Youchi Soga*. Hōshō
10. Atsumori's ghost narrating the fate of his clan; in *Atsumori*. Hōshō
11. The god Inari assisting at the forging of a sword; in *Kokaji*. Hōshō

PLATE II NŌ DRAMA

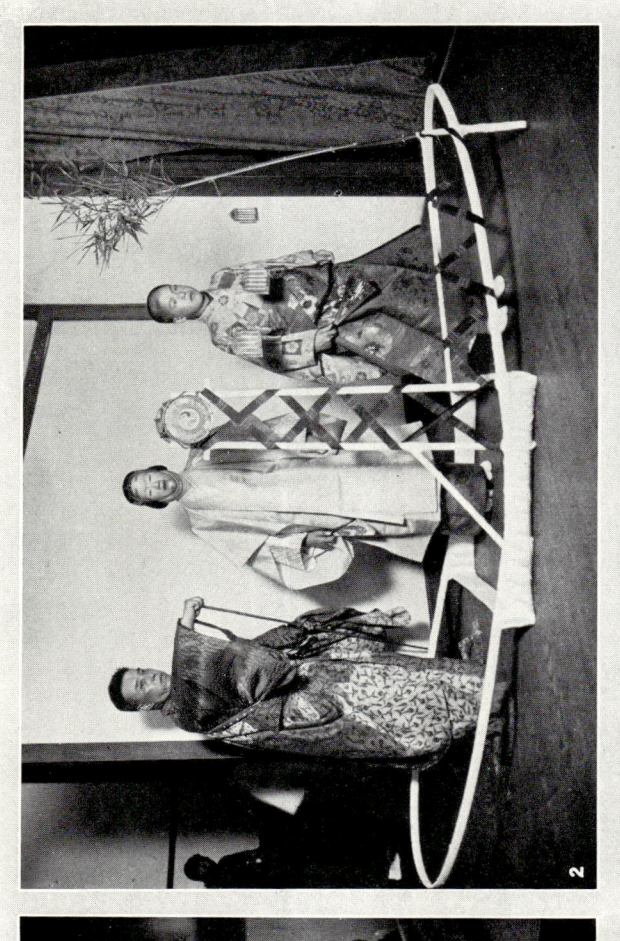
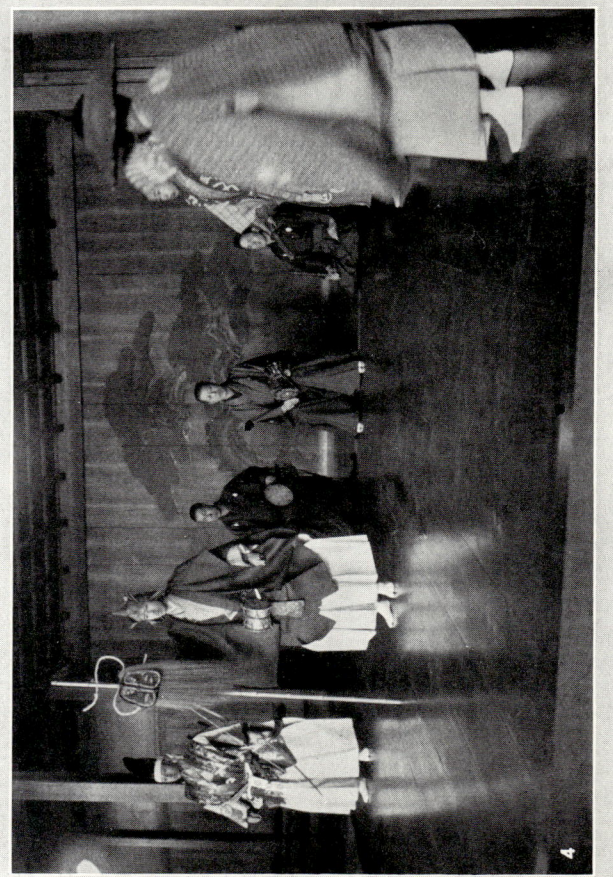

BY COURTESY OF JIRO HARADA

SCENES FROM THE NŌ DRAMA

1. Soga brothers taking leave of their mother before setting out to avenge their father; in *Kosode Soga*. On the Hōshō stage
2. Out in a boat to scare away birds from rice fields; in *Tori Oi*. Hōshō school
3. Benkei and Ushiwaka on the Gojō bridge in Kyoto; in *Hashi Benkei*. Hōshō school
4. Two brothers discussing Buddhistic principles with their enemy; in *Hōkazō*. Kongō school

NŌ DRAMA

PLATE III

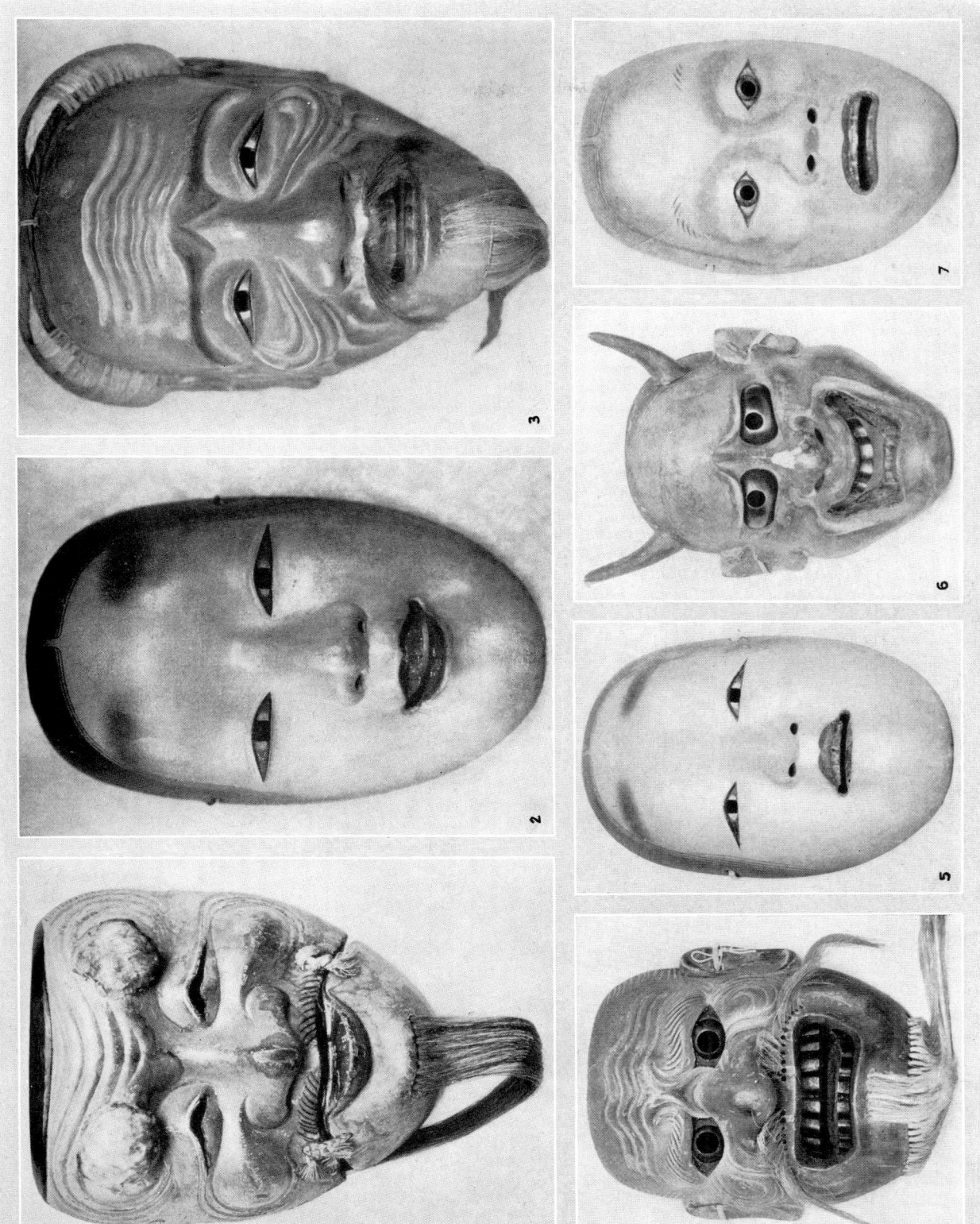

BY COURTESY OF JIRO HARADA

MASKS WORN IN THE NŌ PERFORMANCES

1. "Okina" used by the principal character in *Okina*. Hōshō
2. "Magojiro" used by a young woman character. Kongo family in Kyoto
3. "Sanko" used for elderly man of common class. Kongo
4. "Daiakujō" used for an elderly man of fierce character. Marquis Maeda's collection
5. "Zō" used for young woman. Marquis Maeda's collection
6. "Hannya" for woman demon. Marquis Maeda's collection
7. "Yamamba" used by the heroine in *Yamamba*. Marquis Maeda's collection

BIBLIOGRAPHY.—Fritz Rumpf, *Spielzug der Völker* (Berlin, 1922); Esther Singleton, *Dolls* (New York, 1927); H. R. D'Allemagne, *Histoire des Jouets* (Paris, 1927); Richard Andree, *Ethnograpische Parallelen* (Leipzig, 1889); J. Walter Fewkes, *Internat. Archiv. f. Ethnog.* vii. 45 (1894); Mrs. F. Nevill Jackson, *Toys of Other Days* (London, 1908). (S. Cu.)

NŌ DRAMA. In Japan in the beginning of the 15th century, the *Saru-gaku* (lit. "monkey music," consisting of juggling feats and comic remarks with actions to suit) of Yamato province was revolutionized by Kan-nami Kiyotsugu and his son Se-ami Motokiyo, and what is now known as *nō-gaku*, or *nō* music or drama resulted. Not only did these two geniuses, under the encouraging patronage of the Shogun Yoshimasa, build on what was best in their own *Saru-gaku*, but they drew freely from *Den-gaku* (lit. "rice-field music") which had much in common with the *Saru-gaku*. What was graceful in them was ennobled to profundity in the *nō*, while their comical elements developed into *kyogen* (comic performance) usually given in conjunction with the *nō*.

The *nō-gaku* constituted the principal form of entertainment among aristocrats and the warrior class in the feudal Japan. It was sometimes given in the presence of the emperors, and there prevailed a custom for a time to invite the common people to the performances given in commemoration of some happy events by the Tokugawa Shoguns, who used the *nō* on all ceremonial occasions.

Staging.—The *nō* is performed on a wooden stage built above the ground, the regular size of which now is 18 ft. square, open on three sides, with a narrow extension on one side for the singers, and another on the back of the stage for the musicians and attendants. To that rear extension is attached aslant a passage called *hashigakari* (a bridge). The players appear from under the curtain at the one end of which the passage slightly slopes down. The stage, too, is very slightly tilted to the front. For acoustic purposes, big ceramic jars are placed, generally seven under the stage and two or more under the passage according to its length. Three pine saplings are planted at intervals along the front of the bridge. The wooden wall called *kagami-ita* (mirror board) on the back of the rear extension, forming a background to the stage, is always decorated with a painting of a pine tree, and the narrow panel adjoining it on the side with that of bamboo. These paintings, together with the saplings, may be taken to indicate that originally the *nō* was performed in the woods.

Character of the Nō Pieces.—The *nō* pieces, which number more than 250, are classified into five groups for convenience: (1) *waki-nō* (pieces in which *waki*, the secondary character, assumes preponderance in the play) generally dealing with Shinto or Buddhist deities; (2) *Shura-mono*, which commonly deals with ghosts of warriors; (3) *Kazura-mono*, with noble ladies acting the main parts; (4) *Genzai-mono*, or present-day piece, dealing with love, insanity and other manifestations of human nature; (5) pieces dealing with demons or goblins as subjects, or those of congratulatory nature with gay and joyous elements. For each programme of *nō* performance, which generally lasts a whole day, one from each of the above-mentioned five classes is given in the order mentioned, with a *kyogen* between each and generally a dance in an ordinary dress in addition. The whole programme is preceded by a piece called "Okina," which is held in special reverence, the person acting its chief character, Okina, symbolizing the radiant sun-goddess.

Construction of Nō Pieces.—The construction of the *nō* piece, though by no means uniform, is generally as follows. A *waki* (the secondary *rôle*), generally a monk or a minister of State, first appears and tells who he is. Then he walks a while, singing, suggesting that he is travelling. Coming to a standstill, he announces his arrival at a certain famous spot and takes his place by the post at the front right-hand corner facing the stage. Then the *maye jite* (the principal character in the first appearance) comes in the form of a farmer, fisherman or priest, etc., describing the scenery of the place, or speaking to *waki* resting at the post. The *waki* questions him, and the *maye jite* gives an historical account of the place and of heroes connected with it, or relates the origin of the temple or shrine as the case may require, thus furnishing the audience with a necessary background to the play. The *maye jite* then retires in a hurry. He was in reality no other than a Shinto or Buddhist deity, or a ghost of a warrior, in disguise. While *waki* is startled by the sudden disappearance, there come to the stage common farmers or wood-choppers and give in plain language, spoken more or less in the ordinary way, all detailed information concerning the place, generally reiterating what was already given in intonation, and retire. This allows a necessary time for the principal character to change for reappearance. While waiting, the *waki* sings, indicating a lapse of time. When it comes to an end, the *nochi jite* (the principal character in the latter appearance) in proper form and attire as a Shinto or Buddhist deity, or a spirit of a hero, comes to the stage and dances as if in a night stroll, revealing some spiritual attributes. In words and in action he recounts his bravery, his death struggle, or his suffering in the underworld, asking for the prayer of the *waki* for the peaceful repose of his soul. The *shite* tells his story as he performs, or he merely dances without any intonation. Generally there is a chorus who intonate either alone or with the performers.

Music and Accessories.—Generally several persons sitting on the side extension sing either in chorus, by themselves, or together with the performer. The musicians on the rear extension consist ordinarily of a player each on the transverse flute, the *tsuzumi* (small drum struck with tips of fingers over the shoulder), the *ōkawa* (a slightly larger drum struck on the knee also with tips of fingers) and the drum beaten with two sticks.

The accessories used on the stage in connection with the play are very simple. A fan is much in evidence in the dance (*see* FANS), the studied use of which is very effective with the manipulation of big sleeves. Costumes used in the *nō* are marvels of textile fabrics, refined taste being revealed in bold yet harmonious designs and colours. Above all, the mask to be worn by the principal character (*shite*) and the assistant (*shite-zure*) is a very important part of the *nō* performance. There have been great masters among carvers of *nō* masks in the feudal Japan whose works still remain in a large number.

Main Schools.—Ever since the great reformation at the beginning of the 15th century, the *nō* has had four main acknowledged schools or houses: Kwanze, Komparu, Hōshō and Kongō, all of which are still thriving. Later, another school, Kita won official recognition, while still another, Umewaka, also has many followers, the variation upheld by each school being but slight. On the whole, the *nō* performance may well be compared to a masterful oriental picture in black monochrome, both being guided by highly idealistic aims and with artistic aspirations with many points in common, possessing alike great impelling qualities that thrill the devotee and weary the uninitiated. It has greatly influenced the Japanese stage and ordinary forms of dance known as *mai*, or *odori*, and it is bound to continue to do so. (See THEATRE; JAPANESE ART; PANTOMIME.)

BIBLIOGRAPHY.—F. Brinkley, *Japan—Its History, Arts and Literature* (Boston and Tokyo, 1901); Marie C. Stopes and Joji Sakurai, *The "Nō" Plays of Old Japan* (1913); N. Peri, *Cinq Nō, Drama Lyrique Japonais* (1921); A. Waley, *The Nō Plays of Japan* (1921); F. A. Lombard, *An Outline History of the Japanese Drama* (Boston, 1929).

(J. HAR.)

HAKO-NIWA (box-garden or box-yard) is a kind of *bon-tei* or *bon-kei* (qq.v.) generally acknowledged to be a development of *hako-niwa*. It is therefore sometimes difficult to distinguish them. *Hako-niwa* is a small landscape garden in a wooden box, which nowadays is often replaced by a more durable concrete with one or two holes in the bottom for drainage, though the vessel is usually larger and deeper than that used for *bon-kei*. Planted with dwarf trees, bushes and grass, and embellished with natural stones and miniature figures, houses, towers, bridges, etc., of baked clay or bronze, it generally has a small pond for tiny goldfishes. The box-garden is usually placed outside the window or at a corner of the veranda. Unlike *bon-kei*, which is quickly made and remade according to fancy, the *hako-niwa* is meant to last longer and some require years for their completion as in the case of the real landscape garden. Though *hako-niwa*, in its varying forms, has existed in Japan for centuries, it has come to be associated more or less with the people, and has not attained the dignity enjoyed by *bon-seki, bon-sai* or *ike-bana* (qq.v.) and is often no more than a childish amusement. Especially since the popularity of *bon-kei*, the *hako-niwa* has declined, though it is still to be seen in shop windows, at the entrance to workshops, in factory dormitories, or in humble homes.

DANCE. The dance in Japan has its origin in her mythical age. According to the 8th century *Kojiki,* when Amaterasu, the sun-goddess, retired in high dudgeon to a cavern, Ama-no-Uzumeno-mikoto danced at the cavern's mouth to lure her out. *Kagura,* the sacred dance of today, is traced back to this incident by the native literati. Records speak of the emperor Inkyō playing on a *wa-gon* (Japanese native *koto*) and the empress dancing at the imperial banquet given in 419 on the completion of their new palace building. In the Orient the dance is as old as history, and when some 7,000 Chinese families emigrated to Japan in 540 it is not to be doubted that they brought with them their cherished national custom. In 552 a Korean monarch sent a Buddhist mission to Japan and the dance formed a part of their religious ceremony. The old picturesque dance of China and Korea is still executed semi-annually, to the sound of flutes and waving of feathers in worship by the followers of Confucius. The dance became definitely established as a Japanese institution by Ashikaga Shogun Yoshimitsu's (1363–94) school for dancing, and the Shogun himself incorporated many historical themes of China into dramatic dances. With the invention of the *Nō* play by Kwanami Kiotsugu (1406) and its development by his equally famous son, Seami Motokiyo, the dance became closely associated with the national theatre. In the 16th century the fame of the beautiful Okuni popularized the dance among all classes of society. But the tradition begun by her was interrupted in 1643 when, for reasons of public morality, women were forbidden to appear upon the stage; male actors and the priests of Buddha continued the ancient custom of Korea and China. Western ballroom dances, such as waltzes and two-steps, were introduced to Japan in the last quarter of the 19th century and became a fashion for a time, but were soon dropped, and then revived again. (Y. K.)

Visitors to Japan generally return deeply impressed with the beauty of cherry blossoms and the charming grace of the *geisha* girl dance. The dance is performed not only by the *geisha* and other dancing professionals, but is given in connection with the classical *Nō* drama, and it plays an important part in the old style of acting known as *kabuki* for, as an eminent actor of the old school has said, "an actor without ability to dance is like a wrestler without strength." Sacred dances called *kagura*, very simple in character, are given by maidens at some shrines, while Buddhist dances, such as *Nembutsu-odori*, may be seen in connection with some religious observances.

Speaking of the native dance of Japan, three terms are used: *mai, odori* and *furi* or *shosa*, all meaning dance, though technically differentiated. The first has been used to designate the older style of dancing which has been in vogue among the upper class and come to be performed by professionals. It is likened to the graceful movements of the crane at sunrise. The second, which does not appear in literature before the 15th century, has been applied to the dance that was born and has become a fashion among the common people. It means the spontaneous expression of joy with gesture of hands and feet common to all people. The third designates the dance woven into the acting on the stage. *Mai* may be said to designate a classical, *odori* a popular and *furi* a dramatic dance. However, the first may also be classified into two: classical and popular. The classical *mai* is preserved in the imperial court in connection with traditional observances, or in Shinto shrines as *kagura*, or in *Nō* drama, while the popular *mai* is practically the same as *odori* but called *mai* according to the custom peculiar to certain localities. It is generally maintained that in *mai* the attitude is characterized by solemnity, the gesture by elegance and refinement, and the movement by an easy and natural flow, while in *odori* the dance is more natural and free in attitude and movement, and the gesture more active and subtle, with a greater freedom for variation, allowing even a comical or a rustic element to creep in. *Furi* is enlivened with dramatic quality. However, in many instances the distinction is hard, or even impossible, to draw. Moreover, the three terms may be said to represent different essential elements in the dance, rather than its kinds.

The dance of Japan may generally be divided into two classes: the popular and the special or professional. The former is for the pleasure of the mass of people who may acquire the art in several days or weeks, and it includes such dances as *Ise-odori* (time-honoured dance in the province of Ise), *Tanabata-odori* (for the festival of the star Vega) and others connected with popular festivals, as well as such religious dances as *Bon-odori* (held in summer in memory of the dead), *Nembutsu odori* (with Buddhist prayers), etc. The professional dances are acquired only by patient and laborious practice, requiring at least several years to master them. Some of these dances consist purely of graceful movements, while others are enlivened with dramatic elements. Those with dramatic elements try to narrate a story in rhythmic movements or to reveal feelings of joy, anger, sorrow, love, hatred, etc., either expressed or suggested in the songs or music played in accompaniment. The songs so used are of different styles, such as *naga-uta, tokiwazu* and *kiyomoto*, all rendered to the accompaniment of *samisen*, the three-stringed musical instrument, and some with drums and flutes in addition. The songs are descriptive of scenery; narrative of historical or traditional events; accounts of heroes; of love or madness; sometimes they deal with ghosts of men and women, or with the spirit of a lion or of a spider, etc., an effort being often made to transport the observer to the realm of dreams.

The dramatic dance was originally taught by actors themselves until about the beginning of the 18th century, when it became an independent profession. The pioneers of that profession in Tokyo were Denjiro Shigayama, who was originally an actor, Kwambei Fujima and Senzo Nishikawa, each the founder of his own school or style, followed by other masters who formulated styles of their own, each with a number of followers. The most influential styles of dancing in Tokyo are *Fujima-ryu, Hanayagi-ryu,* and *Wakayagi-ryu* (*ryu* meaning style or school). Those of Kyoto are *Inouye-ryu* and *Shinozaki-ryu;* those of Osaka are *Nishikawa-ryu, Yamamura-ryu* and *Umemoto-ryu,* while Nagoya is dominated by *Nishikawa-ryu.* Broadly speaking, the dances in vogue in Tokyo are those with a dramatic element, being bold and active, cheerful and witty in style, more fitting to be performed by men on the stage than in a room, while those of Nagoya, Kyoto and Osaka, which lay great stress upon the grace and charm of movement, are more appropriate to be seen in a room than on the stage, and performed by female rather than male dancers.

According to a rule, the dancer begins at a point one step behind the centre of the stage, and brings the dance to a close at the centre with a stamp of the foot. The first step is to be taken with an "active" effect and the last with a "passive" feeling. Generally the dancer, in the course of the performance, describes a shape of a folding fan, which symbolizes prosperity as it spreads out toward the end. In pose, the face or the head of the dancer is considered to stand for heaven, the shoulders for the earth, and the waist for the man, indicating the three most important points to be considered in the dancing, and suggesting the relation of the one towards the others in the order of the universe. However, all part of the body are used to make the dance well balanced, graceful and effective. While limbs, chiefly arms and hands in an endless variety of graceful sweeps and powerful flourishes, are mainly relied upon for the rhythmic movement, the waist keeps the equilibrium. A fan or a *tenugui* (scarf) is often used in dancing, being manipulated to suggest all sorts of things as the occasion may require. To give a few examples in common practice: an open fan raised gradually in front signifies the rising sun; used in a drinking attitude it may represent a wine cup; a closed fan may be used to suggest a stick, a bow, an arrow, or a gun, etc.; a scarf may be doubled and thrust into the sash to indicate long and short swords worn by a *samurai;* when redoubled and held on the palm in a smoking attitude it may serve as a pipe; or it

DANCE

PLATE II

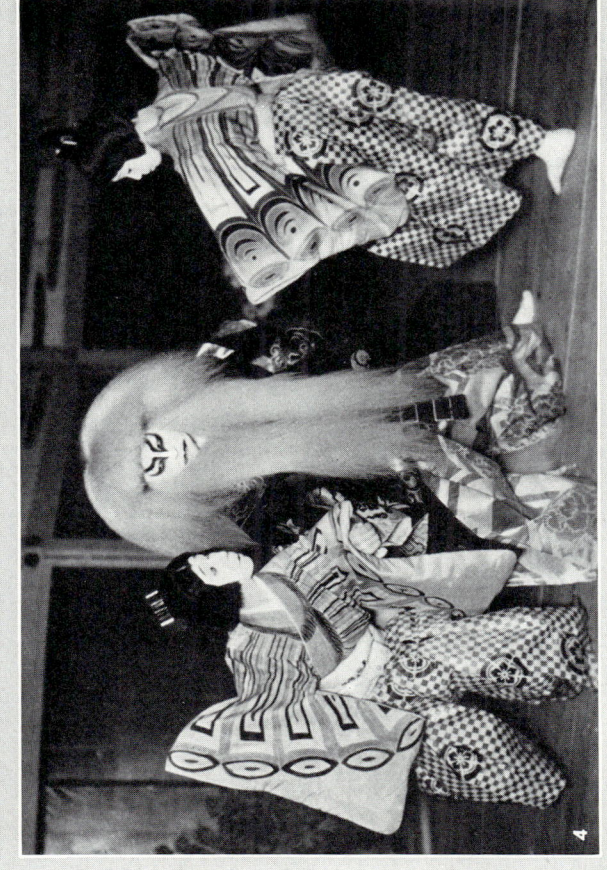

BY COURTESY OF JIRO HARADA

JAPANESE DANCES AS DANCED BY GEISHAS AND ACTORS

1. "Mochizuki," danced by geisha girls of Nagoya
2. Togashi in "Kwanjinchō," danced by an actor
3. "Dojoji," danced by geisha of Nagoya (Naga-uta)
4. Dance of the Lion with Butterflies, danced by actors

PLATE III DANCE

BY COURTESY OF JIRO HARADA

CHARACTERISTIC DANCES OF JAPAN

1. Ghost of umbrella in "Hyaku Monogatari," danced by an actor. 2. Dance called Manzai in "Noriai-bune," danced by actors. 3. "Kagami-jishi," danced by an actor. 4. "Fuji-musume" (wistaria-maid), danced by a girl dancer. 5. "Dojoji," a favorite dance, named after the monastery where it originated. 6. Fox in "Tadanobu," danced by a geisha of Nagoya. 7. "Dojoji," danced by a geisha of Nagoya. 8. Dancing with a *tenugui* (scarf) in "Kisen." 9 "Dojoji," by a girl dancer. 10. "Sagi-musume" (heron-maid) danced by a geisha of Nagoya

SEALS

PLATE II

BY COURTESY OF (1, 3) YAMANAKA AND COMPANY, (2) ALAN R. PRIEST, (4, 5, 6) MRS. ALFRED E. COHN

CHINESE SEALS

1. Ivory seal with lion handle, probably late 19th century. Inscription, Mu-Ch'en, evidently an intimate name of Chang En-Jung. 2. Contemporary soapstone seal with lion handle. Inscription, P'u Ai-Lun. 3. Late 19th century ivory seal, lion handle. Inscription, Chang En-Jung. 4, 5, 6. Set of three seals made of soapstone with lion handles. 4 and 6 give the full name of original owner, T'ai Na-Fu. 5 gives only the given name, which probably in this case was used as the tzu or intimate name. The name appears to be Manchu

may be made to describe running water by holding one end of it and giving it a quick succession of jerks from side to side.

It has been the ideal of some great master dancers of Japan to give the dance dignity, refinement and charm by investing it with idealistic, rather than realistic, quality; to make it suggestive, rather than merely explanatory; to create an interesting design, rather than a conglomeration of decorations. The dance of Japan is unique, and rich in beauty and tradition as the cherry blossoms that adorn the country in spring. (J. Har.; Y. K.)

SEALS. The use of seals for the purposes of identification and ornament has existed in China since earliest times and was emulated in Korea and in Japan from the inception of her imitation of Chinese usages and manners. The word seal may be applied with equal propriety to the stamped impression and the object with which the impression is made. These impressions appear in an infinite variety of shapes and sizes, the more common shapes being square, oblong, elliptical, round and gourd-shaped. In size they run from the huge imperial seals (sometimes as large as $4\frac{7}{8}''$ by $6\frac{5}{8}''$) to miniature seals which are often as small as $\frac{1}{8}$ in. square or in diameter. The ink used is usually a vermilion red, but black and purple are also employed.

Seals have two general uses: one is for identification, the equivalent of a personal signature or guarantee; the other, while it often identifies, is almost purely ornamental and has no legal significance whatever. The identification seal must bear the *hsing* (姓) or family name of its owner, and the *ming* (名), which is the equivalent of our Christian name. It must be understood that the Chinese use several varieties of individual names, so that when we translate the *hao* (號) or intimate name as nickname, we are incorrect, nickname being properly the translation of what the Chinese call *wai-hao* (外號), which is very rarely if ever used on seals. The *hao* is an intimate name often selected by the bearer himself or given to him by his friends as being appropriate to his pursuits or character. The Chinese also use another intimate name, the *tzŭ* (字) (sometimes absurdly and meaninglessly translated as "style") which is created in much the same manner as the *hao*, except that it properly carries some direct literary allusion to the *ming*, and is in its use somewhat more elegant and formal than the *hao*. On ornamental seals the *hao* or *tzŭ* may be used with or without the *hsing*, but in practice usually without. The *ming* may be employed on ornamental seals without the *hsing*. A painter is much more likely to sign his *hao* or *tzu* and stamp his ornamental seal or seals underneath his signature than he is to use his full legal name and seals.

It is very difficult to generalize about Chinese seals because of the frequent departures that Chinese writers and artists indulge in, especially with their ornamental seals. An artist may have as many as, say, 50 to 100 seals, bearing his *ming*, *tzŭ*, *hao* or *wai-hao*, the name of his studio, the name of his native district with his family name, etc. These different names, with such characters as *yin* (印), *chang* (章), *chih yin* (之印, seal of), etc., present an almost inexhaustible possibility for variations. Sometimes the identical inscriptions are duplicated or triplicated in different styles of writing. Saito Ken's *Signatures and Seals of Chinese Artists* (支那畫家落欵印譜, *Shina Kwaka Rakkwan Infu*, Tokyo, 1906), gives reproductions of 38 seals used by Tung Ch'i-ch'ang (董其昌), an artist of the Ming dynasty, and these do not purport to be exhaustive. As well as personal and official seals, there are countless seals bearing the names of temples, public offices, palace halls, personal libraries, manufactories, shops, family seals, and even, on occasion, small houses.

The materials of which seals are made are as varied as the seals themselves. Practically any hard, fine-grained stone may be used, with the semi-precious stones preferred. Metals are used also, most commonly bronze but, on occasion, gold and silver, either solid or plated. The cheapest and most common materials in general business and private use are wood and soapstone, the latter often as beautifully carved as the rarest jade.

The type of character most used is the *chuan* (篆), which we translate as "seal character," but there is great latitude in the arrangement and period of the characters employed, archaic and historic forms being very popular. Flourishes, embellishments and variations are often indulged in (in spite of the fact that the practice is frowned upon by writers on the subject), making it exceedingly difficult to read or decipher the inscriptions. See Hsüeh Ku Pien (學古編), *Studies in Antiquities*, a work on seals written by Wu Chi-ch'eng of the Yüan dynasty, quoted in the *Ku Chin T'u Shu Chi Ch'êng* (古今圖書集成), the K'ang Hsi Encyclopaedia. The lines of the characters may be raised or depressed, giving, in the first instance, vermilion lines against a white background, and in the second, white lines against a vermilion background. The first are variously known as *yang wên* (陽文) or "male" writing, and *chu wên* (朱文) or vermilion writing; the second as *yin wên* (陰文) or "female" writing, and *pai wên* (白文) or white writing. In describing seals, writers invariably mention which of these two styles is used. Seals usually have only one inscription, but early seals, usually made of brass, with inscriptions on both ends or on all six sides, were not uncommon.

There are references to seals in the Four Books (四書) and Five Classics (五經). The *Chi Chia Chou Shu* (汲冢周書) (history of the Chou dynasty unearthed in the 4th century A.D. at Chi, quoted in the K'ang Hsi Encyclopaedia) tells us that when T'ang (湯), the founder of the Shang dynasty (1767–1122 B.C.) deposed Chieh (桀), the last of the Hsia (2205–1767 B.C.) emperors, and convened the feudal princes, he placed the imperial seal at the seat of the emperor. The first report of the use of seals in what we would call authenticated history is in the *Tso Chuan* (左傳, the commentaries of Tso-ch'iu Ming, 左丘明, on *Spring and Autumn Annals*, 春秋 of Confucius, quoted in the K'ang Hsi Encyclopaedia) which tells us: "In the 29th year of Duke Hsiang of Lu (魯襄公, 544 B.C.) the Duke was at Ch'u (楚) for the funeral of Prince K'ang (康王). When he was at Fang Ch'eng (方城) Chi Wu Tzŭ (季武子 the minister of Lu) took possession of Pien (汴) and sent Kung Yeh (公冶) with a sealed document (*hsi shu*, 璽書) to report the matter to Duke Hsiang." We must not infer, however, that this was the beginning of the use of seals, for if it was, the philosopher Chuang Chou (莊周, 4th to 3rd century B.C.) would not have attacked its vogue, declaring that men would return to simplicity and virtue if "tallies were burned and seals destroyed." In fact, it is safe to assume from this pronouncement of Chuang Chou that seals were in general use centuries before his time, probably throughout the Chou dynasty (1122–256 B.C.).

From then on the use and classification of seals became exceedingly complicated. In general seals may be classified as *yin* (印) and *hsi* (璽). The latter character has come to be applied to the seals of the emperor and other important members of the imperial family, such as the empress, the crown prince and ex-emperors; and the former to seals of officials and private individuals, though in ancient times, as late as the Han dynasty, the two characters were used synonymously. It must be observed, however, that during the Han dynasty the distinction began to apply.

In the *Han Chiu I* (漢舊儀, a work on the organization of the governmental machinery by Wei Hung [衞宏] of the Han dynasty) the following regulations were provided for the use of seals: (1) Seals of feudal princes, *chu hou wang* (諸候王), are to be known as *hsi* (璽), to be made of yellow gold with camel knob or handle. (2) Seals of nobles, *lieh hou* (列侯), are to be known as *yin* (印) and are to be made of yellow gold with tortoise knobs. (3) Seals of ministers or generals are to be known as *chang* (章), to be made of gold with tortoise knobs. (4) Seals of officials with a pension of 2,000 piculs of grain or more are to be known as *chang*, to be made of silver with tortoise knobs. (5) Seals of officials with pensions from 400 to 1,000 piculs of grain are to be known as *yin*, to be made of brass with nose (*pi*, 鼻) knobs.

At the present day such regulations if they exist at all are completely disregarded by the average Chinese, who uses any form he chooses on his personal seals even to representations of landscape. The broadest classification is perhaps the one followed by the *Chi Ku Yin P'u* (集古印譜, *Collection of Ancient Seals* by Wang Chang 王常, 1575) which divides all seals into two main categories: (1) *Kuan Yin* (官印), official or public seals, or, in other words, seals that indicate rank or office. (2) *Ssu Yin* (私印), private seals, used by individuals. Under each main classification the material and the type of knob are mentioned. Private seals may be further classified, as in the *Chieh Tzŭ Yüan Shu Hua Chuan* (芥子園書畫傳, *The Mustard Seed Garden Cyclopaedia of Painting and Calligraphy*, by Li Li-weng, 李笠翁, 1679) which gives six classifications with suggestions as to how each class is to be made: (*a*) *Ming yin* or name seal (名印) used as means of identification. Only such words as *yin*, seal (印), *hsin* (信, faith), *yin chang* (印章, seal), *chih yin* (之印) and *chih chang* (之章), seal of; *ssŭ yin*, private seal (私印) should be used after the *hsing* (surname) and *ming* (given name) without other embellishments. (*b*) *Tzŭ yin* or intimate name seal (字印), originated during the T'ang and Sung dynasties, should be used only for ornamentation and not for identification. It should not contain such words as *yin* and *hsin*. The character *shih* (氏), family, alone should be used. (*c*) *Ch'en yin* or subject seal (臣印). All under heaven are the subjects (臣) of the emperor. Therefore anyone can prefix the character *ch'en* to his name, omitting the surname. It was extensively used during the Han dynasty. (*d*) *Hao yin* (號印), another intimate name seal may include *wai hao*. Such terms as *tao jen* (道人), Taoist person, *chü shih* (居士), resident, *i shih*, retired scholar (逸士), *chu jen* (主人), master, may be used with one's *hao* or the name of one's "retreat." (*e*) *Chien shu yin* (箋書印), or letter seal. During the Ch'in and Han dynasties only the name seal was used after one's signature but lately seals bearing inscriptions such as "so-and-so discourses affairs," "so-and-so announces affairs," etc., are beginning to be used. (*f*) *Shou ts'ang yin* (收藏印) or collector's seal. This class of seals also had their origin in the T'ang and Sung dynasties. Either the name, the *tzŭ* or the *hao* may be used followed by such expressions as *chien shang chang* (鑒賞章, seal of critical examination and enjoyment), *chên ts'ang* (珍藏, treasured and guarded), etc.

The first seal to have much historical backing was the imperial seal made by Chin Shih Huang Ti with a piece of Lan T'ien (藍田) jade of rare quality, with a *li* (螭, one-horned dragon) knob and the following inscription: *Shou t'ien chih ming huang ti shou ch'ang* (受天之命皇帝壽昌, by the command of heaven, long-lived and glorious the emperor). This seal was handed down to the Hans. Since then it has come to be known as the *ch'uan kuo hsi* (傳國璽, seal of succession of the empire) and looked upon as the essential symbol of imperial authority. Six additional imperial seals were made, according to the *Han Chiu I*. The first was used for creating princes, etc., the second for letters and documents to the feudal princes, the third for orders for mobilization, etc., and the fourth for treaties, etc., with tributary States. In succeeding dynasties various forms of imperial seals were made, but it is beyond the confines of this article to enumerate them. We might observe, however, that Empress Wu Tse T'ien (武則天) of the T'ang dynasty changed the character *hsi* to *pao* (寶, treasure) and that this character has since prevailed as the name of the imperial seal with the exception of the two T'ang emperors immediately following the empress. During the reign of these two emperors the imperial seal was again known as *hsi*. We might observe further that the *ch'uan kuo hsi* of Ch'in Shih Huang Ti survived, through many vicissitudes, to the reign of Emperor Fei Ti (廢帝 A.D. 934-936) of the Posterior T'ang dynasty (後唐) who perished with the seal in the flames rather than surrender to the Posterior Chin dynasty (後晉). In 1098 a seal purporting to be the genuine *ch'uan kuo hsi* was discovered and offered to Emperor Che Tsung (哲宗) but this was later discredited as was a still later seal discovered (A.D. 1295) in the Yuan dynasty. (*See also* FAR EASTERN ART.)

See also essays, monographs, memorials, etc., by writers of the Sung Yüan and Ming dynasties reprinted in the K'ang Hsi Encyclopaedia.
(A. R. PR.)

DRESS. In A.D. 283 two women weavers were sent from Korea to Japan to teach the making of figured silks and brocades. The *ho*, or ceremonial garment of the Japanese emperor and nobles, has an ancient origin; the Chinese seamstresses came to Japan, about A.D. 300 and made this with silk imported from China. Emperor Yuryaku (A.D. 457-479) reformed the national dress and, in the reign of Emperor Suiko (A.D. 593), rank was signified by distinctive head-gear, a custom imitated from that of the Chinese T'ang dynasty (A.D. 618-906). Costumes were evolved for civilians, ecclesiastics and the militia, differing in colour, patterns, the length of sleeves and the style of hairdressing.

The *kasane*, or loose tunic, was worn with a short lower garment called the *akome*. The *hakama* was a loose skirt reaching only a few inches below the knees over the *shita-gutsu*, or socks. The whole style of head-gear was called *suberakashi*. *Kammuri*, a ceremonial headdress, was secured by *kanjashi*, or pins and the *yeboshi*, or cap, was worn over it. The court ladies wore the *goi*, a garment of embroidered silk, and over it the *karaginu*, which was a short tunic. Over this again, but at the back only, was another smaller garment known as the *mo*. These persisted until the Meiji era (1868-1912), when the emperor himself began to wear Western dress and in 1885 ordered his court to do the same.

The ladies always wear the *kimono*, a loose gown with a neckpiece called an *eri*, and long sleeves, the garment being fastened by a belt. Since the Heian period (794-1159) women have in general dispensed with the *hakama*, and to-day the female dress for social occasions consists of an underskirt, two or three outer garments and a *haori*, or interlined silk coat, over the upper part. The *obi*, a belt about 3 yd. long and 10 in. wide, winds about the figure two or three times. A silk band or gold buckle keeps the bow from shifting at the back. *Tabi*, or socks, are secured above the ankle. The cord by which sandals, or *zori*, are fastened passes between the first and second toes. Coco-nut oil is used by women as a pomade in rolling the hair.

Men in rural districts are barefooted, seldom wear *zori* or the wooden clogs called *geta*, and in the hot season almost no clothing. The common-jacket and trousers of cotton crêpe, blue or white, a large grass hat called *kaza* and straw *zori* are the ordinary dress.
(Y. K.)

TEA CEREMONY is a time-honoured institution in Japan—an institution rooted in the principles of Zen (a sect of Buddhism) and founded upon the adoration of the beautiful in the daily routine of life, such as preparing a meal and tea, cleaning the house and garden, etc. The Japanese word for tea ceremony, *Cha-no-yu*, literally hot water of tea, means an aesthetic way of entertaining guests, usually five at a time with thick and weak tea of pulverized tea-leaf whipped in hot water, preceded by a meal, according to the established rules of etiquette. The entertainment takes place in the tea-room (*chaseki*), usually a small building constructed to suggest a refined poverty, though with great forethought and after endless trouble in the choice of the material and in the construction. The room in which the guests are entertained is generally about 9 ft. square, or smaller, containing an alcove for ornaments and a small fire-place for boiling the kettle, sunk into the floor. Into that room each guest in humility crawls through a small opening less than 3 ft. square. It is connected with the waiting room by stepping stones through a garden path (*roji*), which should contain a water basin (*tsukubai*) for the guests to rinse mouth and wash hands before entering the tea-room.

In this ancient institution which still continues to influence the life of the Japanese people and all their art, the spirit of old Japan still lives.

BIBLIOGRAPHY.—E. S. Morse, *Japanese Homes and Their Surroundings* (1885); F. Brinkley, *Japan—Its History, Arts and Literature* (1901); Kukuzo Okakura, *The Book of Tea* (1906). (J. HAR.)

SCREEN. Because of their fragile nature, no screens of great antiquity have survived, but references to them are not wanting in ancient literature. Folding screens were known in China as early as the 2nd century B.C., at which period glass or mica panellings for them are noted as of value, their transparent nature affording both enjoyment of an outdoor view and shelter from the elements. Then, in the century preceding the Christian era, screens carved and inlaid with jade and other precious materials seem to have been produced. Already in this early period the art of painting screens was practised, for it is recorded that

TEA CEREMONY

PLATE I

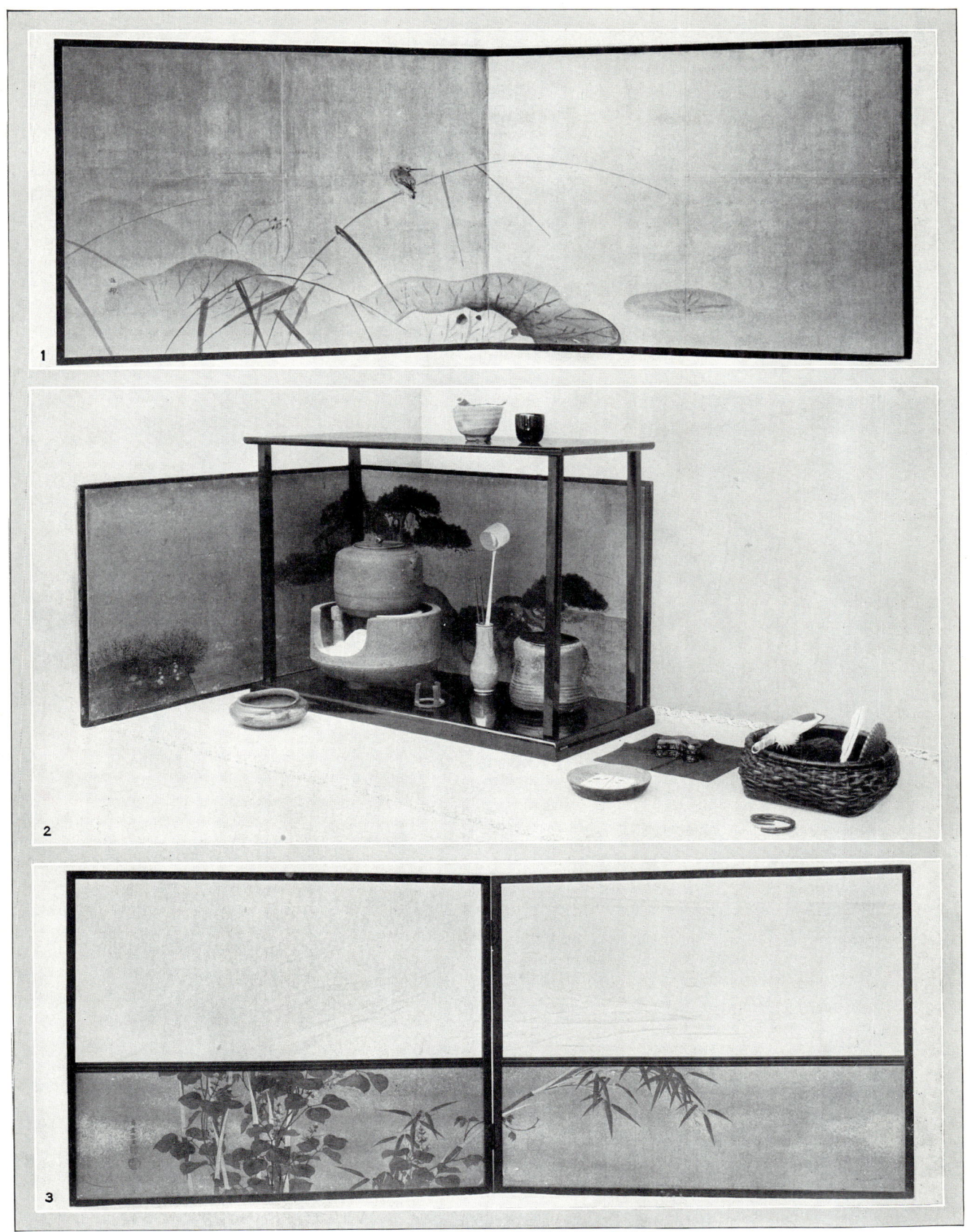

BY COURTESY OF (1, 3) THE TOKYO IMPERIAL HOUSEHOLD MUSEUM, (2) THE METROPOLITAN MUSEUM OF ART, NEW YORK

TEA SET AND SCREENS USED IN THE TEA CEREMONY

1. Furosaki-byobu tea screen painted by Hashimoto Gahō, 20th century. Height, about 2½ ft.; length of each panel, 3 feet
2. Daisu (shelf) with tea ceremony utensils
3. Tea screen by Kō Sūkoku

PLATE II
TEA CEREMONY

BY COURTESY OF JIRO HARADA

METHOD OF PREPARING TEA FOR THE TEA CEREMONY

1. The host has just brought in a basket of charcoal to replenish the fire in the brasier and a case of incense to perfume the room. There is an art and science in making the fire; a rhythmic motion in manipulating the charcoal with a pair of iron sticks, and the placing of the charcoal is well thought out to enable it to ignite and blaze up quickly
2. Having brought in everything to the cha-seki (tea-room) and sitting in front of the iron kettle, which murmurs tranquilly like the lone pine tree by the sea, the host is making obeisance before proceeding to prepare the tea
3. Picking up the dipper made of bamboo, which he holds before him as if he were holding a mirror, the host is shown in a pose just before proceeding to remove the lid of the kettle

4. Having removed the lid of the kettle the host is pouring hot water into the tea bowl to rinse it and also the bamboo whisk to be used for stirring the pulverized tea in hot water
5. The host is about to take the lid off the water jar. Of the infinite number of ways in which the lid may be removed, only one, the most beautiful, way is insisted on. Each movement must be beautiful, not only in itself, but in its relation to that which precedes and that which follows it
6. Having placed a quantity of pulverized tea in the bowl, the host is taking up the dipper to get hot water from the kettle and to pour it over the tea to be whipped with a bamboo whisk already rinsed. The pulverized tea is kept in a keramic or lacquered caddy, and a bamboo or ivory scoop is used for taking out the tea

TEA CEREMONY

PLATE III

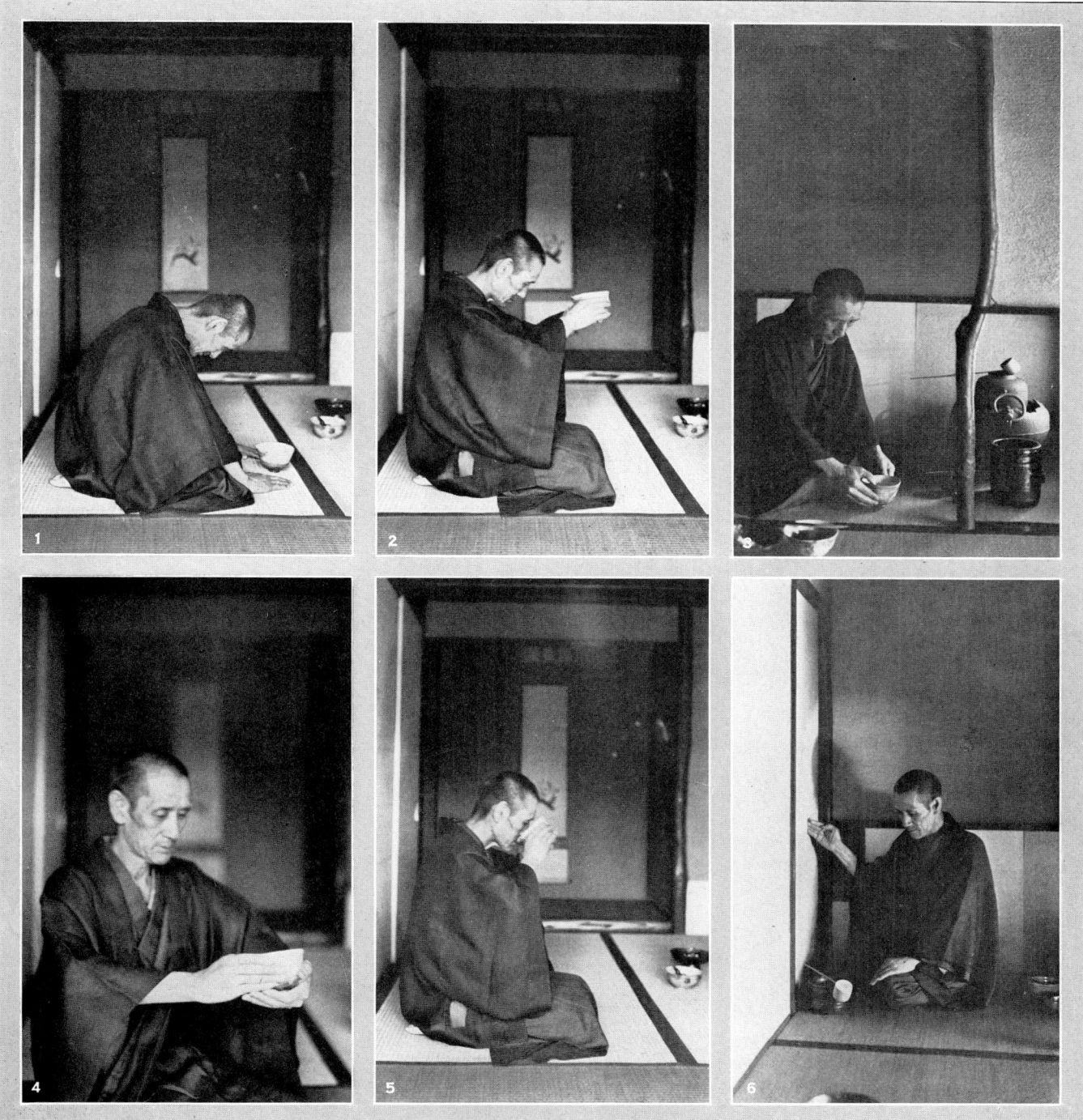

BY COURTESY OF JIRO HARADA

ETIQUETTE OBSERVED BY HOST AND GUEST IN THE TEA CEREMONY

1. After having eaten the sweet, the guest receives the bowl of tea, places it on the mat upon which he sits, and makes obeisance to the host before taking it up to drink
2. The guest holding up the bowl of tea to his forehead in token of respect before proceeding to drink. His mind should be so perfectly calm and attuned to higher things of life that it may be susceptible to any aesthetic suggestion the bowl of tea may bring
3. The host about to offer a bowl of tea to the guests who, having finished their tea, persuade him to partake of it, having placed the sweets near him. This pose shows the host in the act of picking up the bowl to place it towards the guests before accepting it for himself
4. The bowl should be held secure in both hands, its perfect balance in the hands being essential to the maintenance of the mental equilibrium. The bowl thus held, the beauty of the green beverage, whose bubbles may suggest the evanescence of life, must not escape notice
5. Drinking the tea in three sips and a half, the last being accompanied by an appreciative sound of drawing the last drop. After wiping the edge where his lips touched, he looks into the bowl for the tea design may perchance give him a clue for an aesthetic contemplation and the beauty of the bowl should not escape his appreciation
6. The host after everybody has finished drinking the tea is about to open the sliding door to take away the utensils from the cha-seki (tea-room). Etiquette requires that he be on his knees when opening or shutting the sliding screens

PLATE IV   TEA CEREMONY

BY COURTESY OF JIRO HARADA

ETIQUETTE OBSERVED BY HOST AND GUEST IN THE TEA CEREMONY

1. *Usu-cha* (thin tea). The host is about to drink tea at the persuasion of the guests after they have finished drinking theirs. In the cha-seki belonging to Mr. Miyazaki, a tea-master in Nagoya. 2. *Koi-cha* (thick tea). The head guest is receiving the bowl of tea from the hostess. In the *cha-seki* (tea-room) belonging to Mr. Miyazaki, a tea-master in Nagoya. 3. The hostess is ready to prepare tea in the *hiro-ma* (large room). 4. *Cha-seki* in the garden of the Katsura detached palace in the suburb of Kyoto. 5, 7. Ceramic tea caddies with ivory lids. 6, 12. Iron kettles used in tea ceremony. They have extra pieces of iron stuck to the inside bottom so that the kettles, when the water becomes heated, may murmur even as the lone pine tree by the sea. 8. A ceramic tea caddy, with three brocade bags belonging to it. Bags contain dummies so as to keep them in shape. 9. Ceramic water jar used in the tea ceremony. 10. Carved lacquer incense case, used in tea ceremony. 11. Ceramic tea bowl for drinking the pulverized green tea whipped in hot water in the tea ceremony

"Figures of Exemplary Women," illustrating the good or evil effects from right or wrong-doing were depicted on a screen. The Chinese artist Ts'ao Pu-hsing (3rd century) having dropped ink upon a screen while painting, turned it into a fly which Sun Ch'üan (A.D. 181–252) tried to brush away. Shih Hu (3rd century) made a folding screen covered with silk and painted with hermits, birds and animals, to which he added a long inscription. Chang Mo (4th century) depicted on screens the Buddhist saint, Vimalakirti, and a scene entitled "Beating Newly-woven Silk." In passing, mention may be made of a 14-fold screen in the scroll attributed to Ku K'ai-chih (4th century), owned by the British Museum, confirming the accuracy of contemporary accounts that screens consisted of numerous leaves, sometimes as many as 40. In the 5th century, Lu T'an-wei painted a lion and Fang Huai-chên the "Paragons of Filial Piety." Landscapes were not unknown in these early centuries as themes for screens, for they are referred to in old poems and other writings. Screens of tapestry, of embroidery, of crystal and of lacquer are also recorded in contemporary literature. Moreover, fine calligraphy inscribing moral teachings or auspicious sentiments was executed on screens from the 5th century, if not earlier. It is said that Fang Hsüang-ling (A.D. 578–648) collected precepts from all sources and inscribed them on screens which he distributed among his children as reminders of proper conduct.

The T'ang Period.—In the luxurious days of the T'ang dynasty (618–906), screens were in constant demand to adorn palaces and mansions. Those which were bedecked with gold and silver, pearl and tortoise shell, or those of fine textiles woven or dyed, bearing characteristic patterns, must have imparted great splendour to the habitations of rulers and princes. Horses sent from foreign tribes to the imperial stables furnished themes for screens, and a fabulous animal called *mo* which is supposed to eat bad dreams was deemed an appropriate subject for boudoir screens. Then, too, such noted painters as Pien Luan (who treated flowers and birds), Chang Tsao (pines and rocks), and Chou Fang (court beauties), and such accomplished calligraphers as Li Yang-ping and Chang Hsü all decorated screens. Some emperors had about them screens setting forth worthy and moral deeds performed by men of the past, in order that they themselves, as well as their subjects, might derive benefit from these constant reminders.

But for actual examples of T'ang art on screens we have to turn to Japan where, in the Imperial repository called the Shōsōin, at Nara, are still preserved relics of the art of that golden epoch. This treasure-house contains principally the personal belongings of the Emperor Shōmu, which were given to the Great Buddha of the Tōdaiji by the Empress Kōmyō, in 756. The list of donations mentions, among other objects, 100 screens, to which several more were added, at three different times, between the years 756 and 758. Among this large number of screens were examples of Chinese, Korean or Japanese origin which included paintings of landscapes, palaces, figures and flowers; others of batik and of block-resist dyeing, figuring birds, animals and flowers; and, in addition, some screens on which Chinese ideographs formed the chief decoration. Of these 100 odd screens but few remain at present, in whole or in part, among them no painted screens. Nevertheless, the pictorial accomplishments of the 8th century may still be seen in this collection in a six-fold screen, in each leaf of which is shown a figure of a woman standing under a tree. The subject was originally worked in birds' feathers which have disappeared, leaving only the preliminary drawings. Despite the sketchy nature of the drawings of the figures, trees and rocks, one may detect the mature brush-strokes, the importance of which is so much emphasized in the art of painting in the Far East. The screen is probably Japanese, yet its conception and execution are based upon contemporary Chinese patterns. There are also two six-fold screens in this imperial collection, the chief decorative features of which are Chinese inscriptions in large characters. One (Plate III., fig. 1) contains a precept for a ruler, consisting of 48 Chinese ideographs, each written twice, once in the *chuan* ("seal") style and once in the *hsing* ("running") style. The backgrounds are of silk dyed in green and red—alternating in the six panels—bearing designs of conventionalized clouds, birds, animals, trees, plants and rocks, all in white reserve. The screen is very likely Chinese, one of many gifts sent to the Japanese court from China, although it is said that at one time there was discovered upon it a Japanese date corresponding to the year 751—a fact lacking substantiation. In the Orient, to use writing on a large scale for a decorative scheme is no less frequent than to employ a picture for the purpose. Indeed, good calligraphy (*q.v.*) is considered an art of as great importance as good painting, both being the result of brush-work and both presenting images of mental conception.

An example of the pictorial art of the T'ang as reflected in the art of Japan may be seen in a screen (Plate III., fig. 2), preserved in the Buddhist monastery of Tōji in Kyoto. It treats a landscape in polychrome: among trees surrounded by hills and water is a rustic abode within which sits a hermit who is being visited by nobles with their servants. According to an old tradition, the screen was one of the treasures brought back by Kōbō Daishi from China in 806. However, some authorities now regard the painting as a Japanese production of the 11th century, based upon a T'ang original. For, despite its Chinese design, in it are discernible certain technical peculiarities of the early Yamato-é (literally "Japanese picture") style which was developed during the Fujiwara period (900–1189) and is characterized by over-refinement of drawings. Such a landscape screen was used in the baptismal rituals of esoteric Buddhism which required a pictorial representation of a mountain scene in lieu of the natural setting in which the religious service took place in old India. No screens of a secular nature dating from the Fujiwara period are now extant, but literary sources disclose the thousands of screens painted for the use of the Japanese court and for the mansions of nobles. As in the preceding epoch, the need for screens was pressing, because of the peculiar style of the architecture of those days—wide openings on the sides of a building which were closed by wooden doors at night but which during the day needed screening arrangements. Regular and occasional State functions also required special screens appropriate to the events. That a large number of screens was produced may be gathered from the record that Yoshichika (11th century) painted 200 screens on Lord Yoshimichi's order. A story is told about Hirotaka (10th century) who delineated a scene of hell containing a demon who proved so lifelike as to convince the artist that the call to the unknown region was immediate. The subjects, some Chinese and some Japanese, mentioned in this period are varied and numerous: landscapes of the four seasons, monthly observances, trees and plants, falconry, picnics, polo-playing, the paragons of noble deeds, the descent of the Amitābha, the ten Buddhist regions, etc. In Japan, during the Kamakura period (1190–1336), in making screens they followed the preceding Fujiwara in the main, both pictorially and technically.

The Sung Period.—In China itself in the Sung period (960–1279), the practice among prominent masters of painting and inscribing screens was not abandoned. On the contrary, painters like Tuan Yüan, Yen Hsiao, Wên T'ung and Hsü Tao-ning are known to have thus expressed their art; and noted calligraphers applied their brushes after the time-honored custom. The most significant branch of the art of the Sung period was the so-called Idealistic school of painting which was closely followed by the artists of the Yüan (1280–1367) and Ming (1365–1643) dynasties. Painters of this school attempted to express in their works certain noble thoughts and ideals. A landscape-painting, for example, was an essay which suggested the sublimity of nature and invited the beholder to identify himself with it. The inherent love of nature of the orientals, coupled with the teaching of *Ch'an* (in Japanese, *Zen*), produced artists who showed remarkable aptitude for depicting natural phenomena. *Ch'an* means "abstract meditation," the chief aim of its followers being to seek to separate the real from the unreal by divesting themselves of earthly thoughts and desires and by communing directly with nature. Inspired by this teaching, the artists developed marked individuality and their paintings were characterized by purity and suggestiveness. For their themes, the painters of the Idealistic school chose, beside landscapes, birds, animals and even withered trees and rocks, all of which ordinarily were treated in monochrome with China ink. Unfortunately there exists no example of the typical art of the Sung as applied on screens, nor are there any screens dating from the subsequent Yüan and Ming dynasties, in both of which it is recorded that painted and inscribed screens were produced. It is possible, however, that some of the paintings coming from these periods, now mounted as single hangings, were once panels of folding screens.

The Ashikaga Period.—Again turning to Japan, one can see an echo of the Chinese art of these three dynasties in paintings by Japanese artists of the Ashikaga period (1337–1573). Sōtan, Nōami, Sesshū, Masanobu and Motonobu are outstanding figures who painted in ink on screens after the Chinese idealists. A screen by Sōtan (Plate IV., fig. 1), who died in 1464, may be taken as a typical specimen of this style. The vigour of the brush, the subtle quality of the ink, the well-carried-out atmospheric perspective—all tell of the master hand which portrays the spirit of majestic nature. This screen is one of a pair which together show landscapes of the four seasons treated as one composition and consequently forming one composite whole. Beside the "Twelve Monthly Observances" and "Landscapes of the Four Seasons," such themes as "Flowers of the Four Seasons," "Farmers of the Four Seasons," "Lives of the 24 Paragons of Filial Piety," the "Eight Taoist Immortals," etc., frequently occur as single designs. The Idealistic school of painting was carried through the next period, the Momoyama (1574–1602), by artists of the Kano, the Unkoku and the Soga schools. In the screen (Plate IV., fig. 2) by Tōhaku (1539–1610) we see a remarkable monochrome; the varied shades of China ink being so used as to suggest the presence of colours, yet with no disturbing element of pigments and no sense of monotony.

A new type of screen introduced some time in the 14th century from Korea contributed much toward revolutionizing the general scheme of composition. Heretofore, a folding screen had consisted of a group of separate panels, each with brocaded borders, tied together by means of cords passing through holes pierced at the vertical edges of the panels (Plate III., fig. 1). In the Korean type the leaves were joined by paper hinges which were built into the body of the screen before the silk or paper for painting was pasted, a brocade border extending over the composite whole (see Plate IV.). Whereas in the former style the continuance of the design was interfered with by the frame and the brocade borders of each panel, in the latter style the tightly joined leaves made one surface for painting a picture.

Screens characteristic of the Momoyama period, the inherent love of the Japanese for simplicity notwithstanding, are more decorative in type, with backgrounds of gold leaf upon which appear bold designs in solid pigments on a massive scale. Eitoku (1545–90), who was the chief exponent of the style, is said to have supplied 100 pairs of screens for the Momoyama palace of the Taikō. He painted in two styles, ink and polychrome; the polychrome screens are very effective; for example, one of a pair in which are shown foreigners bringing tribute to the Chinese emperor, Tai-tsung, of the T'ang dynasty; the subject—"Barbarians Presenting Tribute"—being symbolic of the peace and prosperity of the country. The popular pictorial motives on screens at this time were "The Dragon and the Tiger," "Lions," "Old Pine Trees" (respectively symbolizing the conflict between spirit and matter, nobility and power, longevity and fidelity).

The Tokugawa Period.—In Japan during the Tokugawa period (1603–1868), a new movement in decorative painting was developed by Sōtatsu (1576–1643) who preserved the vigorous and broad brush-work practised by the masters in monochrome, but in place of ink used pigments on a gold ground. Even as he adopted the coloring of the old Yamato-é, so he took many themes from old sources, such as the romances of Genji and Isé, the wars of the Hogen and Heiji Eras, the wind and thunder gods. He was also a genius in the impressionistic treatment of flowers and waterscapes on screens. Following Sōtatsu's style, Kōrin (1658–1716) further enlarged upon decorativeness by introducing more brilliant colours and more daring composition. In the twofold screen (fig. 6) depicting violent waves is apparent this artist's largeness of conception and power of technique. In the Tokugawa days, artists in all schools—the Kano, the Tosa, the Genre, the Literary, the Realistic—exerted their artistic efforts on screens. In principle, the pictorial scheme for screens by these painters of varied styles had changed little from that of the preceding Ashikaga and Momoyama periods and it is still continued to-day. A bold design is treated in dissymmetry, yet is well balanced and effective; at the same time it bears a certain moral, historical, legendary or auspicious significance. The subjects treated were many and varied, including those which have already been referred to and also such themes as the "Eight Views of Hsiao Hsing," the "Ten Snow-Incidents," the "A-fang Pleasance," the "Four Gray-beards of the Shan Mountain," the "Seven Sages of the Bamboo Grove," the "Four Accomplishments," "Floating Fans," "Phoenixes," etc. Generally Japanese screens are six-fold, about 6 ft. in height and 12 ft. in width when stretched, and they are usually executed in pairs. Among the smaller type we may count "pillow" screens with brightly coloured pictures, which are placed about beds, and low, two-fold screens with simple decoration, or none at all, which are used in connection with the tea-ceremony (q.v.).

The Ch'ing Dynasty.—During the Ch'ing dynasty (1644–1911) in China, painting on screens was practised, as indicated by the presence of occasional examples dating from the last few centuries. But it is in screens of applied art that the period excels. It has already been said that the application of the minor arts to screens began in ancient China. The best known among such screens of recent centuries are the so-called "Coromandel screens" which are made of wooden panels finished with a coat of lacquer, through which designs—landscapes, figures, flowers, auspicious emblems, etc.—are incised and filled with various thick, opaque water-colours; a technique known from the Ming dynasty. A large portion, however, of the existing specimens are of the 17th to 19th centuries (Plate I., fig. 1). "Coromandel" has no bearing upon their provenance, but indicates that these screens of Chinese origin were shipped to European countries from the coast of Coromandel. Other screens in the category of lacquer are those with lacquered panels (sometimes coated with white oil paint) decorated in gold lacquer; and those of red carved lacquer. Screens of carved teakwood construction set with jade and porcelain plaques, or panelled with silks, tapestries or embroideries, are occasionally seen. (See Plate II.). (See also INTERIOR DECORATION, ORIENTAL; JAPANESE PAINTING AND PRINTS; CHINESE PAINTING; FLOWER ARRANGING; BATIK.)

Furniture.—As an article of furniture, the screen is an ornamental frame, usually of wood, but sometimes of metal, for protection from observation, draught or the heat of a fire. Screens are made of all shapes and sizes, and may consist of leather, paper or textile materials fastened to the framework; they may have several leaves or only one—thus a fourfold screen has four leaves. Fire screens are usually small, with a single leaf—indeed in the Georgian period of English furniture they often took the form of a circular, oval, heart-shaped or oblong piece of framed embroidery fixed to a wooden pole or upright, upon which they could be raised or lowered. This variety, which was called a pole-screen, was more effective as an ornament than as a protection. The hand-screen was light and portable, as the name implies. At the present time fire-screens are often of glass set in metal frames. The larger type of screen, with several leaves, is of uncertain origin, but probably first came into use towards the end of the 16th century. The earlier examples were of stamped or painted Spanish leather or of some rich stuff such as tapestry; at a later date lacquer was extensively used. They were tall enough to conceal the person sitting behind them, and were frequently exceedingly handsome and stately. (K. T.)

TEXTILES AND EMBROIDERIES. Woven Fabrics of China.—The origin of silk-weaving in China is lost in the region of myth and legend, and nothing remains to show what the earliest stuffs were like. The oldest Chinese patterned stuffs known to exist were unearthed by Sir Aurel Stein in the Lop desert, Chinese Turkestan, in 1914. The site lay on the route opened

SCREEN

PLATE II

BY COURTESY OF THE METROPOLITAN MUSEUM OF ART, NEW YORK

JAPANESE "WAVE SCREEN" OF THE 17TH CENTURY, PAINTED BY OGATA KORIN

This screen, with its design of waves dashed on a gold ground between stretches of smooth water, is one of the most prized productions of Korin. It is characteristic of the artist in its combination of simplicity with daring composition. Korin painted folding screens, fans and lacquers of great beauty. The "Wave Screen" is signed "Hokkyō Kōrin," accompanied by one of his seals "Dōsū"

SCREEN

PLATE IV

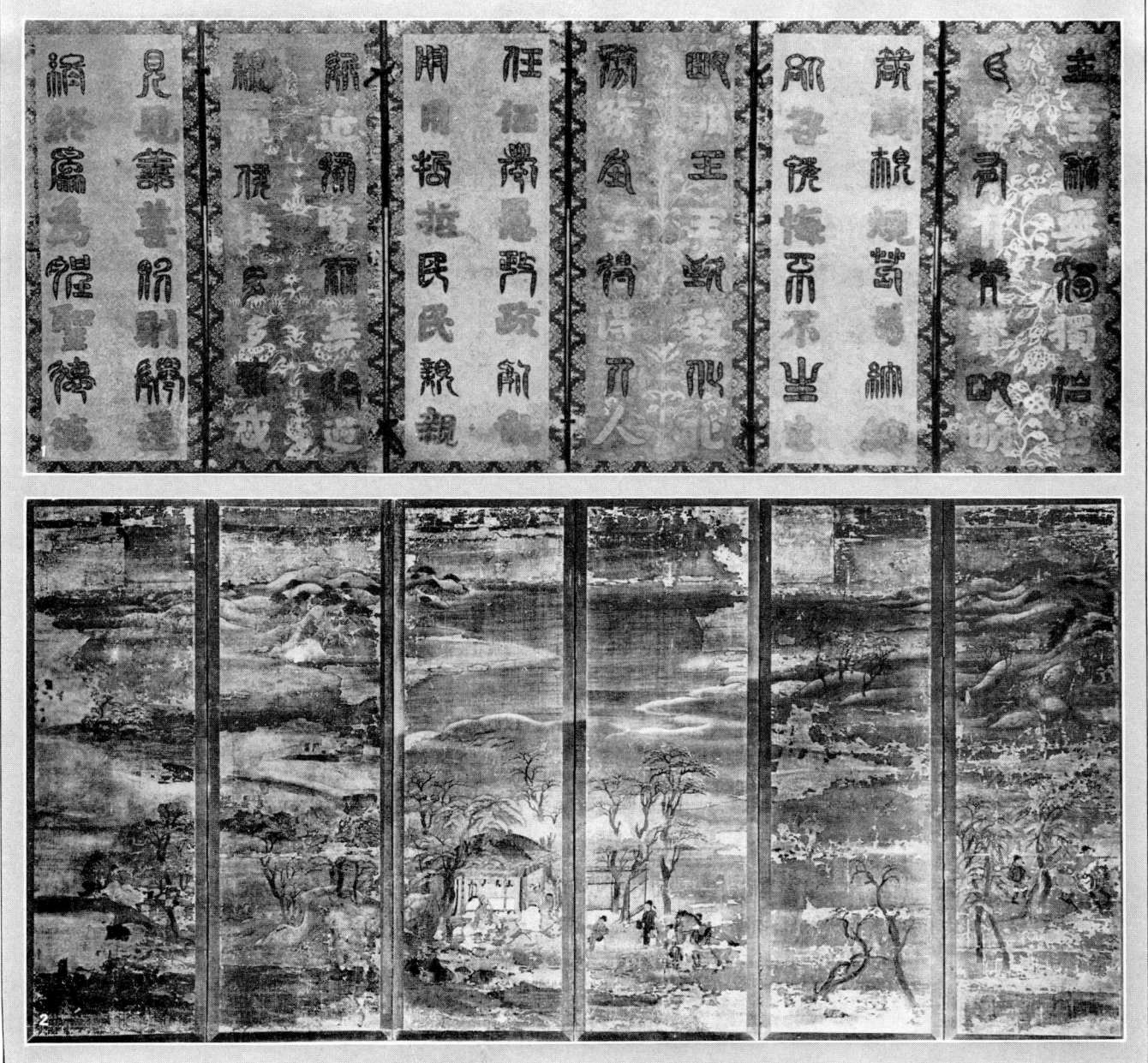

BY COURTESY OF (1) THE DIRECTOR OF THE IMPERIAL HOUSEHOLD MUSEUM, JAPAN, (2) (SHIMBI SHOIN, LTD.) FROM "THE MASTERPIECES SELECTED FROM THE FINE ARTS OF THE FAR EAST"

A CHINESE AND A JAPANESE SCREEN IN THE T'ANG STYLE

1. Chinese screen of the eighth century painted with a precept in 48 ideographs, each character written both in the "seal" and in the "running" style. The panels, which are joined with cords, are coloured alternately red and green, with designs of clouds and other conventionalized forms in white. From the Imperial Collection in the Shosoin, Nara, Japan

2. Japanese landscape screen of the 11th century, probably after a T'ang original, depicts the visitation of a noble and his servants to a hermit's house set in a landscape of trees, hills and water. The over refinement of the drawings is characteristic of the "Japanese picture" style of the Fujiwara period (900–1189). From the Buddhist monastery of Toji at Kyoto

SCREEN

PLATE V

BY COURTESY OF THE MUSEUM OF FINE ARTS, BOSTON

TWO JAPANESE SCREENS

Above: Landscape, by Oguri Sōtan (1398–1464), painted in monochrome, with gold wash, on paper. It is one of a pair of six-fold Japanese screens in the Fenollosa-Weld collection

Below: Spider-monkeys, by Hasegawa Tōhaku (died 1610), painted in monochrome on paper. It is one of a pair of six-fold Japanese screens in the Bigelow collection

PLATE IV   # TEXTILES AND EMBROIDERIES

PHOTOGRAPHS, (1) HERBERT G. PONTING F.R.P.S., (2) BURTON HOLMES FROM EWING GALLOWAY, (3) PUBLISHERS PHOTO SERVICE

EMBROIDERERS AT WORK

1. Japanese embroiderers at work in Kyoto, Japan. These workers show great skill in rendering the pictorial effects favoured by their countrymen
2. Swiss embroiderers working on embroidery-frames outside a shop in Lucerne, Switzerland: Customers are thus enabled to see how the work is done
3. Hungarian needle woman displaying a sample of brightly coloured embroidery characteristic of that country. Heavy thread is used to create many of the effects produced

TEXTILES AND EMBROIDERIES

PLATE XII

JAPANESE COVERS

1. Japanese cut and uncut velvet; fowls with their chicks; the plumage rendered in cut and uncut pile, 19th century
2. Embroidered satin cover used for covering a ceremonial present. Japanese landscapes are worked in gold thread, 19th century

BY COURTESY OF THE DIRECTOR OF THE VICTORIA AND ALBERT MUSEUM, LONDON

out by the Chinese for the silk trade with western Asia in the 2nd century B.C., and replaced by an easier route in the 4th century A.D. The stuffs are attributed to the 1st century B.C., during the Han dynasty, and they are undoubtedly influenced by earlier traditions. The patterns of dragons, griffins, animals, birds, scrolls and diapers are archaic in form, though at the same time they have a remarkable resemblance to later work. The next Chinese dynasty especially associated with the output of artistic wares is the T'ang (A.D. 618–906). Considerable numbers of textiles attributed to this period have been preserved. The Chinese were then in contact with Persia both by land and sea, and this western intercourse is reflected in the art of the time. It is conspicuously seen in a silk banner said to have been used by the Japanese Prince Shotoku (A.D. 572–623), and now removed from Nara (the old imperial capital) to the Tokyo museum. The design is a typical Sassanian hunting-scene, with the king on horseback attacking a lion; the manner of representation is, however, Chinese and Chinese characters are introduced. Many other silk weavings of this epoch are preserved in the royal treasure-house at Nara in Japan.

A characteristic type of Chinese weaving, done by the tapestry method in fine silks and gold thread, and known as k'o-ssu, is first met with under the T'ang dynasty. The specimens which have been found in the Gobi desert region differ remarkably little from those of modern times. The same very fine silk warp is used, and the weft of bright coloured silk enhanced by the use of gold thread. On the other hand there can be no reasonable doubt that these examples woven more than a thousand years ago were the heirs of a far greater antiquity—perhaps assignable in its origin to the dim period when Chinese handicrafts first assumed a civilized form. The patterns are less archaic than those of the "Han" silks already mentioned, but they are similar in their scope —including dragons, symbolic "lions," phoenixes, and various animals, birds and flowers.

Under the Yüan dynasty, founded by a Mongolian conqueror about 1280, Marco Polo (besides other travellers from Europe) found his way across the Asiatic continent to China. He speaks of the silk brocades woven in many parts of that country. Numbers of Chinese silk and gold fabrics were brought to the West at that time and under the Ming dynasty which followed in the 14th century. Some are at Regensburg and Danzig and in other church treasuries of Europe. Occasionally Arabic inscriptions are inwoven into these stuffs showing that they were intended for the use of a Mohammedan ruler of western Asia.

With the arrival of the Portuguese at Canton in 1517 a new era begins for Chinese textiles. "Chinoiserie" soon came into vogue in Europe, and the trading ships of Portugal, Spain, England, France, Holland and other countries brought home vast quantities of Chinese textiles often made specially for export. During this time the weaving of fine silk fabrics, uninfluenced in design by Western associations, went on as before. Dragons, phoenixes, clouds, waves and symbolical ornaments were reproduced on official garments, temple hangings and other stuffs. In China a landscape or a figure subject becomes a "pattern" almost as naturally as any other kind of ornamentation. Landscapes including rocks, rivers, boats, buildings, trees and figures were rendered by the tapestry-weaving process already described. A panel belonging to a series representing a popular commemorative festival held annually by the Chinese, is reproduced in the Encyclopædia Britannica.

Woven Fabrics of Japan.—Textile art in Japan owes a great deal to the Chinese. The ancient royal treasure at Nara, already mentioned, contains some of the most remarkable early Chinese stuffs in existence. The inference that Japan was then very largely dependent upon the more ancient civilization of her neighbours for the richer sort of textiles is confirmed on more general grounds. In the early centuries of the Christian era large numbers of Chinese weavers settled in Japan. They usually worked under Japanese control, and became distributed through the country.

In the year 1584 a Japanese embassy arrived in Europe, visiting Pope Gregory XIII. in Rome, and King Philip II. in Spain. They brought with them silk weavings as presents, receiving in return velvets and brocades. From this time onwards European influence may be discerned here and there in the textiles of Japan. But before the 17th century was well advanced, Japan closed her doors entirely to the foreigner, until in 1858 the country was reopened to European and American trade by Com. Perry, U.S. Navy.

Japanese textile-design displays an acute perception of natural forms, seizing the salient features and transforming them with a light touch to the fabric. Ducks are shown floating on the rippling water, irises growing in the stream, fowls with their chicks (Plate XII., fig. 1), cranes on the wing; with these are landscape effects —lakes and streams, clouds, pine trees, castles and bridges. Symbolic ornaments and small diaper patterns are also common. Different methods of ornamentation are frequently combined in one fabric. A silk stuff may have a woven pattern helped out by printing and completed with a few deft touches of embroidery.

(See LACE; INTERIOR DECORATION, ORIENTAL; FAR EASTERN ART; SCREENS, CHINESE AND JAPANESE; EASTERN DRESS.)

BIBLIOGRAPHY.—Victoria and Albert Museum, *Catalogues;* "Chinese Art" (*Burtengten Magazine Monograph,* 1925); A. Von le Coq, *Chotscho* (1912); Sir A. Stein, *Scrindia* (1921). (A. F. K.)

BY COURTESY OF THE YOUNG WOMEN'S CHRISTIAN ASSOCIATION
WHEEL BY WHICH THE JAPANESE FARMER IRRIGATES HIS RICE LANDS*

JAPANESE GARDENS. The art of garden-making was probably imported into Japan from China or Korea. Records show that the imperial palaces had gardens by the 5th century, their chief characteristic being a pond with an islet connected to the shore by bridges—as is shown later by mentions of the emperor Shōmu's (724–748) three gardens in Nara. During the Heian period (782–1185), when the symmetrical *shinden* style of architecture prevailed, the main garden (as often, even to-day) was laid out on the southern side of the house, always with hills and a pond with an island. However, with the change in domestic architecture of the Kamakura period (1186–1335), came modifications of the garden. Learned Zen priests, who assiduously studied the art of garden-making, gave Buddhistic names to different rocks in the design, and linked religio-philosophic principles with the rules governing it. Other cults and superstitions crept in also, further complicating the design.

With the supremacy of the Ashikaga dynasty (1394–1573) came popularization of gardens, which were designed to be enjoyed from within as from without, opening a new era in the development of garden-making. The subjective mood became dominant, and the gardens reflected individuality. People demanded *shibumi* in their gardens—an unassuming quality in which refinement underlies a commonplace appearance, appreciable only by a cultivated taste. Aesthetic priests, "tea-men," and connoisseurs devised new forms of gardens for *cha-seki*, the little pa-

*From the article "Japan" from the Encyclopædia Britannica.

GENERAL KEY TO GARDEN DESIGN OF LANDSCAPE TYPE
BY COURTESY OF JIRO HARADA

vilions or rooms built for *cha-no-yu* (tea-ceremonies), and a special style developed which revolutionized Japanese garden art.

Styles in Gardens.—The vogue of designing in the three degrees of elaboration—*shin, gyo* and *so* (elaborate, intermediate and abbreviated)—was adopted also for gardens. Many splendid gardens were produced in the Momoyama (1574–1602) and Edo (1603–1868) periods. However, the centre of garden activity gradually shifted from Kyoto to Edo, the seat of the Tokugawa Shōgun. One development was a utilitarian phase; *e.g.*, the duck pond in the Hama detached palace in Tokyo, and the cultivation in the Kairaku-yen at Mito of reeds for arrow-shafts, and plums for military supplies. Feudal lords generally had fine gardens in their provincial homes as well. Quite a number of gardens have survived the abolition of the feudal system after the Restoration of 1868, when so many celebrated gardens perished through neglect or were sacrificed. The establishment of public parks, which were not unknown even in feudal times, has been specially encouraged throughout the country since 1873. Gardens of Western style came with other Western modes but made little headway. The great earthquake and fire of 1923 demonstrated the utilitarian value of the Tokyo gardens. Tens of thousands found safety in the parks and in the large private gardens scattered throughout the city.

Classes of Gardens.—Japanese gardens are generally classified, according to the nature of the ground, under two heads: *tsuki-yama* (artificial-hills) and *hira-niwa* (level-gardens), each having special features. *Tsuki-yama* consists of hills and ponds, and *hira-niwa* of a flat piece of ground so designed as to represent a valley, a moor, and so on, and *tsuki-yama* may embrace a portion laid out as *hira-niwa*, both types being treated in the three degrees of elaborations already mentioned. Hill-gardens as a rule include a stream and pond of real water, but in the *kare-sansui* (dried-up landscape) style, while rocks are composed into the form of a waterfall and its basin, and of a winding stream and pond, gravel or sand is used to symbolize water, or to suggest the temporary phase of a naturally dried-up landscape. In extreme examples, where prime importance is given to rocks, and trees are absent, a real "rock garden" may be said to result. There are also styles known as *sen-tei* (water-garden) or *rin-sen* (forest-water), and, in level gardens, *bunjin-zukuri* (literary men's style), a very simple and small type, originated by dilettanti in Chinese literature. The tea-garden or *roji* (dew-ground or passage) as it is called, is another distinct style evolved to meet the requirements of the tea ceremonies, as already mentioned. *Genkwan-saki* (front of entrance) or house-approaches have always claimed special treatment—a simple curve, wherever possible, partially to conceal the entrance to the house and give character to its front view.

Characteristic Features.—The characteristic features of a Japanese garden are the waterfall, of which there are ten or more different modes of arrangement, the spring and the stream to which it gives rise, the lake, the hills built up from the earth excavated when its basin is dug, the islands with many varieties of bridges, and the natural stones which constitute the skeleton of the garden. The selection and effective distribution of these stones are the prime consideration and have been endlessly experimented with and deeply pondered, the cream of such experiments in composition being handed down by means of drawings. The studied irregularity of the arrangement of the stepping-stones in the *cha-no-yu* garden, wherein beauty and use are combined, is a noteworthy element of garden-design. In modern Japanese gardens flowers are few and evergreens popular. The significance here is that simplicity, restraint and consistency are sought rather than gaiety, showiness or the obvious variations of the seasons, and subtle gradation in the tones of the foliage is preferred to the changing aspect of deciduous trees, though with some exceptions such as maple trees. As in the case of stones, trees must be distributed in the garden in harmony with their natural origin and habit of growth. Of garden furniture and accessories, the well, decorative and useful alike, the stone water-basin, endless in variety, stone lanterns, figures and pagodas, arbours and summer-houses, are the most characteristic, together with gateways and fences, particularly the widely varying *sode-gaki* (sleeve-fence) attached to the side of the house to screen certain portions, and used to blend harmoniously the natural beauty of the garden with the human art displayed in the architectural features of the house.

Ideals and Aims in Garden Design.—The ideals of garden-designing have often been modified during its long history, being influenced by the prevailing thought of each period. At one time eminent Zen priests designed gardens in accordance with the principles which lay at the base of their philosophical teaching; at another, painters became deeply interested and designed gardens as though they were painting landscapes on silk. In the course of history the objective standpoint in garden-making gave place to a subjective impulse. Various philosophic principles and religious doctrines were embodied in the making of gardens, not so much to interpret those particular principles and doctrines as to explain the aesthetics of garden design, and more particularly of the distribution of natural rocks, by illustrations drawn from familiar philosophic principles. Long after such principles have ceased to sway the mind of the people, the terminology survived, preserving a repertory of symbols. The laws of direction, of harmony, of the five elements, the principles of cause and effect, of the active and passive, of light and shadow, or of the nine spirits of the Buddhist pantheon, as well as superstitions of all sorts, still continue to

JAPANESE GARDENS

PLATE I

BY COURTESY OF JIRO HARADA

CHARACTERISTIC JAPANESE GARDENS

1. Garden of the Tenryuji, Buddhist Temple, Kyoto; designed by Musokokushi (14th century)
2. Koraku-yen, Okayama (17th century)
3. Garden of the Dempo-in, Tokyo
4. Crane and Tortoise Islands, in the garden of the Kinkaku-ji, Kyoto
5. Garden of the Ryoanji, Kyoto, attributed to Soami

PLATE II — JAPANESE GARDENS

BY COURTESY OF JIRO HARADA

IMPERIAL AND OTHER JAPANESE GARDENS

1. Kenroku-yen, Kanazawa
2. Garden of the Ginkakuji, Kyoto, attributed to Soami
3. Garden of Shisenkaku, designed by Ishikawa Jodan, Kyoto
4. Imperial Garden of Shukaguin, Kyoto
5. Imperial Garden of the Katsura palace, Kyoto
6. Imperial Garden at Shinjuku, Tokyo

FLOWER ARRANGING

BY COURTESY OF JIRO HARADA

JAPANESE STYLES OF FLOWER ARRANGING

1. Flowers arranged in Seizan-Ryu style. The Seizan-Ryu school is an outgrowth of the Ikenobō cult (see figs. 4 and 5)
2. Flowers arranged in Tozanko-Seiryu style (see figs. 7 and 8). The triangular grouping, characteristic of all Japanese flower-arrangement, symbolizes Heaven, Earth and Man
3. Another arrangement of flowers in Seizan-Ryu style (see fig. 1)
4. Pine, plum and bamboo arranged for a happy occasion, in Ikenobō style
5. Autumnal flowers arranged in Ikenobō style, in combination with a kakemono (hanging picture), suggesting the singing of autumn insects
6. Arrangement in Mori-bana style
7 and 8. Further examples of Tozanko-Seiryu style (see fig. 2). The grouping with all the stems together at the base is typically Japanese
9. Lotus arranged according to Soami style. Soami (15th century) is reputed to have been the originator of the three-element style
10. Rikka, or standing flowers, grouped to suggest a landscape, a style peculiar to the Ikenobō school
11. Flowers arranged in Tensho-Koryu style. As in all Japanese arrangements, an effect of even symmetry is avoided
12. Flower arrangement according to Shogetsudo-Koryu style, originated by Myōye-Shonin in 1171–1231

influence to some extent the general design of gardens.

The aim is to bring man closer to Nature, and all manner of means have been resorted to in the effort to realize it. Some of the master-designers reproduced in miniature famous scenes of China and Japan. They planned the garden and planted trees to give the illusion of a view extending over and beyond its own immediate confines, but at the same time they so designed it as to be a secluded and sylvan retreat from the world, great ingenuity being displayed in both directions. In some instances, with only a few stones in a narrow strip of ground, a great expanse of landscape has been included as a background. In another instance, Rikyu, in his garden at Sakai, obstructed the open view of the sea in such a way that only when the guest stooped at the stone water basin to wash his hands and rinse his mouth preparatory to entering the *cha-seki*, did he catch an unexpected glimpse through the trees of the shimmering sea, thus being suddenly made to realize the relation of the dipperful of water lifted from the basin to the vast expanse of sea, and of himself to the universe. The Japanese have tried to emphasize in their gardens the charm of restraint, and of beauty so concealed that it may be discovered individually, thus providing that thrill of joy to the soul which comes from doing a good deed in stealth. Thus, at least in its ideals, the Japanese garden, which has always been part and parcel of the home, by no means stops at merely creating and arranging beautiful spots, but aims at being natural that it may satisfy the human craving for nature, and, by supplying peace and repose, may be a retreat in which man's spirit can wander and find spiritual recreation and sustenance. (*See also* BON-KEI; BON-SAI; BON-SEKI; HAKO-NIWA; JAPANESE ARCHITECTURE.)

See J. Conder, *Landscape Gardening in Japan* (1893); J. Harada, *The Gardens of Japan* (1928). (J. HAR.)

PUBLISHERS' NOTE

The articles in this booklet are all taken *verbatim* from the new 14th Edition of the Encyclopædia Britannica except that in a few unimportant instances certain material has been omitted or condensed for mechanical reasons. The plates too are reproduced unchanged but the numbering is not always consecutive because the original numbering has been retained so as to agree with the text. A certain number of cross references to articles not in this booklet are also retained for the benefit of those who possess the Britannica.

Following the Britannica custom, we have retained at the end of signed articles the initials and not the full name of the author. The reader, however, can always identify the author by referring to the Table of Contents where the full names of the authors are given together with the initials.

FLOWER ARRANGING in Japan is an old art of composing natural flowers, foliage or fruit-bearing branches in a vessel for the decoration of a room. Its important position in the home was established in the middle of the 15th century, when the tea-ceremony (*q.v.*) became a fashion, and so popular did it grow that it soon became independent of the tea-room to be taught by flower-masters. By the 17th century there arose many schools or styles which held competitive exhibitions of their art. Such exhibitions are still being held and there are more than 100 styles, the number still increasing. Private lessons are given by numerous flower-masters and a course on flower arranging, or to use the Japanese term, *ikebana*, is included in the curriculum of nearly all the girls' schools in Japan.

Common to practically all the styles is the principle guiding the fundamentals. There is to be a tall spray representing the "leading principle," Heaven. Another branch should be kept low down to denote the "subordinate principle," Earth. And there is to be another branch between the two which stands for the "reconciling principle," Man. Thus an effort is made, besides aiming at a beautiful form, to indicate man's relation to the universe. There should always be these three prominent features, however many other branches of minor significance may be added, the joining of these principal points forming a triangle. However, the *rikka* (standing flowers), a special art of the Ikenobo school, may be considered an exception: it denotes the universe with actual suggestions of landscapes by the branches and flowers. In each style the highest artistic value of a vase of flowers is brought out in its relation to the season, the occasion, and the other objects of ornament, chief among which is the *kakemono*, the hanging picture. As the arranged flowers are to be placed on the *tokonoma* (an alcove in the guest room) they are so composed as to be best seen from the front. Now that there are so many foreign styled rooms in the Japanese houses, it has become necessary to have flowers so arranged as to be appreciated from all sides, and there is a tendency to develop a style to meet this requirement.

BIBLIOGRAPHY.—J. Conder, *The Flowers of Japan and the Art of Japanese Floral Arrangement* (Tokyo, 1891); F. Brinkley, *Japan—Its History, Arts and Literature* vol. iii. (Boston and Tokyo, 1901); Mary Averill, *The Flower Art of Japan* (1926). (J. HAR.)

ENAMEL. Enamels do not appear to have reached China until long after they were to be found throughout Europe. The Chinese make no claim to their invention; but, on the contrary the native term, "*Fu-lin* ware" (hence *Fa-lan*), directly suggests an origin in the eastern Roman provinces, that name having been applied to the Byzantine empire by Chinese historians as early as the 7th century. The derivation of the word has been the subject of controversy and is uncertain; but all authorities are agreed as to the western origin of the art; which was, in all probability, introduced into China by Arab traders, or by travelling craftsmen working their way eastwards as opportunity arose of plying their craft profitably. Glass, which in China was also of alien origin, was imported from the Roman empire certainly as early as the 3rd century A.D.; but it was not until the reign of T'ai Wu (424–452) of the northern Wei dynasty that craftsmen from an Indo-Scythian kingdom on the north-west border of India came to the Wei capital in Shansi and succeeded in making excellent opaque glass of various colours from local minerals.

Although the Chinese were thus informed as to the production of an essential material for the making of enamels and were already most highly skilled in the working of bronzes and other metals, it is remarkable that there appears to have been no development of the art of enamelling at least until the 13th century, when the Mongolian conquests introduced into the Far East so many arts hitherto unknown. A record exists, in the *Ko ku yao lun*, a book on antiquities published in 1387, of the production on a large and varied scale of enamelled ware which "resembles the cloisonné work of Fo-lang." This is herein termed also *Kuei kuo yao*, ware of the devils' country. It also states that natives of Yunnan have established factories for this ware in Peking and that the enamels made at the provincial capital, Yunnan-fu, are "fine, lustrous and beautifully finished." It appears therefore that the *Ta shih yao* or Arabian (so-called) enamel ware was well established in China at this period; and that Byzantine work of similar character was also so well known as to invite comparison with the native product and that, as pointed out by M. Paléologue, "the workmanship (of the Chinese enamels) presents occasionally, in fact, striking resemblances with certain enamels of the Byzantine School: the mixture of different enamels inside the wall of the same cell, the employment of gold encrustations in the treatment of the figures and hands, etc."

From the technical point of view, Chinese enamels fall into three categories—cloisonné, champlevé and painted. In none does the technique vary appreciably from that employed in western countries.

Cloisonné.—In *cloisonné*, the outlines of practically every detail of the design are defined with narrow bands or ribbons of metal—copper, silver or gold—soldered edgewise to the base, in such a way as to cover the whole surface to be decorated, with shallow cells sometimes called *cloisons*, but this term is more correctly employed to designate the bands themselves. These are then filled with the appropriate enamel colours, ground to a fine powder, moistened and tightly packed into their respective cells. "The piece," says Dr. S. W. Bushell, "is usually fired in the open courtyard, protected only by a primitive cover of iron network, the charcoal fire being regulated by a number of men standing round with large fans in their hands." This process has to be repeated several times, on account of the shrinkage, under heat, of the enamel, and the pitting which also takes place. When the whole surface is thus satisfactorily covered in this manner it is ground down to an even texture with pumice stone and polished with charcoal; the metal surfaces of the cloisons, now clearly visible being gilded, as well as those parts of the object which have not been adorned with enamel; for instance, the neck, rims and foot of a vase as well as any decoration in relief which projects beyond the enamelled surface.

The earliest examples of cloisonné enamel that can be authentically associated with the Far East, are mirrors in the Shōsō in ("lonely building"), at Nara in Japan. The backs of these have cloisonné work, somewhat crude in character. There is no doubt that these and other objects in the collection were deposited in the Shōsō in in the year 756 by Kōmyō-Kōgo, widow of the Emperor Shomo-Tennō (724–749), with other treasures collected during his life. We have here, therefore, authentic examples of the art that must date back at least to the T'ang dynasty, and may, as is certainly the case with some other objects in the collection, be of Chinese workmanship. It is generally agreed that they are neither Japanese nor Byzantine. So far as is known at present, the sequence of Chinese enamels with which we are acquainted begins, however, only in the Yuan period; and the earliest recorded marks belong to the reign of the last emperor of that dynasty (1341–1367). The great period of the production is certainly that of the Ming dynasty which followed and existed until 1643.

The mark most commonly found within this epoch is that of the Ching T'ai reign (1450–1456); so Dr. Bushell suggests that there must have been a great revival of the art at this time, as even in his day, the term Ching T'ai Lan was "commonly used in Peking as a general synonym for cloisonné enamels." He points out the significance of the fact that this reign covers the time of the last siege and capture of Constantinople by the Turks (1453) when some of the craftsmen then dispersed may have even penetrated to China. However this may be, the Ming enamels, bold in design, with fine depth and purity of colour, were never surpassed in later epochs. The two shades of blue, a dark lapis-lazuli tone and a pale sky-blue with a very slight tinge of green, are particularly excellent. The red is of dark coral tint and the yellow full-bodied and pure. Greens derived from copper are sparingly used and Dr. Bushell states that rouges d'or (reds made of gold) do not come into the colour scheme at all. The black and white are the least successful; the former shallow and dull, the latter clouded and muddy. At the same time, an imperfection of technique is noted, a close examination revealing minute pitting in the enamels, due to inadequate packing of the material, and some want of polish in the surface. These technical defects, however, do not appreciably detract from the artistic value of the Ming enamels and, indeed, serve as a clue to their identification.

To the patronage of the Emperor K'ang Hsi (1662–1722) was due a great revival of art industries. In 1680 he established a whole series of imperial factories for this purpose, of which that devoted to the manufacture of enamels was No. 6 on the official list. Here he had made sets of incense vessels of cloisonné enamel for presentation to the numerous Buddhist temples in the neighbourhood of Peking, founded under his auspices and other objects for the honorific gifts which were characteristic of his enlightened reign. The enamels of his time were marked by an improvement in technical quality as compared with those of the Ming period, while the finer qualities of the latter are still, to a considerable extent, in evidence. In many cases the forms of ancient bronze vessels were revived for these purposes, with the addition of enrichments in enamel. The style of this reign persisted during that of K'ang Hsi's successor, Yung Chêng (1723–1735); while the long period on the throne occupied by Ch'ien Lung (1736–1795) was marked, as in the case of many other industrial arts, by a further perfection of technique, but with the loss of much of the vigour of design and breadth of execution that distinguished the products of earlier periods. Modern enamels, chiefly imitations of older work, are more hurriedly made and not so well finished. The quality of the gilding especially is far below that of the older productions.

Champleve.—In *champlevé enamels*, cloisons are not used, the hollows to be filled with colour being cut out of the metal with graving tools. Otherwise the process is similar to that last described. It is probably the oldest method of enamelling known, and there is no evidence as to the date of its introduction into China, though some of the most ancient examples extant belong to this class. The general trend of design and execution, historically, is much the same as that of cloisonné. Examples in which both methods are employed are not infrequent.

Painted Enamels.—The *painted enamels* of China, generally known from the principal seat of their manufacture as *Canton enamels*, are practically identical in technique with the Limoges and other painted enamels of Europe. Specimens of these are known to have been taken to China by the missionaries of the late 17th and 18th centuries, and not only to have exercised direct influence on the Chinese ware, but also, in some cases, to have been copied. Representations of European subjects, copies of engravings and armorial decorations, are also found there. Painted enamels are termed by the Chinese *Yang t'zu* (literally "foreign porcelain"), the palette of colours used being the same as with enamelled porcelain though, in the case of enamels it is termed *Yang ts'ai* (foreign colours). A ground of opaque enamel, generally white, is laid on the copper; and on this the colours are superimposed and fired. Owing to the soft nature of the ground, these sink in and are incorporated with it, producing a loss of brilliance, which, as admitted by the Chinese, renders them inferior to enamelled porcelain with which they may well be compared. The earliest dated example of Canton enamel consists of a set of objects inscribed *Yung chêng yu chih* (1723–1735) made to imperial order. Although imitations have continued to be made, nothing of real quality in this style was produced after the termination of the reign of Ch'ien Lung in 1795. The method has always been looked upon by the Chinese as in alien taste; a writer of 1782 (quoted by Bushell) remarks, "They are only fit for use as ornaments of ladies' apartments—not at all for the chaste furniture of the library of a simple scholar." Enamels of this kind were also made, with characteristic decoration, for the Siamese market.

Translucent (as opposed to opaque) enamels were occasionally made by Chinese artisans. Important pieces are rare, but sometimes of fine quality, a deep blue, obtained from a native cobaltiperous ore of manganese, and a pale turquoise blue from copper being especially successful. This method more often appears in conjunction with gold and silver in Chinese jewellery; in which, also, imitations, in enamel, of real gems are frequently employed.

Japanese Enamels.—The examples of enamel in the imperial treasury at Nara, Japan, have already been referred to; and it may now be repeated that they cannot be attributed to Japanese craftsmanship. No examples of authentic enamels of Japanese origin that can be dated earlier than the end of the 16th century seem to exist. The western influence which promoted the art in China does not appear to have penetrated to Japan; the first Japanese appearance of the art seems to have been in the form of the decoration of sword furniture by the founders of the Hirata family who worked at Kyōto under the patronage of the Tokugawa Shōgun, Iyeyasu about the year 1611. They made use, on a small scale, both of the cloisonné and champlevé methods. A dull green was one of the first colours obtained. The range of colours was afterwards extended with a white of good quality. There was no further development of importance until the 19th century, when Kaji Tsunikichi (born A.D. 1802) of Nagoya established in that city an important and successful manufacture of cloisonné which obtained a considerable vogue especially among foreigners. On this basis further developments have taken place of considerable interest.

Modern Japanese artists have modified the cloisonné process with remarkable ingenuity and have produced work of great interest, in which the cloisons are sometimes completely veiled, the resultant effect being that of enamelled porcelain with realistic designs of flowers, etc., and a wide and almost unrestricted range

ENAMEL

PLATE III

PHOTOGRAPH, HERBERT G. PONTING, F.R.P.S.

THE PROCESS OF CLOISONNÉ

A cloisonné artist of Japan at work. The details of a design are outlined on a vase, with narrow bands or cloisons of metal (copper, silver or gold), which are soldered edgewise to the surface so as to make a pattern of shallow cells. Enamel colours, ground to a fine powder, and moistened, are then tightly packed into the cells, to complete the design

PLATE IV · ENAMEL

PHOTOGRAPH, HERBERT G. PONTING, F.R.P.S.

FIRING THE ENAMELS

Japanese cloisonné artists firing enamels in a charcoal fire. This process is repeated several times because of the shrinkage of the enamel under heat and the pitting which takes place. When the firing has been satisfactorily completed the surface of the vase is ground down to an even texture with pumice and polished with charcoal, and the metal surfaces of the cloisons, now clearly visible, are gilded

ENAMEL

PLATE V

BY COURTESY OF (1) S. AND G. GUMP COMPANY, (3, 4, 5, 6, 8) THE METROPOLITAN MUSEUM OF ART, NEW YORK, (7) THE DEPARTMENT OF FINE ARTS, BROOKLYN MUSEUM

PAINTED, CLOISONNÉ AND CHAMPLEVÉ CHINESE ENAMELS OF THE XVIII. AND XIX. CENTURIES

1. Imperial teapot of Peking enamel painted, Ch'ien Lung period (1736–95)
2. Round screen of Peking enamel, with a landscape design
3. Incense burner of cloisonné on copper, in three parts, bowl, ring and cover. It is decorated with floral designs and openwork on turquoise blue ground; height, 16 inches. 19th century
4. Incense burner in cloisonné with stand and cover of same material and design. Turquoise blue ground; 24½ x 12½ inches. Ch'ien Lung period
5. Large dish of Peking enamel decorated with Taoist sages walking. Ch'ien Lung period
6. Cloisonné snuff bottle of turquoise blue and white enamel ground, with coral stopper; height, 2-3/7 inches. Ch'ien Lung period
7. Seated figures and tripod censer of cloisonné. The figures, 37 inches in height, are on garden seats, also in cloisonné, and represent an empress (left) and a princess, probably of the Ch'ien Lung period. The robes of the former are executed with designs on chocolate colour ground and those of the latter on a ground of blue and imperial yellow. Faces and hands are gilt. The censer is enamelled in both cloisonné and champlevé on turquoise blue ground. The handles are of archaic sceptre-shape and the cover is surmounted by a gilt bronze finial; height 36 inches. Era of Tao-kuang (1821–50)
8. Gourd-shaped cloisonné snuff bottle, with metal and enamel stopper, on wood stand; height, 2⅞ inches. Ch'ien Lung period

PLATE VI · ENAMEL

BY COURTESY OF (1, 2, 7) THE METROPOLITAN MUSEUM OF ART, NEW YORK, (3, 4, 5, 6, 8) THE DEPARTMENT OF FINE ARTS, BROOKLYN MUSEUM

THE CLOISONNÉ PROCESS AND CHINESE CLOISONNÉ ENAMELS OF THE XV.–XVIII. CENTURIES

1 and 2. Stages in the process of cloisonné enamelling, showing first, the metal plate on which the design is executed by soldering thin metal bands or *cloisons* to the base to form shallow cells (second step). These cells are filled with powdered enamel colours, and the piece is then fired and polished. 3. Beaker-shaped imperial vase with gilt bronze dragon and phoenix handles. Turquoise blue ground sustaining flowers and vines; height 41½ inches. Reign of Ch'ing Tai (1450–56), Ming dynasty. 4. Trumpet-shaped vase decorated with eyes and cloud forms on turquoise blue ground; height, 14½ inches. Ming dynasty. 5. Beaker-shaped vase with floriated ornament, scrolls and palmettes; height; 21½ inches. K'ang-hsi period (1662–1722). 6. Twin vases enamelled in green and joined by bronze ornaments, signifying the unity of the universe; height, 25½ inches. Era of Yung-Cheng (1723–35). 7. Jui sceptre (repaired); length, 15¾ inches. K'ang-hsi period. 8. Dove-shaped altar wine vessel on wheels, patterned after a type of ancient vessel used at rituals. Besides the conventional ornamentation, the decoration consists of scrolls and various designs, such as monsters' heads, copied from very old bronzes; height, 22 inches. K'ang-hsi period

of colour. Namikawa of Tōkyō has been one of the most successful of these. A Kyōto artist of the same name has worked with credit in true *cloisonné*. J. Ando of Nagoya has obtained novel effects by the use of translucent enamel on a silver basis. These developments have carried the art of enamel very far from the old traditions, but, while the skill and ingenuity of technique they evince may be appreciated, it cannot be said that in decorative value they compare with the older Chinese tradition. During the 19th century, the Japanese produced many imitations of the latter; which, for a time gave rise to quite a false appreciation of their place in the history of the art.

BIBLIOGRAPHY.—F. Brinkley, *Japan and China*, vol. vii. (1904); Brooklyn Museum of the Institute of Arts and Sciences, *The Avery Collection of Ancient Chinese Cloisonnés* (1912); S. W. Bushell, *Chinese Art*, vol. ii. (1919); R. L. Hobson, *Chinese Cloisonné Enamels*, in *Burlington Magazine*, vol. xxi., pp. 137, 202, Ibid. *Canton Enamels*, in *Burlington Magazine*, vol. xxii., p. 165. (E. F. S.)

JAPAN. Weapons.—The bow was always the chief weapon of the fighting-man in Japan. "War" and "bow-and-arrow" were synonymous terms. Tradition tells how Tametomo shot an arrow through the crest of his brother's helmet, in order to recall the youth's allegiance without injuring him; how Nasuno Michitaka discharged a shaft that severed the stem of a fan swayed by the wind. Still better authenticated were the feats performed at the "thirty-three-span halls" in Kyōto and Yedo, where the archer had to shoot an arrow through the whole length of a corridor 128 yards long and only 16ft. high. Wada Daihachi, in the 17th century, succeeded in sending 8,133 arrows from end to end of the corridor in 24 consecutive hours, being an average of over 5 shafts per minute; and Masatoki, in 1852, made 5,383 successful shots in 20 hours, more than 4 a minute. The lengths of the bow and arrow were determined with reference to the capacity of the archer. In the case of the bow, the unit of measurement was the distance between the tips of the thumb and the little finger with the hand fully stretched. Fifteen of these units gave the length of the bow—the maximum being about 7½ft. The unit for the arrow was from 12 to 15 hand-breadths, or from 3ft. to 3¾ft. Originally the bow was of unvarnished boxwood or *zelkowa;* but subsequently bamboo alone came to be employed. Binding with cord or rattan served to strengthen the bow, and for precision of flight the arrow had three feathers, an eagle's wing being most esteemed for that purpose.

Next in importance to the bow came the sword, which is spoken of as the samurai's chief weapon, though often during long ages it ranked after the bow. It was a single-edged weapon remarkable for its three exactly similar curves—edge, face-line and back; its almost imperceptibly convexed blade; its admirable tempering; its cunning distribution of weight, giving a maximum efficiency of stroke. The 10th century saw this weapon carried to perfection, and in every age numbers of men devoted their whole lives to acquiring novel skill in swordsmanship. Many of them invented systems of their own, differing from one another in some subtle details unknown to any save the master himself and his favourite pupils. Not merely the method of handling the weapon had to be studied. Associated with sword-play was an art variously known as *shinobi, yawara* and *jujutsu*, names which imply the exertion of muscular force in such a manner as to produce a maximum of effect with a minimum of effort, by directing an adversary's strength so as to become auxiliary to one's own. It was an essential element of the expert's art not only that he should be competent to defend himself with any object that happened to be within reach, but also that without an orthodox weapon he should be capable of inflicting fatal or disabling injury on an assailant. Were he caught weaponless by a number of assailants, his art of yawara was supposed to supply him with expedients for emerging unscathed. Nothing counted save the issue. The methods of gaining victory or the circumstances attending defeat were scarcely taken into consideration. Out of this perpetual effort to discover and perfect novel developments of swordsmanship, there grew a habit which held its vogue down to modern times, namely, that when a man had mastered one style of sword-play in the school of a teacher, he set himself to study all others, and for that purpose undertook a tour throughout the provinces, challenging every expert, and, in the event of defeat, constituting himself the victor's pupil.

The sword exercised a very potent influence on the life of the Japanese nation. The distinction of wearing it, the rights that it conferred, the deeds wrought with it, the fame attaching to special skill in its use, the superstitions connected with it, the incredible value set upon a fine blade, the honours bestowed on an expert sword-smith, the profound study needed to be a competent judge of a sword's qualities—all these things conspired to give the katana an importance beyond the limits of ordinary comprehension. A samurai carried at least two swords, a long and a short. Their scabbards of lacquered wood were thrust into his girdle, not slung from it, being fastened in their place by cords of plaited silk. The short sword was not employed in the actual combat. Its use was to cut off an enemy's head after overthrowing him, and it also served a defeated soldier in his last resort—suicide. In general the long sword did not measure more than 3ft., including the hilt; but some were 5ft. long, and some 7. Considering that the scabbard, being fastened to the girdle, had no play, the feat of drawing one of these very long swords demanded extraordinary aptitude.

Spear and glaive were also ancient Japanese weapons. The glaive (*naginata*, long sword) was a scimitar-like blade, some 3ft. in length, fixed on a slightly longer haft. Originally the warlike monks alone employed this weapon, but from the 12th century it found much favour among military men. Ultimately, however, its use may be said to have been limited to women and priests. The spear, however, formed a useful adjunct of the sword, for whereas the latter could not be used except by troops in very loose formation, the former served for close-order fighting.

Armour.—Japanese armour (*gusoku*) may be broadly described as plate armour, but the essential difference between it and the European type was that, whereas the latter took its shape from the body, the former neither resembled nor was intended to resemble ordinary garments. Perhaps the easiest way of describing the difference is to say that whereas a European knight seemed to be clad in a suit of metal clothes, a Japanese samurai looked as if he wore protective curtains. The Japanese armour was, in fact, suspended from, rather than fitted to the person. Iron and leather were the chief materials, and as the laminae were strung together with a vast number of coloured cords—silk or leather—an appearance of considerable brilliancy was produced. Ornamentation did not stop there. Plating and inlaying with gold and silver, and finely wrought decoration were freely applied. On the whole, however, despite the highly artistic character of its ornamentation, the loose, pendulous nature of Japanese armour detracted greatly from its workmanlike aspect, especially when the *horo* was added—a curious appendage in the shape of a curtain of fine transparent silk, which was either stretched in front between the horns of the helmet and the tip of the bow, or worn on the shoulders and back, the purpose in either case being to turn the point of an arrow. A true samurai observed strict rules of etiquette with regard even to the garments worn under his armour, and it was part of his soldierly capacity to be able to bear the great weight of the whole without loss of activity, a feat impossible to any untrained man of modern days. Common soldiers were generally content with a comparatively light helmet and a corselet.

The Japanese never had a war-horse worthy to be so called. The misshapen ponies which carried them to battle showed qualities of hardiness and endurance, but were so deficient in stature and massiveness that when mounted by a man in voluminous armour they looked painfully puny. Both stirrups and the wooden saddle-frame were often of beautiful workmanship, the former covered with rich gold lacquer, the latter inlaid with gold or silver. In the latter part of the military epoch chain-armour was adopted for the horse, and its head was protected by a monster-faced mask of iron.

PRINTED IN U. S. A.
BY R. R. DONNELLEY & SONS CO., CHICAGO

THE
Encyclopaedia Britannica

FOURTEENTH EDITION
IN TWENTY-FOUR VOLUMES

READERS of this book, made up of articles and illustrations taken from the latest Fourteenth Edition of the Encyclopaedia Britannica, will appreciate the authority and the beauty of text and illustration throughout the twenty-four volumes of the Britannica. The excellence of the materials published in this book is a measure of the excellence of that used in the original volumes themselves.

More than 3,500 authorities as distinguished as those represented here contribute to the pages of the Britannica. More than 15,000 illustrations as beautiful in colour as the colour plates in this book and as rich in tone as the photographs, are to be found in the Britannica.

AN INCOMPARABLE SOURCE BOOK
OF HUMAN KNOWLEDGE

The obvious care devoted to the articles within these covers in the hope of making them not only entertaining but thoroughly instructive indicates the care bestowed upon the thousands of other articles which make up the Britannica. Neither effort nor money was spared to bring into this standard encyclopaedia of the world the latest authoritative information in text and picture on every conceivable subject of human interest. And all this material was designed to meet the needs of men, women and children in the home, in business and in the school.

The Encyclopaedia Britannica carries in its twenty-four volumes no less than 35,000,000 words written by more than 3,500 world authorities. This text is richly illustrated with 15,000 pictures, many in colour and with 500 maps, 200 of which are in colour. Considering the completeness and authority of its text and the quality of its illustrations the new Britannica is the least expensive encyclopaedia you can buy.

As little as $5 down and $5 a month for a few months will bring the set to your home for your immediate use and enjoyment.

Literature describing the Britannica, its four beautiful bindings, and its prices and plans of easy payment may be had by sending a post card or a letter to either office listed below.

ENCYCLOPAEDIA BRITANNICA, Inc.
342 Madison Avenue, New York City

The ENCYCLOPAEDIA BRITANNICA CO., Ltd.
80-86 Regent Street, London, W.1.

Out of the finest of all encyclopaedias
—this enriching book you hold in your hand

AS A RESULT of unusual popular demand such books as the one you are now holding in your hand are being prepared by the editors of the Encyclopaedia Britannica. The books are made up of the authoritative text and the beautiful illustrations, appearing in the latest Fourteenth Edition of the Encyclopaedia Britannica and each one of them covers exhaustively a single subject.

The books are designed for the use of students and laymen who wish a single reading course, as well as an authoritative and beautiful volume covering singly the whole of a specialized topic. They represent absolutely authoritative text written by the greatest authorities from all over the world. They are designed to meet the needs, also, of teachers and curators of museums.

Nowhere else can you obtain a small book of such absolute and diverse authority, giving all the facts for beginning a study of specific subjects.

AT AN UNUSUALLY LOW PRICE

The books are inexpensive only because it has been possible to save the cost of resetting by making use of the Britannica type and plate pages. Colour plates, alone, of the same quality as those in these books, if bought separately from dealers, would cost at least twice as much as the book itself.

The books are sold at museum desks, general bookstores and through teachers to their classes or may be ordered from the office of the Encyclopaedia Britannica.

BOOKS OF THIS SERIES NOW READY FOR SALE OR ON THE PRESS ARE:

1. *Chinese Art*
2. *Painting*
3. *Mammals and Birds*
4. *Graphic Arts*
5. *Botany, the Science*
6. *Botany: Plants and Gardening*
7. *The Earth, the Seas and the Heavens*
8. *Theatre and Motion Pictures*
9. *Fishes, Reptiles and Insects*
10. *Japanese Art*

Others scheduled will cover such a variety of topics as "Architecture", "Literature", "Biographies of Famous Women", "Travel", "Sports", "How to Do and Make Things", "Geography", and "Mediterranean Arts". The new Britannica offers an exhaustive supply of material for such books and the Britannica publishers invite suggestions for additional subjects.

WHAT THEY SAY ABOUT THESE BOOKS

"It is in every way an admirable volume and places for the first time within easy reach of students a comprehensive study of the subject. I can safely say that I consider your plan for similar books one of the real contributions toward popularization of art appreciation in recent years."
HORACE H. F. JAYNE, *Director of The University Museum, University of Pennsylvania*

"It was a very happy and excellent idea to issue these books in a separate and so attractive a form. I am convinced that they will make a ready appeal to art students and the public in general and that there will be a great demand for them."
BERTHOLD LAUFER, *Field Museum of Natural History, Chicago, Illinois*

"I congratulate you on the idea of collecting the articles by your learned collaborators in the Encyclopaedia Britannica and making them available in single volumes. I believe these books will prove most useful, both to students and to the general public, and that museums will welcome them as valuable additions to the study bibliographies of trustworthy material that can be recommended to the thousands of people who ask for guidance."
LANGDON WARNER, *Fogg Art Museum, Cambridge, Massachusetts*

"I cannot tell you how much good this volume will do. There is a very great need among a large portion of the American Art world for books of this sort."
GEORGE PEARSE ENNIS, *George Pearse Ennis School of Painting, New York City*

ENCYCLOPAEDIA BRITANNICA, Inc.
342 Madison Avenue, New York City

The ENCYCLOPAEDIA BRITANNICA CO., Ltd.
80-86 Regent Street, London, W.1

PUBLIC LIBRARY
ROBINSON, ILL.